BUHARI:
THE MAKING OF A PRESIDENT

Buhari:
The Making of a
President

by

Jimi Adebisi Lawal

Safari Books Ltd.
Ibadan

Published by
Safari Books Ltd.
Ile Ori Detu
1, Shell Close
Onireke
Ibadan.
Email: info@safaribooks.com.ng
Website: http://safaribooks.com.ng

© 2017, Jimi Adebisi Lawal

First Published 2017

All rights reserved. This book is copy right and so no part of it may be reproduced, stored in any retrieval system, or transmitted, in any form or by any means, electrical, mechanical, electrostatic, magnetic tape, photocopying recording or otherwise, without the prior written permission of the author, except for brief quotations in critical reviews, articles or academic work. In the latter instance full citation must be provided.

ISBN: 978-978-54785-4-9 - PAPERBACK
978-978-54785-5-6 - CASED EDITION

Dedication

This book is dedicated to all the *Talakawas*, the downtrodden, who not only saw the need for change ahead of the elites, but also struggled (with some paying the supreme price) for the actualisation of their dream.

Table of Contents

Dedication... *v*
Foreword.. *xi*
Acknowledgements... *xvii*
Timeline of Events.. *xix*
Introduction... *xxix*

CHAPTER 1: The Man Buhari................................... 1
CHAPTER 2: The 2003 and 2007 Presidential Efforts.. 15
CHAPTER 3: New Direction for Nigeria: El-Rufai, Bakare and Author Meet...................... 25
CHAPTER 4: The 2011 Elections................................ 37
CHAPTER 5: Reversing a Decision/ The CPC Renewal Committee............................ 47
CHAPTER 6: Science as Winner: 2014 Voters Register and the PVC............................ 55
CHAPTER 7: Enter the APC....................................... 63
CHAPTER 8: Choosing the National Chairman and the work of the APC Strategy Committee... 81
CHAPTER 9: Welcoming the 'New PDP' Entrants... 89
CHAPTER 10: The 2014 Presidential Primaries and Choice of Running Mate...................... 105

Chapter 11:	Election Planning and Monitoring Directorate and the Campaign Trail.	137
Chapter 12:	Technology as a Game Changer: The Card Reader	155
Chapter 13:	Dealing with the February 14 Postponement	169
Chapter 14:	Drama at the National Collation Centre	183
Chapter 15:	Transition Matters	195
Epilogue:	Beyond Buhari: How Nigeria is governed; Significance of the Buhari Presidency and the Future of Nigeria	203
Appendixes		209
1.	CPC Renewal Committee (Interim Report)	211
2.	CPC Renewal Committee (Final Report)	225
3.	Puritanism vs Pragmatism	237
4.	Author's Letters of Appointment – Presidential Campaign Committee 2011 and 2015	247
5.	Presidential Election Results: 2003, 2007, 2011 and Predictions for 2015	249
6.	Letters Exchange: Ikimi and Tinubu	257
7.	APC Platform Document	285
8.	Buhari's Speech Declaring to Contest the 2015 polls	287
9.	Strategy Committee's Report	291
10.	Picture of Jonathan seeking for prayers from Pastors and Obas	299

11.	Campaign pictures with Mammoth Crowd..	303
12.	Colour Coded Surveys on Buhari's Chances	311
13.	Time to Rebuild Nigeria	313
14.	Buhari's Inaugural Speech Given at the Eagle Square, Abuja	321
15.	Offer of US$ 5.1 million from Ifegwu's Solicitors in London	329
Postscript:	About the Author: Baptism of Fire	333
Index:		365

List of Tables

Table 1:	Comparison of Results for 2011 & 2015 Presidential General Elections	192
Table 2:	DaMina Advisors VERITAS Frontier Markets Electoral Forecast Statistical Model Nigeria 2015 Presidential Election Comprehensive State-by-State Forecast	252

Foreword

The first four months of the year 2015 will be remembered by many as some of the most apprehensive days ever in the history of our nation. As political gladiators took to the arena, the atmosphere was palpably foreboding to Nigerians as well as the international community. The destiny of Nigeria was hanging in the balance. In the centre of this political theatre were two personalities with significantly different trajectories: one, the incumbent president, Goodluck Ebele Jonathan of the People's Democratic Party (PDP) who had enjoyed an unprecedented, almost meteoric rise, to the apex of political power, and the other, then General Muhammadu Buhari of the All Progressives Congress (APC), whose patience and persistence amid consecutive defeats rivalled, if not trumped, that of the legendary Abraham Lincoln. As one who had the rare privilege of earning the trust of both candidates and listening to their expectations and concerns, I could feel the tension in the atmosphere. The duo had met in electoral contest four years earlier and the outcome had left hundreds of casualties in days of post-election violence. Many feared that 2015 could be more catastrophic.

In the climax of his penultimate attempt at the presidency in 2011, Muhammadu Buhari had broken down in tears, grieved by the country's paradoxical underdevelopment despite her abundant resource endowment, a shameful condition sustained by years of corruption. At that time, Buhari had declared that campaign as the last one for him, indicating that he would never again present himself for the office of the president. However, by the end of the 2011 elections which left the nation largely divided, it was clear to some of us who had worked closely with Buhari in that election campaign that the man still had a role to play in stabilizing the nation and in laying a new foundation for her greatness. The mammoth crowds and cult following I had seen around Buhari as his running mate in the 2011 elections, combined with his rare leadership qualities in a nation that had, for long, suffered severe trust deficit, reminded me of my childhood political hero, Chief Obafemi Awolowo of blessed memory. We did not want this rare breed to go down in history as "the president Nigeria never had." Therefore, after the elections, we embarked on a mission to bring him out of "retirement". Central to this persuasive mission were a trio described in this book by the author as "The Three Musketeers", namely the author himself, Jimi Lawal, Mallam Nasir El-Rufai and yours truly, Tunde Bakare. This book describes the journey that led to the eventual emergence of President Muhammadu Buhari in 2015.

Buhari: The Making of a President is a story of intrigues, suspense, betrayals, reconciliations, collaborations and strategic concessions, one which only an insider could have told to such detail. The book commences from the President's early life and narrates his earlier contributions to the nation as a highly disciplined military officer who was to distinguish himself in public administration as a military governor, a minister for petroleum resources and a military Head of State. The persuasive force of Buhari's integrity is highlighted in the details of his negotiations with the Abacha administration prior to accepting the role of Chairman of the Petroleum Trust Fund (PTF). His political journey from the All Nigeria People's Party (ANPP) to the Congress for Progressive Change (CPC) is narrated in Chapters 2-5. The story of the merger that birthed the APC and the subsequent strides gained by the party is told in considerable detail in Chapters 6-9 while the intrigues surrounding the 2015 elections are presented in Chapters 11-15. The unprecedented role of the Permanent Voters Card (PVC) is not left out in this narrative. In the book, the author also describes, from his perspective, the close shove Nigeria had with a post-election conflict that could have left the nation in disarray as well as the factors that turned the tide in favour of democracy. There are a number of high points in the book but one stands out – the heart-touching story of the victory of principles over money in the convention that led to the emergence of Muhammadu Buhari as candidate of the APC. This is told in Chapter 10. In the postscript, the author introduces himself to the reader and describes the events that trained him to deal with sharks in the waters of business and politics.

I first met Jimi Lawal in 2010 in the course of convening like-minded patriots in a movement to save and transform Nigeria on the platform of the Save Nigeria Group. That meeting is alluded to in this book. Jimi struck me as a very intelligent person right from the first day I met him because of his highly cerebral contribution during that first meeting in Dubai. But I must admit that I pulled back a bit when Jimi gave me his complimentary card and I saw four addresses for his organisation's operational bases: Lagos, London, Toronto and China. However, as time went on, I discovered that each location was real, not imaginary. Apart from Lagos, I have since stayed with Jimi in his homes both in the UK and Canada. The "three musketeers" (Mallam Nasir El-Rufai, Jimi and I) had a ball in China, with his staff in China at our beck and call, while we were there on a business trip. His ideology of pragmatic puritanism and his inclination to scientific analysis of threats and opportunities thrusts him into the league of thought leaders in political strategy, the same class as David Axelrod who facilitated the rise of President Barrack Obama.

Of course, we have had our differences in political persuasions particularly in the period leading to the 2015 elections when the other two of the "three musketeers", Jimi and El-Rufai, could not relate to my position on the transition process. Influenced by nothing other than my God-inspired persuasion as regards what is best for Nigeria, I had enumerated well-defined steps towards addressing the fundamentals, the most important of which was the restructuring of our nation, prior to elections. To buttress this point of difference, Jimi has reproduced, in Chapter 12, excerpts from my January 4, 2015 address to the nation titled "The Gathering Storm and Avoidable Shipwreck: How to Avoid Catastrophic Euroclydon." Two years after the elections, our positions still differ on this issue as it is clear to me that, despite the narrow escape we experienced in the 2015 elections, the ensuing governance challenges in the political, economic and social landscapes are pointers to the inevitability of a return to the restructuring imperative.

Finally, *Buhari: The Making of a President* is laden with inspiring lessons especially for young and aspiring politicians: lessons in election campaign management; lessons in trustful give-and-take as the way forward for Nigeria; lessons in collaboration guided by the ideal of contact without contamination; lessons in politics of character and the eventual triumph of principles; and lessons in what the author identifies as the "G-Factor", that is, the God-factor in politics. It is also a wake-up call to Nigerian politicians especially those in the two major political parties, the APC and the PDP. While the PDP should be convicted by the indicting narrative in this book, the APC should be sobered by the personal example of the man, Buhari, and must return to the sense of purpose that birthed his election victory, knowing that election victory was just a step to the real deal, which is governance, as those who fail to learn from history will themselves become history.

Dr. Tunde Bakare
Lagos, Nigeria

Acknowledgements

In expressing gratitude to all those that worked with me in preparing, researching, writing and bringing this book to fruition, I felt obliged to step back and start from the beginning.

I never contemplated being actively involved in politics. In fact, the reverse was the case; as I was expressly forbidden by my parents from partaking in active politics. Yet, our nation was not moving forward and the words of Plato - the legendary Greek Philosopher that "One of the penalties for refusing to participate in politics is that you end up being governed by your inferiors" would not leave my mind. Thus, when the three of us (along with other like minds) decided to embark on the task of nation building, I had to get my dearest *Egbon* - Pastor Bakare to lead Mallam El-Rufai and me in 2010 to convince Kabiyesi (the Awujale of Ijebu Land) to rescind the restriction and support our endeavours. Kabiyesi was convinced, so my debts of gratitude must start with him. In the same vein, the political odyssey of the past seven years would neither have commenced nor amounted to anything without Pastor Bakare and Mallam El-Rufai. Indeed, this book is as much theirs as it is mine. They pushed and reminded me on several occasions to expedite action in ensuring its timely completion.

I had written articles and lengthy reports before. But this is my first book. So, I shall be the first to admit it was a major challenge. The initial target was to complete the work by the first anniversary of President Buhari's Administration. So, this finished product came about a year late with two editorial assistants having been fired in the process. I had never settled for an inferior quality work, as a result of which the two previous attempts had to be abandoned and completely destroyed. The search for a competent hand took me to Chief Tunde Fagbenle, who introduced me to Richard Mammah. Thus, I am immensely grateful to Chief Fagbenle and Richard for their invaluable contributions; even though the errors and omissions remain mine.

As previously stated, a couple of deadlines for the completion of this work had been missed. I must express profound gratitude to my Publisher – Chief Joop Berkhout of Safari Books Limited, for putting enormous pressure on me by calling day and night to get us through the finish line.

Finally, this would not have been possible without a tolerant and supportive better half - Hajia Maryam. Having to combine this task with a hectic full time public service in the past two years meant sleepless nights and the sacrifices of quality family time. I was rightly accused of being anti-social and unfair by her and our children during the last Christmas holiday. I was guilty as charged and words alone cannot express my gratitude to them for being nonetheless caring and understanding. This is the result of our collective sacrifices, in the hope that the end justifies the means.

Jimi Lawal
Kaduna, February 2017.

Timeline of Events

April 2002

A few months before his 60th birthday, former military Head of State, General Muhammadu Buhari, rtd, bows to pressure and picks up a membership form of the opposition All Peoples Party, APP; enlisting in the world of partisan politics for the first time.

2003

Buhari contests the 2003 Presidential Elections on the platform of the APP and proceeds to challenge his defeat in court after losing to his former boss and People's Democratic Party, PDP candidate, General Olusegun Obasanjo, rtd.

El-Rufai, Nuhu Ribadu, Oby Ezekwesili and Chukwuma Soludo serve alongside others in the Ngozi Okonjo-Iweala-led Economic Management Team, EMT within the Obasanjo presidency.

2006

El-Rufai meets Buhari for the first time on political issues, and they talk on improving his relations with Obasanjo, the Third Term agenda and the future of the country.

Buhari participates very actively in efforts at the National Assembly to scuttle the Third Term bid.

2007

Buhari contests the 2007 presidential elections on the platform of the ANPP and loses to Governor Umaru Yar 'Adua of the PDP.

January 2009

Nuhu Ribadu, El-Rufai and Jimi Lawal in exile hold talks on either El-Rufai or Ribadu running for president in 2011.

June 2009

In Harvard, Ribadu, Jimi Lawal and El-Rufai meet with the Dr. Isa Odidi-led Nigerian diaspora organisation, Change Nigeria Project (CNP) to discuss areas of political cooperation.

July 2009

The political advocacy initiative, Good Governance Group, 3G is established in Nigeria. In addition to its Nigerian members like Saliu Lukman, Yinka Odumakin and Uche Onyeagocha, the exiled trio of Nasir El-Rufai, Nuhu Ribadu and Jimi Lawal are also involved.

November 23, 2009

President Umaru Yar 'Adua suffers a stroke and is flown to Saudi Arabia for treatment.

December 2009

To take on the cabal that is insisting on governing on behalf of Yar 'Adua, the G53, G57 and Save Nigeria Group emerge. First it was G53 which was then expanded to

G57, before merging with the Save Nigeria Group (SNG) under the leadership of Pastor Tunde Bakare. The arrowhead behind the formation of G53 was Yinka Odumakin, Publicity Secretary of the Afenifere Renewal Group (ARG) and member of the 3G Steering Committee.

December 2, 2009

G53 issues a statement calling on Yar 'Adua to resign or be impeached.

December 16, 2009

Buhari moves on politically, founds CPC.

December 20, 2009

G57 makes statement asking for Vice President Goodluck Jonathan to be sworn in immediately as Acting President.

January 2010

Pastor Bakare steps into SNG leadership and physically leads Save Nigeria Group protests in Lagos and Abuja to enforce the clamour to swear in Jonathan as Acting President.

February 2010

Jonathan becomes Acting President and Yar 'Adua is flown back to Nigeria from Saudi Arabia.

March 2010

SNG, 3G meet in Dubai. They agree to open political relationship talks with AC and Labour Party and to also 'keep in view' the prospect of discussing with the just registered CPC.

El-Rufai, Pastor Bakare and Jimi Lawal consult further on 'who we are building this house for?!'

April 25, 2010

AC, 3G (including El-Rufai and Jimi Lawal) meet in Accra. Lai Mohammed leads AC team. AC wants 3G to merely provide 'Northern presidential candidate.' 3G insists on a better defined democratic environment and properly constituted grassroots structures within the arrangement.

May 1, 2010

El-Rufai and Jimi Lawal return from exile to Nigeria.

May 5, 2010

NSA Gusau informs that President Umaru Yar'Adua has died.

May 6, 2010

Jonathan sworn in as substantive President.

June 1, 2010

PDP Reform Forum produces document on 'Democratising the PDP Primaries System: Proposals for Reform.' Ken Nnamani, Aminu Masari, El-Rufai are active in the group. Obasanjo endorses proposals.

June 18, 2010

Jonathan disappoints; fails to rally PDP NEC and Reform Forum's proposals are thrown out at the Governors - dominated session.

June 2010

Ribadu privately meets with AC on being its presidential candidate and to work at committing 3G to an alliance.

July 2010

Pastor Bakare hosts 'Arrowheads' meetings in his Lagos home. Participants fail to follow through with initiative. Ribadu notably continues with AC deal which 3G, SNG and Arrowheads would not endorse.

September 2010

Buhari, CPC make outreach to SNG.

September 28, 2010

Last formal meeting between SNG and Jonathan; $50,000 'transport' gift upsets Pastor Bakare.

October 2010

El-Rufai comes under fire for comments on Buhari being too old.

December 2010

SNG decides to collaborate with CPC.

January 15, 2011

Buhari asks Bakare to be his running mate on the CPC platform.

January 2011

Alliance talks between ACN and CPC collapse, with the former's demand for a post-dated letter of resignation by Bakare rejected.

Obasanjo proposes Buhari-Okonjo Iweala ticket for CPC and merger with ANPP, Labour Party and ACN. El-Rufai signs Buhari/Bakare's INEC Nomination Form.

February 2011

Bakare appointed Chair of CPC Presidential Campaign Council.

Buhari appoints Jimi Lawal as member of Campaign Finance Committee

Obasanjo abandons Buhari, renews support for Jonathan.

April 2, 2011

Elections begin with legislative contests only to be aborted by INEC after early CPC upsets in the North.

April 2011

CPC participates in 2011 Presidential Elections with General Buhari and Pastor Bakare as running mates.

Saddened by how much Nigeria had changed for the worse during his lifetime, Buhari weeps on the last day of the presidential campaign in Abuja.

June 2011
Buhari, Bakare, El-Rufai and author participate in Chatham House post-mortem on the 2011 elections.

November 3, 2011
Nasir El-Rufai appointed Chairman of CPC Renewal Committee, with leave to nominate members subject to confirmation by party leadership.

December 2011
Nasir El-Rufai as Chairman of CPC Renewal Committee along with Jimi Lawal and others as members inaugurated by the party leadership.

January 2013
El-Rufai and Sarki Abba persuade Buhari to visit Tinubu in his Ikoyi residence to discuss prospects for future political cooperation.

January 16, 2013
ACN, CPC Alliance/Merger Committee set-up.

February 5, 2013
First formal meeting between ACN-CPC merger committees with Author appointed as one of the members representing CPC.

February 6, 2013
First formal merger meeting between CPC, ANPP and ACN takes place.

February 13, 2013

First formal merger meeting between CPC, ANPP, ACN and a faction of APGA is held.

February 2013

Three major opposition parties in the country, the Action Congress of Nigeria (ACN), the Congress for Progressive Change (CPC), the All Nigeria Peoples Party (ANPP) and a faction of the All Progressives Grand Alliance (APGA) decide to merge to more robustly take on the PDP in the 2015 polls. Their choice of name is the All Progressives Congress, APC.

May 11, 2013

As part of the conditions pursuant to the registration of the new party, a special CPC Convention to formally ratify the merger is held at the Eagle Square, Abuja.

June 2013

Interim National Executive set-up for the new party; APC with erstwhile ACN chief and former Governor of Osun State, Chief Bisi Akande emerging as Interim National Chairman.

July 31, 2013

The APC is formally recognised by the Independent National Electoral Commission (INEC).

August 31, 2013

Dissatisfied with the state of affairs in the ruling People's Democratic Party, PDP, seven of its governors, along with several other leaders of the party and their supporters, walk out of the National Convention of the party. The disaffected governors include Rotimi Amaechi of Rivers State, Rabiu Musa Kwankwaso of Kano, Sule Lamido of Jigawa, Babangida Aliyu of Niger and Abdulfatah Ahmed of Kwara.

September 2013

The seven governors (G-7) who had walked out on the PDP, formally announce that they are leaving the People's Democratic Party (PDP) and proceeding to form the 'New PDP.'

November 2013

Five Governors of the 'New PDP' formally join APC. The Interim National Chairman of the APC, Bisi Akande, in a joint statement with the "new PDP" chairman, Kawu Baraje, announces a merger of the two parties.

March 2014

APC National Election Planning Committee headed by Rivers Governor, Rotimi Amaechi goes to work.

April 2014

Pastor Bakare makes case for National Reconciliation and Integration Committee as part of the National Confab.

August 2014

Ekiti APC Governor, Kayode Fayemi concedes defeat to PDP candidate, Ayodele Fayose.

November 2014

APC wins first major election, with Ogbeni Rauf Aregbesola being re-elected as Governor of Osun State.

December 2014

Muhammadu Buhari emerges as flag-bearer of the APC, beating former Vice President Atiku Abubakar, Governors Rabiu Musa Kwankwaso and Rochas Okorocha, and *Leadership* Newspaper publisher, Sam Nda-Isaiah.

January 6, 2015

The Buhari Presidential Campaign visits Rivers State.

February 2015

The Election Planning and Monitoring sub-committee of the Buhari/Osinbajo Campaign swings into action, with Author serving as a member.

INEC postpones presidential election slated for 14th February.

March 28, 2015

In the first ever upset of its kind in modern Nigerian history, opposition flag-bearer, Muhammadu Buhari defeats incumbent President, Goodluck Jonathan; who conceded and called to congratulate Buhari a couple of days later on March 30th.

May 29, 2015

Muhammadu Buhari sworn in as President of the Federal Republic of Nigeria.

Introduction

The decision to write this book was taken to ensure fidelity to the truth. As things are today, a lot of stories are flying around as to how General Muhammadu Buhari got to be elected President of Nigeria. And some of them are just not correct. Underscoring this point, even the seemingly straightforward nomination of Vice President Osinbajo became a major national controversy some months ago .

Taking liberties with facts and history in our view is not just dishonest, it is also the wrong approach to follow in our desired path of nation-building. Equally, being the simple man that he is, President Muhammadu Buhari is not one to personally strive over records. But as avid students of history and front-row participant-observers in the making of this landmark event, some of us have insisted that history must be correctly rendered. This is what we have sought to do here.

Furthermore, the story of the making of President Buhari is that of the typical saga of perseverance that ultimately results in success. This is another reason why it is even more compelling that we wrote this book so that virtually everyone who reads it can be persuaded to imbibe the lesson of not giving up if you do not succeed the first, second or even the third time.

And in addition to simply not giving up, it is also of critical importance to keep in mind the definition of "insanity" by the Alcoholics Anonymous: 'To do the same thing again the same way and expect a different result.' No, you would need to thoroughly examine why you had not succeeded earlier, adopt a new course and take practical steps that would result in your desired goal. This, in a nutshell, is what this book is all about.

And this is where we come in.

About twelve of us had met in Dubai, in the United Arab Emirates during the final days in office of President Umaru Yar'Adua and decided that something had to be done about the future of Nigeria. Other very seriously concerned patriots at the meeting were Pastor Tunde Bakare, Jimi Agbaje, Yinka Odumakin and Mallam Nasir El-Rufai. It is this process that led to a series of engagements over the next half-decade, that along with the efforts of several others, resulted in the first ever party-to-party transition in our recorded democratic history, and realised the long-running goal of electing Muhammadu Buhari as President.

But our journey did not begin with Buhari himself. Rather it was a more all-encompassing effort to join other patriots in the struggle to make Nigeria great again after the chicanery of the Third Term campaign, the deeply flawed 2007 "elections" (through the imposition of Umaru Yar'Adua as President) after that gambit was defeated, and the manipulations to prevent the rightful elevation of then Vice President Goodluck Jonathan coming into office, first as Acting President and later as substantive President after Yar'Adua's demise.

We will take it from the beginning.

JAL
Kaduna, February 2017

CHAPTER ONE

The Man, Buhari

Muhammadu Buhari is many things to many people. But one thing that almost everyone is agreed upon is that this is one Nigerian statesman and leader that is clearly not given to the lifestyle of ostentatiousness and vain opulence that is characteristic of many an 'African big man.'

Born on December 17, 1942 in Daura - one of the frontline Hausa towns, which is located in today's Katsina State - to a Fulani father and a mother of mixed Hausa and Kanuri parentage, the young Muhammadu was enrolled in primary schools at Daura and Mai'adua. He also attended the Katsina Model School between 1953 and 1956 and then the Katsina Provincial Secondary School (now Government College Katsina) from 1956 to 1961.

As a foretaste of Muhammadu's latter rise to the leadership heights, it is to his credit that while in school in Katsina, he was a class monitor from the second form, house prefect in the fifth form and during his sixth form, was both house prefect and head boy of the school. In that sense, he had held the main leadership positions a student could occupy at that stage of his life and development.

This exposure did come in handy when at age 18, he was selected as the Northern Region beneficiary of the countrywide merit-based competition, organised by the famous old British shipping line, Elder Dempster. The prize was an all-expense paid holiday in the UK, and that most significantly also was to be the first time that he would be travelling out of the country. It is equally to his credit and that of the Nigerian system at that time that he had competed alongside children of federal and state ministers and senators, including the late Shehu Musa Yar'Adua and Abdul Malik Isa Kaita, whose fathers, Alhaji Musa Yar'Adua and Al-Haji Isa Kaita, were then the ministers of Lagos Affairs and Education in the country.

Equally noteworthy was the fact that he was also not studying at the more upscale Barewa College where the children of the northern elite were to be found in those days.

Called to be a Soldier

From his infancy, Muhammadu Buhari had clearly shown a preference for outdoor activities. As a young growing lad, he would after returning from school go over to the family farm to help out with taking care of the animals. He was so comfortable with outdoor activities that the decision to send him to boarding school came in most handy as it provided a fitting environment for him to blend academic and outdoor activities in a composite mix.

Also auspicious was the introduction of a cadet corps in his school in Katsina. As a paramilitary institution, the drills, parades, camping tours and related exercises carried out in the cadet corps served as a teaser for someone like Muhammadu who was later to elect on a full career in military service.

Enlisting in the Nigerian Army in 1961, Muhammadu Buhari was trained at the Nigerian Military Training College (NMTC), Zaria from 1962 to 1963, underwent officer cadet training at the Mons Officer Cadet School in Aldershot in England.

From November 1963 to January 1964, he attended the Platoon Commanders' Course at the Nigerian Military Training College, Kaduna and later in 1964, the Mechanical Transport Officer's Course at the Army Mechanical Transport School in Borden, United Kingdom.

He also benefitted from a training stint at the Defence Services Staff College, Wellington, India in 1973. To cap his training regimen, from 1979 to 1980, the then Colonel Buhari attended the US Army War College in Carlisle, Pennsylvania, in the United States where he obtained a Master's Degree in Strategic Studies

A LEADER EMERGES

After cutting his teeth in the first years of training within the military, it soon emerged that in Muhammadu Buhari, the Nigerian Army had indeed been blessed with a very conscientious soldier who would indeed excel over time.

Some of the initial attributes and character traits that were noticed about him this early and which were to stand him out in succeeding years included his capacity for hard work, commitment to duty, natural penchant for service, respect for his seniors, devotion to teamwork and loyalty to his men.

In report after report, his instructors at the various military academies where he trained; recorded these attributes in their testimonials on the young officer and these were to be later corroborated also by his field commanders and other superior officers that he served under.

Further evidence of the remarkable carriage and grooming of this officer came in the flurry of roles that he was invited to take on overtime. Among other postings and deployments, he served as a peace enforcer during the post-independence crisis in the Congo (now Democratic Republic of Congo) and also fought valiantly for the Federal Forces during the Nigeria civil war.

Other than the basic inconvenience of prosecuting a 'police action' against fellow Nigerians during the war, so remarkable was Buhari's professional commitment to discharging his duties as a soldier at this time that though he was only a lieutenant when the war started in July, 1967, he was subsequently promoted to captain and then major by the time the crisis had been contained in January, 1970. Of course, these promotions did not just entail more money in his pockets, but they also came with greater leadership responsibilities which he was equally able to discharge most meritoriously.

A further testament of Buhari's professional and leadership capacities came in the slew of post-war deployments that he was handed. Accordingly, he served as Platoon Commander at the 2nd Infantry Battalion, Abeokuta and Military Administrator for the defunct North-Eastern State which has since been further divided into six states between the Murtala Muhammed era and the last State creation exercise in 1996.

Equally underscoring the very high professional regard in which he was held, when the February 13, 1976 coup that terminated the life of General Murtala Muhammed took place, Buhari's name emerged in the shortlist of two possible successors for the position of Chief of Staff, Supreme Headquarters that General Olusegun Obasanjo was vacating to be sworn in as replacement Head of State.

With that position eventually being given to his friend and colleague, General Shehu Musa Yar'Adua, he went on to serve as Federal Commissioner for Petroleum and Natural Resources and Chairman of the Nigerian National Petroleum Corporation (NNPC).

During Buhari's stint at the petroleum ministry, it is to his credit that, among other achievements, the nation was able to build two refineries at Kaduna and Warri, about twenty depots, more than 3,200 kilometres of pipelines and numerous pumping stations.

Again, given the close nexus between petro-dollars and national wealth, it has not been uncommon for the integrity of petroleum ministers to be questioned during the period of their service. For Buhari, this was to come one day after the Economic Department of the Petroleum and Natural Resources Ministry had briefed the government on the cost and fluctuation of commodities, currencies and other market indicators while he held sway at the ministry. After the session was concluded and everyone was walking out, Obasanjo reportedly called him back and asked: "Are you sure not even five cents of any of this is sticking to your fingers?"

At this point, Nigeria was exporting 2 million barrels of oil a day and the going price was about $18 a barrel. There was indeed a lot at stake. However, Buhari's response was cryptic: "Sir, you can investigate me." And then he saluted and went back to his work.

Not only did Obasanjo not carry out any such investigation, indeed, when the opportunity for Buhari to attend the War College came up, the Head of State was not too keen on letting him go on out of fear that anyone else he would put in charge of petroleum would undo all the progress that had been made there! And the facts reveal that upon Buhari's consequent departure, Obasanjo wound up not putting anyone else in the position of minister of petroleum and natural resources but rather took on the duties himself till the end of the regime's time in office.

Also at this time and as a further demonstration of Buhari's growing leadership stature, other than Obasanjo and Shehu Yar'Adua, he was the only military officer who sat in the three final decision making councils in the country. These were the Supreme Military Council, the Council of States and the Executive Ministers' Council.

And to cap his record of strategic endorsements at this time, his nomination to proceed for further training at the US Army War College, Carlisle, Pennsylvania, ahead of the return to civil rule in October 1979, was made by none else than his immediate boss in service, Army Chief, General Theophilus Danjuma.

A CHAD ENCOUNTER

On returning from his training stint at the United States War College, Buhari was posted to Lagos as a General and team leader of the Commanding Forces Division, later to Ibadan as Commander of the 2nd Division and then to Jos to take over command of the fledgling 3rd Armoured Division. It was while at Jos that he was to be confronted with one more definitive moment in his service life.

Soldiers from the neighbouring Chad had crossed over into Nigerian territory in 1983, occupied nineteen islands abutting the Lake Chad, and in the process made a mockery of the territorial integrity of the Nigerian nation. In a very specific sense also, this incursion in particular was putting mud on the face of the officers and men of the 3rd Armoured Division, within whose jurisdiction the particular transgression was being carried out, a situation no self-respecting commander would condone.

A grossly incensed Buhari as field commander of the affected areas acted fast. He ordered the border with Chad to be closed, cutting off food and fuel supplies to the rebels. And then, not only did he lead his troops to chase the rebels out of every inch of Nigerian soil that they were occupying, but for further assurance, they pushed the battle further into Chad and in the process, occupied some 50 kilometres of Chadian soil.

Terrified, the Chadian President telephoned Nigeria's President, Shehu Shagari to please get his General and his troops out of his country! Shagari gave the command and Buhari and his men retreated.

While the immediate result of that act of muscle-flexing was that there was peace and calm on that border for very many years, a corollary fall-out however was that Buhari's colleagues in the armed forces took very appreciative notice of the no-nonsense mien and courage exhibited by this particular officer, even as his composite popularity profile also rose further within the rank and file of the armed forces.

When the coup that ousted President Shehu Shagari was carried out on December 31, 1983, no doubt this brave Chadian campaign by Buhari was to come into reckoning and he was unanimously chosen by his colleagues in the Armed Forces to assume the office of Head of State.

While the jury on his years of service during this period is still out, the administration's attempts to tame the excesses of the political players it had removed from office, combat the scourge of corruption, tackle growing social disorder through the "War Against Indiscipline" campaign and stabilise the national economy rank as some of its most noble ambitions.

In his book, *The Accidental Public Servant,* Nasir El-Rufai remarks about this time and its consequent political fall-outs:

> We have had a few leaders, like General Murtala Muhammed between 1975 and 1976 and General Mohammadu Buhari between 1983 and 1985, who had huge followings because they were perceived to be honest, straightforward, nationally-minded people that applied rules to the big man and the small man evenly and did not care about status, religion or ethnicity. Part of the reason General Buhari is still popular with many Nigerians and part of the reason he could contest the presidency and can win is because as a military head of state, he was perceived to be tough on corruption, and tough on the big men. Every Nigerian knows what the problems are in Nigeria, and it is the big men and women who believe that rules should apply to everyone except them. The ordinary Nigerian –the common man and woman struggling to survive illiteracy, poverty and disease will line up and do the right thing under good leadership.

True to this thesis, 'the big men' soon struck back. After twenty months in power, a palace coup was executed against the Buhari administration, which led to his removal from office. The coup was at the behest of his former Chief of Army Staff, Ibrahim Babangida, who subsequently replaced him in office. He was then committed to house arrest, first in Akure and later Benin City, before finally being released in December 1988 to return to his family and farm in Katsina.

Back in Katsina, Buhari just wanted to stay under the radar and rest. But his people would not just let that be. Pressure was mounted on him and he was soon involved with the non-governmental community development aspirations of the Katsina Foundation, an initiative put together by the elite of his home state and in which he was to serve most commendably for many years as Chairman.

The foundation had five priorities:
1. To provide potable drinking water especially to the rural areas worst hit by water shortage.
2. To support and encourage health and educational development in the best possible ways.
3. To lay a solid foundation for the establishment of a sound economic base, through setting up of viable industries.
4. To fight desertification and enlighten the people on tree planting and the dangers of desert encroachment.
5. To serve as an instrument for social, economic, moral and cultural development.

True to his upbringing, Buhari administered the affairs of the foundation most scrupulously even when there were very clear odds stacked against him.

In one such instance, a military governor of the state had requested him to sign off ₦38.5 million or about 92% of the total funds in the foundation's coffers to him to administer. This was most unacceptable but even when the board sent a delegation to explain to the government on how best the board had intended to run the foundation, he would not budge and sent his deputy to Buhari's house to collect the cheque. The governor also went on to make embarrassing and unguarded utterances to the press, full of unfounded allegations, and threatening to remove the chairman if the funds were not released to him.

When the entire board met to review developments, it resolved to turn down the governor's request as they were likely to vitiate the achievement of the primary objectives of the fund; go ahead with its action plan to allow the four extant committees on water, health, education and projects to submit their reports for consideration with a view to meeting the foundation's set objectives, and condemned the unfortunate and unguarded utterances made by the governor and resolved to never succumb to any form of blackmail or intimidation.

The no-nonsense stand of the board further infuriated the governor and he purportedly dissolved the board of trustees and appointed a sole administrator for the foundation. In response, some donors to the fund headed for the Lagos High Court to challenge the purported dissolution of the board. Subsequently, an order was issued by the Court restraining the governor from tampering with the foundation's funds and fixing a date for hearing. This stalemate persisted until a civilian governor took over the administration of affairs and withdrew the purported dissolution notice.

That was indeed the first and last time anyone tried to interfere with the affairs of the Katsina Foundation under Buhari's watch, and he went on to run the foundation for seventeen years before stepping down as chairman.

Indeed, so enamoured were his people with his service that even when he was otherwise engaged with other schedules in Abuja during some of this time, the board of directors would rather move meetings to Abuja to accommodate his schedule.

In the wake of the annulment of the results of the June 12, 1993 elections by the Babangida regime, the hibernating General was once again dragged onto the front-lines from where he participated as one of the leaders of the Association for Democracy and Good Governance in Nigeria (ADGN), an initiative that had been convened by his former boss, General Olusegun Obasanjo to resolve the crisis.

The PTF challenge

With General Sani Abacha subsequently taking over power in those politically charged circumstances, and the decision by his administration to set-up a Special Fund to manage and deploy buffer funds collected following an increase in fuel prices, Buhari was tapped to serve as Executive Chairman of the Petroleum (Special) Trust Fund, PTF.

Given his long-running inclination to serving the popular interests of the people at all times while ensuring the preservation of his integrity, probity and good name, Buhari proceeded to discuss in detail the terms of his engagement with the Abacha junta before making any commitment on the offer.

As he reasoned, under the circumstances, he was on very good negotiating ground because it was he that, upon acceptance, would really be helping the administration and not the other way round.

And he had his facts. First, it was common knowledge that the administration was having a challenge of securing acceptability with the people in the light of the circumstance of its emergence. On account of Buhari's popularity, his acceptance was going to register as a plus for the regime.

Second, all over the world, it was a well-known fact that fuel price increases had never been palatable and as such the plan by the government to raise fuel prices at the pump from 3.25 naira per litre to 11 naira per litre was going to attract negative reactions.

Third, given the foregoing, about the only way to get the policy through entailed putting someone like himself who had immense goodwill with the public in charge of the additional funds that would be coming in. In doing so, the administration would gain some credibility from the public and on the basis that they trusted him to actually use the revenues accrued to improve social development and infrastructure, they would be persuaded to tolerate the increase.

And fourth, he was not even looking for a job! But in the interest of the nation, he was yet willing to take up the challenge.

With all these in mind, he told Abacha's envoys to arrange for him to have a meeting with the Head of State where he gave Abacha the following key terms and conditions for accepting the offer. When that meeting took place, Buhari proceeded to put all of his cards on the table.

Firstly, while the government would write the decree governing the PTF's purpose and mission and powers, he (Buhari) would be the one with the final say over its final draft form. Secondly, the law had to necessarily state his name explicitly as chairman of the PTF. Thirdly, that as chairman, he would have the final say over who would sit on the board of directors. In addition, only three people would have the authority to sign cheques on behalf of the PTF: one being himself, the second being the PTF's director of finance and the third being the member secretary; and for any cheque to be disbursed, a minimum of two of these three people must sign the cheque. And finally, no invoice could be approved without his signature, even if it was for a mere 100 naira worth of office supplies!

There were several other integrity safeguards that also needed to be met. Any payment greater than 15 million naira would have to be taken to the board of directors for approval before being issued. An experienced consulting firm was to be signed on to conduct cost-benefit analyses, market surveys and comparison studies to accompany all the major projects being undertaken and these reports would inform project specifications when tenders are to be received. A competitive process in which companies with proven experience and with similar projects under similar working conditions bid for projects would be put in place. An insurance programme to ensure what was delivered was what was agreed upon would also be implemented. Any company securing a job worth between one and 10 million naira would have to bring a bond from an insurance company undertaking to reimburse the government if the job was not done according to specifications, and any company securing a job worth between 10 million naira and one billion naira would have to bring a bond to the same effect, certified by the Central Bank of Nigeria.

When Abacha obliged all of his requests, Buhari then accepted to take up the offer after these conditions precedent that he had listed were fulfilled and ran the organisation for several years before going on a well-deserved rest from the national scene.

Overall, many are agreed that the PTF experiment has been one of the most impactful on our national infrastructure climate. For example, the first billion naira on projects went straight to Lagos for a 43-kilometer road connecting the port, as well as water works and drainage systems to, among other places, Victoria Island.

It was indeed the classic case of 'men at work, everywhere' such that by the time it was rested, the fund had built more than 12,000 kilometres of roads, including the ones from Abuja to Port Harcourt and Port Harcourt to Enugu.

In the arena of education, the scheme undertook the refurbishing of schools, the building of laboratories, workshops and university libraries, and also purchased fleets of school buses which went a long way toward improving the transportation needs of Nigeria's young people.

The activities of the PTF were later wound down when Obasanjo returned to lead as civilian President in 1999.

CHAPTER TWO

The 2003 And 2007 Presidential Efforts

If Buhari thought that the PTF stint was going to be his last time in the arena of public service in Nigeria, he was not reckoning with the fact that in the considered view of many, the emergence of the People's Democratic Party, PDP as the new ruling house in the land, along with the return of his former boss, Obasanjo, as President was already proving not to be the silver bullet that the nation was looking for to put its biggest troubles behind it.

Indeed, in several critical respects, things were getting even worse on the leadership turf in the country and under these circumstances, the intervention and involvement of other tried and tested national leaders like Buhari - who were few and far between - was still seriously needed to help steer the ship of state correctly.

The expression 'a goldfish has no hiding place' could not have been truer; and so the private and public calls on the unassuming leader from Daura to reconsider his stance to stay on in the shadows in order to get involved once again in the nation's political and governance processes were growing louder and louder by the day.

Looking back, there is indeed a sense in which Muhammadu Buhari could not really have held out for much longer. Growing up at a time in Nigeria when the family, community and nation still made a lot more sense than we know it today, he had been raised with virtues and values that he also wished would be part of the bequest to successive generations. It was the family that rose to the gauntlet of ensuring his continuing education and growth after his father had died when he was just four years of age. He was seventeen when Nigeria gained its independence and as such was able to take in the clamour and fervour of nationalism and independence. As a twenty-four-year old army lieutenant when the Civil War began, he had no other option but to do all that he could to ensure that the unity of the young nation was sustained and upheld. Ten years later, he was stepping down as governor of what was then the Northeast Region (now comprised of six states: Adamawa, Bauchi, Borno, Gombe, Taraba and Yobe) and going further to lead the Ministry of Mines and Petroleum Resource during General Olusegun Obasanjo's term as military Head of State. And less than a decade after that, his colleagues had unanimously chosen him to serve as Head of State and Commander-in-Chief of the Armed Forces when the Shehu Shagari presidency was truncated. And then to cap it all, he had been brought back from retirement to serve as Executive Chairman of the omnibus Petroleum Trust Fund, PTF at a time when the nation was in dire political straits and when the ruling Abacha junta needed every help that it could find. Indeed, he had tasted and seen Nigeria in its heyday and risen to the challenge now and again to help put things aright. Now once again, that the nation yet required help that he had successfully stepped in to provide on previous occasions, could he really continue to remain on the outside?

Finally, deferring to this avalanche of pressure to join in the political field from where he could respond to the aspirations of millions of Nigerians who saw in him the veritable answer to the gnawing leadership void in the country, at age fifty-nine, Muhammadu Buhari in April, 2002 picked up a membership card and formally became a member of the All Peoples Party, APP (which was later to be renamed the All Nigeria Peoples Party, ANPP).

A lot can and will yet be said about Buhari's personality going forward. For me however, his personal summation is that there are indeed two very critical variables that are at the centre. The first is Buhari's unwavering commitment to helping to solve problems that he sees around him, albeit, within the ambits of his resources and the law and the second is his insistence on not going out there to seek to get anything that he is not ordinarily qualified for, or entitled to.

As his life story and personal disposition readily bears out, joining the world of partisan politics for Buhari was then not an expression of vaunting personal ambition, a pathway to amassing wealth, a means of self-aggrandisement or the working out of an internal ego problem as is the case with many a Nigerian politician. Rather, he was coming to politics in the same way and with the same motivations with which he always approached issues: an overriding commitment to join others in a world of service that will make the society better for all.

On account of his long-established commitment to accountability and probity, it was really going to be very difficult for anyone to 'shoot down' Buhari from his high moral perch. As a young military officer, he would not drive a car to impress someone. When he needed a house of his own, he borrowed from his bank in Kaduna to build it. He could have asked any of a number of contractors to build him a house as others had done but he did not. He could also have awarded himself plots in the six states that comprised the Northeast Region when he ran the zone as its governor; or even one or more oil blocks during his sojourn as Petroleum Minister. To his enduring credit, he did none of these.

With this kind of attitude that was long ingrained and which he was even now also clearly unwilling to soft-pedal on, it was therefore him and not the original 'founders' of the party that soon began to dictate the pace of affairs therein. And just as had been the case in his dealings with Abacha during the PTF era, his high moral standing and solid grassroots appeal made it impossible for the 'founders' to cut him to size as they would have wanted! The facts of the matter were that he was not desperate to be there and as would be demonstrated later in the course of this narrative, it was they in fact, that needed him more than he needed them!

On the platform of the APP/ANPP, he contested to become president but this was not to materialise as he was twice defeated by Olusegun Obasanjo in 2003 and Umaru Yar'Adua in 2007. In both instances, he formally approached the courts to democratically contest the declared outcomes and for him to be declared winner, but on both occasions this was not to be.

Buhari's entry into the race on the two occasions sought to build upon the popular appeal and folk hero status that he commanded even then. The results of both elections demonstrated that despite the structural and logistical inadequacies of the ANPP platform upon which he ran, and the fact that he was standing as an opposition candidate in a political climate that did not have a massive reputation for electoral fairness and which was dominated by one political party, he was able to garner several million votes respectively in both outings.

Indeed, literally every Buhari political outing in notably the northern states of Nigeria was the literal equivalent of a breathtaking and hair-raising exercise in crowd appeal. He is the veritable man of the people, one with whom they totally identified with, and for whom they would spare almost nothing to be with whenever he came calling. He was their leader and they were his people.

It is to be stated that during these years when Buhari was involved with the All Nigerian Peoples Party, ANPP, and while all of these contests and contestations were taking place, Mallam Nasir El-Rufai (whom I had first met in 1989 while running the now defunct Alpha Merchant Bank) and I, to an insignificant extent were part of the People's Democratic Party, PDP administration that held the reins of government at the centre. And just like many other Nigerians, we were very much aware of the retired General's high record of probity as well as the large crowds that followed him each time he stepped out on the campaign trail. We therefore also knew that under other circumstances, he could one day be sworn in as an elected president of Nigeria. But we could also see that there were in those two attempts in 2003 and 2007, several missing links that needed to be addressed if that desire was ever to come to fruition.

The first of our concerns had to do with the relative lack of ambition and ideological confusion of the leadership of his adopted platform, the ANPP. As the second largest political party in Nigeria for some eight years, and one which at a point had seven of Nigeria's thirty-six governors, the ANPP was in a good position to very tactically drive a process that could see it become the leading political party in the nation at a point. To do so however, it had to more robustly define its mission and then reach out to other political actors in other formations to work out practical alliances. When it failed to do this in a succinct and pro-active manner, the road was then left open for the ruling behemoth, the PDP, to make its own alternative pitch that further reduced the ANPP's size and span.

Second, the absence of a well-defined ideological core left the party with a situation where selfish and self-aggrandising governors practically splintered the party, with each holding a chunk of it in real terms. Opportunism and factionalism was therefore the order of the day and in all fairness, it was really the high moral pedigree with which Buhari had come in that was the single most evident restraining factor for the crass debauchery that was playing out underneath.

This opportunism got to its peak in the 2007 polls when different interests in the party literally sold out to the PDP, and to put the icing on the cake, its then National Chairman and vice-presidential candidate, Chief Edwin Ume-Ezeoke jumped ship and accepted to be part of the Yar'Adua administration. This occurred even when the party was yet embroiled in a suit, challenging the reported outcome of that election that would have made him (Ume-Ezeoke) the Vice-President of Nigeria!

Third, within the core of The Buhari Organisation (TBO) at this time, very little complementary work was really being done to overcome these limitations and then go on to the larger task of scientifically determining why their candidate was not winning. Going forward there was a need to put together a revamped brand proposition that had a better chance of resisting the PDP's shenanigans, sweeping the polls nationally and ensuring that the vote counts. All over the world, making this transition usually involves tough and rigorous work but we were not seeing this in this case. In the United Kingdom, New Labour did it for Tony Blair to emerge Prime Minister, while The Clinton Democrats did same to get Bill Clinton into the U.S White House. And here in Nigeria, MKO Abiola, who had been rejected by the NPN in the 1980s also did a strategic make-over whose result was the June 12, 1993 electoral victory whose successful conclusion was however to be stalemated by the military. The TBO did its best but was not playing at these elevated levels then.

BUHARI AND OBASANJO'S 3RD TERM DRIVE

In my subjective view, the beginning of the shift in strategic thinking on the part of Buhari may have begun with the events of the Third Term debacle.

In his reported account of his visit to Buhari to sound out his views on the landmark move, El-Rufai in *The Accidental Public Servant* recounts that the atmosphere he was confronted with at that time was a largely impractical one: Buhari was rightly enraged over the effrontery of the Third Term gambit in the first place but being cocksure that the attempt would not fly, was also not really doing anything to stop it!

As El-Rufai – who like me, had differed with Obasanjo on the subject – recounted in the book, he had to painstakingly discuss with Buhari the reality that if enough external pressure was not privately and publicly brought to bear on the political class, Obasanjo could in all probability yet have his way! Another point which was raised in that parley was the need to ensure that when the third term move was eventually defeated, ample damage control initiatives should be in place to ensure that the nation would yet be spared the 'bull in a china shop' scenario that could follow.

It is to his credit then that Buhari not only began to take a front-row seat in the opposition to the Third Term Agenda but also sent a delegation consisting of Dr. Mahmood Tukur, Adamu Fika, Wazirin Fika and Senator Saidu Kumo, the ANPP National Secretary, to meet with Obasanjo and express the fact that Buhari's view on the subject was 'that he had derailed, and that the tenure elongation project would be defeated.'

El-Rufai continues with the narrative:

> Buhari remained available to engage with Obasanjo while making repeated trips to Abuja to visit legislators in their houses, or call them, making a pitch for them not to support the third term attempt. His first basic argument was that the American Constitution, which is what we modelled our constitution on, started without a term limit provision, but over time the Americans realised these term limits were necessary and this is why it is in our Constitution and we should not change it. Secondly, if we amend the Constitution to allow a third term, what stops Obasanjo from trying to get a fourth term, or a fifth or a sixth? Where will it end? When does the work of government end? When does the work of a leader stop? At some point, one must draw a line and hand over to a successor. General Muhammadu Buhari had considerable moral authority and was completely disinterested in the outcome of the third term debate, so having him available and physically in Abuja to oppose it helped a lot in defeating Obasanjo, Tony Anenih, Ahmadu Ali, Ojo Maduekwe, Senators Mantu, Dalhatu Tafida and other third term protagonists. What was impressive about Buhari is that he did this all very quietly and effectively without the desire to claim any credit.

With the Third Term gambit being defeated, the coast was now clear for the conclusion of the 'electoral process' that saw Buhari being defeated for the second time and which brought in Umaru Yar'Adua as President.

While Buhari did not win the resultant elections, the conclusion of the polls process however did help to bring to light the fact that there were indeed very glaring limitations within the ANPP that would continue to hobble his aspirations as long as they were not fixed. It equally brought to the fore the critical point that Buhari was inadvertently losing more and more of his political capital by staying within an ANPP that was doing nothing to fix these limitations.

This last point is patently evident from the fact that, only one year into the political circuit in 2003, Buhari had garnered as much as 12,710,022 or 32.19 percent of the votes against a nationally very well-known second term opponent like his former boss, General Olusegun Obasanjo, rtd. Now, in 2007, the troubles within the ANPP had reduced his tally of votes to a mere 6,605,299 or 18.66 percent even when he was running against a very troubled PDP that was also fielding a nationally less popular, Umaru Yar'Adua!

Of course the resultant post-defeat recourse to the tribunal did not yield any desired results, particularly when his own vice-presidential candidate in that election, Chief Edwin Ume-Ezeoke, had alongside a sizeable rump of the party's leadership, shockingly accepted to join the very dubiously contrived 'Government of National Unity'. Underscoring the patently unacceptable conduct of the poll, it had taken the Chief Justice of Nigeria, Idris Kutigi, to cast a deciding vote in favour of the PDP even as the proposal to the leadership of the ANPP by the victorious President Yar'Adua was coming at the same time as he was also publicly acknowledging that the elections that had brought him into office had been deeply flawed.

Why then did the eager-to-move-on ANPP leadership not build on this self-indicting admission to insist on a rerun?

THE BIRTH OF THE CPC

After a careful evaluation of his political fortunes in the seven years that he had been engaged with the ANPP, Buhari now came to the decision that it was time to move on.

On December 16, 2009, the Congress for Progressive Change, CPC was founded and by March 2010 had successfully scaled all the pre-registration formalities to enable it to formally receive a certificate of registration from the Independent National Electoral Commission, INEC.

CHAPTER THREE

'The Three Musketeers': El-Rufai, Bakare and Jimi Meet

It was not only Buhari that was disappointed with the perfidious conduct of the political class. Across the nation and beyond, scores of patriots were now very seriously disenchanted with the system and seeking solutions to the problem as best as they could. It was now becoming very clear that something had to give as we could no longer continue to do things in the same way while basking in the false hope that the results would indeed be otherwise! As the adage goes: it is the way you make your bed, that you would lie on it!

At this point also, the attacks by the system on dissenters like Mallam El-Rufai, former Economic and Financial Crimes Commission, EFCC chairman, Mallam Nuhu Ribadu and I, had resulted in a situation where all three of us had been forced out of the land of our birth even when we still had an undying commitment to continue to seek its betterment. We would not be restrained and went in search of like-minds with whom we could engage in cooperative political action to redeem our land.

While in exile then and thinking of what to do about our country, we adopted the strategy of setting up and collaborating with a number of pro-democracy initiatives through which we would continue to make the case for change in Nigeria. One such early initiative which we were associated with was a group known as Change Nigeria Project, CNP. It was set up with like-minded Nigerians in the Diaspora that included Professors Isa Odidi, Idris Dag-Ellams and Joseph Igietseme, Dr. Victor Ozieh and Timothy Modu to name but a few.

To its credit, CNP organised a few conferences and programmes in North America and the United Kingdom amongst other public engagements. But perhaps the most noteworthy achievement of the group was the production of a party manifesto, which was subsequently adopted by the Congress for Progressive Change and used for the 2011 Presidential election.

In July 2009, we inaugurated yet another group, the Good Governance Group, 3G through which we continued to similarly push for change in the country.

Things however began to take a more urgent dimension when on November 23, 2009, President Umaru Yar'Adua suffered a stroke and had to be flown to Saudi Arabia for treatment. A cabal that included his wife, Turai, former Delta State Governor, Chief James Ibori, and a few cabinet ministers such as Adamu Mohammed Aliero and Mike Aondoakaa came up with a grand plot to disguise the true details of his medical condition and in the process deceive Nigerians that the incapacitated President was yet carrying out the duties of state!

To take on the Yar'Adua cabal at this time, a flurry of groups such as the G53, G57 and the Save Nigeria Group, were also emerging on the scene and with the active support and involvement of El-Rufai and I. First it was G53, which then became G57; and in turn G57 was to subsequently merge with the Save Nigeria Group, SNG. The arrowhead behind the formation of G53 was Yinka Odumakin, Publicity Secretary of the Afenifere Renewal Group, ARG and member of the 3G Steering Committee, while Pastor Tunde Bakare, the Convening Overseer of the Latter Rain Assembly, a Christian congregation, was the undisputed leader of the SNG.

On December 2, 2009, G53 issued a statement calling on Yar'Adua to resign or in the alternative for the National Assembly to formally commence impeachment proceedings against him. This was some two weeks before Buhari left the ANPP to found the CPC. By December 20, 2009, the expanded G57 made a statement urging that, in the continued absence of President Umaru Yar'Adua, Vice President Goodluck Jonathan should be immediately sworn in as Acting President.

When this call was still being resisted, by January 2010, Pastor Bakare physically led Save Nigeria Group advocacy and protests to pressure the Federal Executive Council and the National Assembly to abide by the Constitution and swear in Jonathan as Acting President. The protests were not to be called off until they had achieved their purpose and in February 2010, Jonathan formally became Acting President even as the cabal simultaneously arranged a late night return of Yar'Adua from Saudi Arabia.

To its credit, the Save Nigeria Group (SNG) really did make its mark in the country, stridently petitioning and protesting for the kicking in of the constitutional provision that the then Vice President and former Governor of Bayelsa State, Goodluck Jonathan, should immediately be confirmed as Acting President of Nigeria given the evidently deteriorated health status of his principal, President Umaru Yar'Adua.

At this point, we knew that Yar'Adua was seriously incapacitated and there was a provision in our Constitution which stated that upon the event of the incapacitation of the president, an Acting President should be declared. But this was not being done and so the SNG loudly insisted that it be done without delay, until this was achieved in 9th February, 2010, with the National Assembly having been compelled to adopt the 'Doctrine of Necessity' as the legal basis for Jonathan's assumption of office as Acting President.

Despite Jonathan's assumption of office as Acting President, his capacity to function was however yet being restrained by 'the cabal' who were at this time insistent on continuing to run a parallel government in the name of Yar'Adua. So the SNG, as the conscience of the nation, would not relent in its advocacy that all things must be properly done.

According to the provisions of Chapter VI, Section 144 of the 1999 Constitution of the Federal Republic, which states:

(1) The President or Vice-President shall cease to hold office, if -

(a) by a resolution passed by two-thirds majority of all the members of the executive council of the Federation it is declared that the President or Vice-President is incapable of discharging the functions of his office; and

(b) the declaration is verified, after such medical examination as may be necessary, by a medical panel established under subsection (4) of this section in its report to the President of the Senate and the Speaker of the House of Representatives.

(2) Where the medical panel certifies in the report that in its opinion the President or Vice-President is suffering from such infirmity of body or mind as renders him permanently incapable of discharging the functions of his office, a notice thereof signed by the President of the Senate and the Speaker of the House of Representatives shall be published in the Official Gazette of the Government of the Federation.

(3) The President or Vice-President shall cease to hold office as from the date of publication of the notice of the medical report pursuant to subsection (2) of this section.

(4) The medical panel to which this section relates shall be appointed by the President of the Senate, and shall comprise five medical practitioners in Nigeria:-

(a) one of whom shall be the personal physician of the holder of the office concerned; and

(b) four other medical practitioners who have, in the opinion of the President of the Senate, attained a high degree of eminence in the field of medicine relative to the nature of the examination to be conducted in accordance with the foregoing provisions.

(5) In this section, the reference to "Executive Council of the Federation" is a reference to the body of Ministers of the Government of the Federation, howsoever called, established by the President and charged with such responsibilities for the functions of government as the President may direct.'

By March 2010, SNG and 3G met in Dubai and after a review of the state of affairs in the country, agreed to hold talks with the Action Congress and Labour Party on the possibility of a political collaboration going forward. The meeting equally agreed to 'keep in view' the prospect of also discussing along the same lines with the just registered CPC at a time in the future.

'WHO ARE WE BUILDING THIS HOUSE FOR?'

Shortly before Pastor Bakare's return to Nigeria, El-Rufai and I had a follow-up meeting with him. The session reviewed our mutual activities and progress made thus far and very importantly, Bakare raised the issue of 'who are we building this house for?' insisting that as a group and as a nation, our best interests would be better satisfied if we had a candidate that we would ultimately be presenting to the nation as our very well-considered leadership option.

At this point, we briefed him of the internal discussions within the group which were concluded as far back as January 2009 in Maryland, to have either El-Rufai or Nuhu Ribadu run in the 2011 elections. His response was that he was personally okay with the candidacy of El-Rufai but took strong exception to Ribadu describing him as 'Obasanjo's attack dog.' We then prevailed on him to yet keep an open mind on the subject before shutting the door on Ribadu.

In line with the resolutions from our 'Dubai consensus' referred to above, we then proceeded on to an April 25th engagement where a 3G delegation - that included Mallam Nasir El-Rufai and I – met in Accra with an Action Congress team that was led by its National Publicity Secretary, Alhaji Lai Mohammed.

I recall that at the meeting, the Action Congress team was unequivocal in its emphasis that what it needed us to do in the alliance was to supply 'a presidential candidate of Northern extraction.' However, one of the things El-Rufai insisted upon was that if the 3G eventually decided in favour of taking up the offer, all the candidates to be presented to the nation must go through a properly conducted and transparent internal selection process.

It was after these series of meetings that El-Rufai and I decided to put an end to our self-exile status and subsequently returned to the country on May 1, 2010. It was indeed a very discreet undertaking as the security situation in the country then was still very shaky, with many within the 'Umaru Yar'Adua group,' still most incensed about the fact that our involvement with the opposition was contributing most significantly in undermining and counteracting their own opportunistic intentions of continuing to rule in Yar'Adua's name, no matter his state of health or incapacitation and in gross disregard of the express provisions that had been outlined in the 1999 Constitution. Subsequent developments were however to make their position grossly untenable even as the balance of power was to be decisively shifted.

Barely four days into our return, had word filtered in that Yar'Adua may have died. I called the security czar, General Aliyu Gusau, rtd.

"Ranka dede Sir, I heard a rumour." He responded before I could finish the sentence that it was true. "I am going to inform the Acting President now before it becomes publicly available," he added.

After seeing our yeoman's role in affirming and promoting his constitutional right to succeed his deceased boss, Goodluck Jonathan upon becoming substantive President, requested to work closer with the Pastor Bakare led group even though we were not too excited over the offer for several reasons that we shall come to later on. We along with other groups however gave him the suggestion that it was most urgent to reform the ruling People's Democratic Party, PDP, that we were still aligned with at this time, and thereafter go on to reform the country.

He gave his nod to the suggestion and a PDP Reform Committee whose membership included, among others, former Senate President, Ken Nnamani, El-Rufai and the former Speaker, Rtd. Honourable Aminu Masari were empanelled to work on the subject of reforming the party. The committee went on and did its work and handed in its findings and recommendations for ratification and implementation. Jonathan accepted it and took it before the Party's all-powerful National Executive Committee which was being dominated by the governors but they dismissed it and rather than defend the submissions, President Jonathan simply gave in and let matters be! He didn't even have the courage to explain why he had literally given in without a fight to the members of the committee that had worked tirelessly on the necessity of reforming the PDP.

In addition to failing on this score, we also knew Jonathan to be completely incompetent and liked his pint. The country was literally being run by the powerful Petroleum Minister, Diezani Alison-Madueke, with most of the other ministers bowing to her! You want to do battle in that kind of government? No, it won't work. El-Rufai, with the tacit support and agreement of our group, wisely stayed away.

Dissatisfied with the continuing poverty of leadership - and the parlous state of affairs in a country that we loved so dearly - we therefore knew that we had to look elsewhere for fresh directions. At this point, the 2011 elections were drawing quite close. We were in the second half of 2010 and under immense pressure to take a stand.

We decided to constitute a small team of concerned and like-minded leaders with a track record of performance to strategise on the way forward. A short list of twelve people which consisted of Dr. Ngozi Okonjo-Iweala, Governor Babatunde Fashola, Governor Danjuma Goje, Mallam Nasir El-Rufai, Oby Ezekwesili, Prof. Pat Utomi, Nuhu Ribadu, Fola Adeola, Donald Duke, Jimi Agbaje, Yinka Odumakin, Hon. Wale Osun and my humble self as the Secretary was constituted, with our non-partisan elder brother, Pastor Tunde Bakare as Convener.

We went to work immediately and had a couple of meetings in the convener's residence in Opebi, Lagos. From these, we adopted a couple of viable options for further consideration.

There was however to be a crack in our ranks going forward as the political tempo of the nation heightened. Nuhu Ribadu was the first to opt out even though he had mentioned at the inaugural meeting that he was in discussions with the leadership of ACN; which we understood to be a continuation of our previous meetings with them in Accra. Overall, this is a story for another day but the core substance was that, contrary to our group's position that we first undertake a very robust and most scientific analysis of the best political options open to the nation at this time before any talk of individual ambitions could be entertained, he unilaterally went behind us to accept to run as presidential candidate on the platform of the then Action Congress of Nigeria (ACN).

Another development at this time was that the leadership of the Labour Party had also intimated us that it was inclined towards reserving its presidential slot for El-Rufai. I went ahead and obliged them in principle on his behalf but El-Rufai declined. He insisted that he was clearly not considering running for office at this time, and that besides, we were yet to finish with our detailed analysis of the best political options open to the country. He also insisted on clearing his name by concluding the frivolous criminal charges against him before considering any public service.

Pastor Bakare and several others within the group nudged him to think through the issue some more but he was adamant. An additional reason was that he also did not think that the Labour Party was very seriously structured and indeed it was not a strong performer at the time. Moreover, he did not want to be seen as competing against Nuhu who at this period was set to pick up the ACN ticket. We saw reason with him and let the matter rest.

Going forward however, the resolution that emanated from several review sessions of our group under Pastor Bakare was a firm decision that we yet had to play a role in the unfolding political scenario. After forming SNG and galvanizing the nation to do what was right by the Constitution, the logical next step then was to resolve that our next task would be to participate most actively in the process of determining the individual that would become the next President of Nigeria.

Voting for Buhari

By that time, four candidates had emerged as possible contenders, namely Jonathan, Buhari, Ribadu and Ibrahim Shekarau. We met in October 2010, evaluated the four candidates, and the majority view was that the only person worth supporting under the circumstance possibly, was Buhari.

For El-Rufai, this conclusion came with a burden as a few weeks before then, while responding to a public media query, he had been quoted as having said that "I have great respect for President Babangida. I think he has done a lot for Nigeria. You won't take that from him. He has made his mistakes like every human being, but people like President Babangida and General Buhari should just disappear. They should give way to a new set of people with new ideas. Young people preferably." Asked to clarify his position, he had continued: "Gen. Babangida, Gen. Buhari, all of them should vacate the stage; they all brought the country to where it is today." That statement now came to haunt us.

El-Rufai admitted this much later on and also put the matter in renewed light. In 'The Man Buhari,' a paper he delivered at a conference organised by the Coalition for Change on March 12, 2015, he affirmed:

> 'I had held the view that Buhari should step down for a younger person to run for president but changed my mind based on reflection and pragmatic assessment of where Nigeria was heading. I therefore joined his party the CPC in order to do all I can to assist Buhari become the president of Nigeria.'

He then went on to describe Buhari as

> 'Nigeria's version of Deng Xiaoping and Nelson Mandela combined –the change agent that will put Nigeria on the path of peace, reconciliation, fairness and justice, with rapid and inclusive economic and social development. These Mandela and Deng in their seventies did for South Africa and China.'

The basis for our choice of Buhari now even as we had not met with him as a group to appraise him of this fact was quite simple. We had surmised that as at that time, there were three major problems facing the country. Firstly, Nigeria was about to fall apart on account of insecurity. Secondly, corruption was becoming endemic and thirdly on the economy, we were borrowing and borrowing and almost not saving anything from the bumper windfall of escalating crude oil prices. We saw him as the most disciplined and determined of all the gladiators that were in the race and thus resolved to reach out to him.

As things were developing, Nuhu Ribadu, who had been counting on getting the support of our group for his aspiration on the platform of the ACN, was not pleased. He openly blamed me; accused me of being the one who didn't allow people to support him and that I had instigated the 'analysis' that gave Buhari the edge and was indeed the brain behind it. But he was off the mark. We had carried out a most objective analysis and seen that all critical indicators had placed Buhari above him and the rest of the pack. We were on a mission and had no choice but to accept the outcome of our unbiased, merit-based analysis. We decided to yet go on with our outreach to Buhari.

Pastor Bakare led us to a landmark meeting with Buhari in Kaduna in November 2010 and we briefed him on our group and why we had come. We informed him that we had carefully and most dispassionately analysed the political situation of the country and came to the conclusion that we should work with him in his bid to be President. He was very pleased. It was just a few of us – Pastor Tunde Bakare, Jimi Agbaje, Yinka Odumakin and I – at this meeting with him, not the entire group.

In his response, Buhari thanked us for accepting to support him but also wondered why we were not as a group going with Ribadu and we then explained to him that Ribadu had betrayed our mutual position on how we were to participate in the unfolding political process and was therefore working on his own in this respect.

CHAPTER FOUR

The 2011 Elections

We were however to meet a very messy situation when we joined The Buhari Organisation (TBO). In essence, TBO was being run by two people: Buba Galadima and Dr. Sule Hamma.

They and a few others were the ones who had formed the Congress for Progressive Change (CPC), in December 2009, before the election of the amiable Prince Tony Momoh as party chairman. They were also chiefly the ones that had been milking the Buhari train since 2002 when he first came out to run for the office of President of the Federal Republic of Nigeria.

Critically, they had built a wall around Buhari that was impenetrable. It was indeed an impossible environment to make real progress in. All the plans the man agreed to with us in the course of our initial engagement could not be pushed through as things stood then. We felt helpless.

I will give some examples.

In one instance, they said they already had a manifesto that had been approved by Buhari for the forthcoming elections. But their manifesto document was very badly written and spanned only about twenty pages. In the ensuing debate, El-Rufai saved the day by convincing them that their approved manifesto was neither a Quran nor a Bible which could not be altered; and more so, that the same Buhari had approved an outline of a manifesto that was tabled by Pastor Bakare in our inaugural meeting. Thus, we eventually worked on modifying the CNP/SNG model manifesto as a replacement document that was ultimately adopted as the CPC Presidential Campaign Manifesto for the 2011 elections.

A second instance was when we wanted to raise money for the campaign effort. They had boasted that they had all of that already covered. However, by February 2011, it became obvious that additional funds were required. They had been hoping for contributions from all kinds of places but unfortunately these were not forthcoming and time was running out!

These incidents were happening with just a few weeks to the 2011 polls. We were frustrated and couldn't do much without some dramatic adjustment of the situation. So, we knew that Buhari's chances were at this point not at the peak.

But there was still something going for Buhari. No matter how much you do to defeat him, he had this hard core of committed supporters that would always give him millions of votes any time, any day. I am talking of the youth and the *talakawa*. Consistently in 2003, 2007 and also in 2011, they always delivered. So, we remained persuaded in the fact that all that was required was to broaden the base by getting the elites to buy in and also expand our candidate's level of cross-regional acceptance.

Back to our troubles within the TBO, it was indeed a very tough run but we soon found a way around it. Anytime we ran into yet another stumbling block, Pastor Bakare would go back to Buhari and tell him: "General, do you want to be President or not? You have failed twice, this is the third time. Are you going to give us a chance or should we just give up?" He would agree with us whenever we called him to order in this manner and we would then continue working with the others on how best to get things done.

President Buhari is a 'hands-off' leader. Once he trusts you and gives you the job to do, he leaves you to go and get it done. When you go back to him on the same issue, he just does not want to listen." Go and do your job," he would charge. And our work was definitely cut out for us.

Given the odds we were faced with, we knew that we needed to cut through the tape to get the desired results. After further analysis, we now came out with several short-cut options, including undertaking discussions with the ACN high command with a view to having a merger or alliance as a way of garnering more electoral votes in the fast-approaching elections. We understood that TBO had negotiated an alliance with ACN previously in 2007 but it was inconclusive so it made sense to revisit the subject.

BUHARI REACHES OUT TO BAKARE

When it became obvious to Buhari in January 2011 that there was a major problem with TBO, he single-mindedly came up with a masterstroke; he requested Pastor Bakare to be his running mate. Clearly, he didn't want to lose our group, even as he was equally conscious of the need to continue to broaden his cross-regional appeal. These in my view were the most logical reasons behind his offer for Pastor Bakare to run alongside him.

The offer came as a most unexpected bombshell to Bakare and at first, he would not take it. I was one of the first people he called when Buhari made the offer to him and when I saw where he was going, I would not give him an inch.

> 'Egbon sir, you have taught us that we have to get involved to change our country for the better. Now the opportunity has come for you to walk the talk and there is no way we are going to let you off. Congratulations, Sir! And please talk to Mallam sir, and we shall compare notes thereafter.'

I was aware that he made several other 'protest' calls to family members, friends and associates and 'leaders of thought' all across the country but at the end of the day, the consensus was for him to accept the offer.

Bakare made one final attempt to get off the ticket. Taking El-Rufai and I along, he appealed to Buhari himself, offering to nominate some other persons in his stead. About this time also, Obasanjo had sent a message to Buhari through El-Rufai to consider running with Ngozi Okonjo-Iweala as his running mate in exchange for his (Obasanjo's) financial and political support. Buhari listened to us and then responded:

> 'Pastor, I thought very long and hard before I made you the offer. Your name came from my heart and so I knew that I did not need to consult many people over it. Are you taking it?

'Bakare had no other option at this point.

When Bakare finally accepted the offer to stand as the vice-presidential candidate of the Congress of Progressive Change, CPC in that election, Buhari was however not done. He said: "Pastor, you will run the campaign so that you guys will have no more complaints." And just like that, he signed off the campaign to us, with Bakare now also serving as Chairman of the Presidential Campaign Council (PCC)!

But it was really late in the day as this was already the end of January, 2011 and the elections were due to be held in literally a matter of weeks!

The odds notwithstanding, we pushed on all fours to get the job done. We started getting more and more contributors in, but we had less than two months to campaign as the election was in March 2011. Indeed, we had only about thirty days to prosecute this massive endeavour!

It was a gruelling run. We needed an aircraft, we were travelling a lot by road on account of the meagre resources we could mobilise at this time. We travelled the roads from Kaduna to Minna to Abuja to Nassarawa. And there was indeed very little money. So, we would finish a tour with Buhari in the North and then race over to join Pastor Bakare in the South West.

We travelled the roads from Lagos to Ibadan to Oshogbo and so on, and then we would meet in Ilorin or in Kogi. So, Buhari would be coming from the North to the South and we would be coming from the South up North and we would meet in the middle. Likewise, as our teams made trips from the East to the West, we would meet in Benin.

It was really a most enervating race and so the fact that the ticket came out second at the end of the contest, with over twelve million votes was indeed a miracle. There was really no money and no solid organisation in the most efficient sense of the word and it is under these circumstances that we would then situate Buhari's frustrations at the end of the exercise itself when he publicly broke down on the final day of the campaign and said he would never run for office again and that he had tried his best. That was it!

At the close of voting, the officially declared results indicated that Buhari had scored 12,214,853 votes, to come second behind President Goodluck Jonathan of the

PDP, who reportedly polled 22,495,187 votes and was therefore declared the winner.

While this result clearly did not give Buhari victory at the polls, it was however to confirm the fact that it was indeed a wise decision for Buhari to have left the ANPP and gone on to found the CPC by December 2009. Even with the relative novelty of the party and its quite apparent financial and organisational constraints, candidate Muhammadu Buhari had scored twice the number of votes he had recorded in the 2007 polls when he had contested on the platform of the supposedly more entrenched ANPP!

However, beyond the mere facts of persisting organisational inadequacies, limited funding and lateness in kicking off the campaign proper, there were also several other critical obstacles which we encountered during prosecuting the campaign that were insurmountable.

For example, the former Governor of Cross River State, Donald Duke, made the point that election rigging was indeed a widespread and regular practice in many of the elections that had been conducted in the country. This was also echoed by Nasir El-Rufai in his book *The Accidental Public Servant*, where he outlined the fact that military and paramilitary intimidation, if not 'occupation', had also been a regular feature of the voting context in the country for some time. So, the election was really neither free nor fair!

Indeed, we knew that there was some rigging in the 2011 polls and we got the data about what had taken place. We had set up an election monitoring platform which showed the states where the PDP rigged big time.

The incidence of rigging was particularly widespread in the South-East and South-South where agents of the

PDP just took out most of the polling infrastructure and declared any number of votes that suited their fancy. It was that brazen. There was no election. It was just thumb-printing and stamping and we had evidence of this. Even the *talakawa* without any empirical evidence were convinced that they had been robbed; hence the results were met with spontaneous but widespread post-election violence on a gigantic scale in several northern states. Lives were lost, properties destroyed and the violence continued unabated for days. It was such that many concerned Nigerians and indeed, the international community had to appeal to Buhari for him to make a public appeal to the enraged masses to sheathe their swords.

AN ALLIANCE THAT WOULD NOT FLY!

Overall however, it was quite unfortunate that we couldn't carry any states in the South. We didn't have the money to mount a strong operation on this turf and we also didn't have the on-ground political muscle relative to our competitors. Under the circumstances, we were then compelled to rely very heavily on the alliance talks we had been having with the ACN, which was then the dominant party in the South-West.

Under the draft terms of the deal, Muhammadu Buhari was to run as the sole candidate of the alliance while both parties would formally merge no later than six months after securing victory at the polls.

This arrangement however fell through when the ACN abandoned us in favour of a covert deal with the PDP even when it was putting up a public face of also contesting the polls in its own right. It was such a cold-blooded move but once Tinubu signed off on it, the road was wide open for us to lose in all ACN-held states (Lagos, Ogun, Osun, Oyo, Ekiti and Edo), such that CPC did not even reach the threshold of 25 percent in any of the southern states including Lagos – Pastor Bakare's base.

When the results of the 2011 elections were declared, there were other interesting revelations also. You recall that Nuhu Ribadu had left us and gone on to run on the platform of the Action Congress of Nigeria, ACN. Well, he secured some 1.7million votes in all in that election. In addition to the fact that he lost to Buhari in Ribadu's own ward, his home state of Adamawa, and indeed all of the North, he was also to be colossally short-changed in most of the South-West where his adopted party had near-absolute control!

Indeed, the only state Ribadu carried, countrywide, was Osun whose Governor, Ogbeni Rauf Aregbesola had temporarily broken ranks with the core of the ACN leadership, insisting that he had a localised interest in ensuring that the ACN did not lose in any elections conducted in that state within that season, irrespective of all of the other deals and intrigues that were being played out at the national level. Aregbesola had a subsisting challenge against his position in the courts and the concern was that any electoral outcome that gave victory to the rival PDP would invariably be pleaded as supporting evidence that should be considered in upturning his election. Critically on account of Aregbesola's brinksmanship therefore, Ribadu was able to secure 58.46 percent of all the votes that were recorded in the presidential contest in Osun state.

Ribadu was not the only casualty. Buhari too also suffered as our discussion with the ACN high command with a view to having a merger or alliance was scuttled at the last minute on the impracticable ground that Pastor Bakare should sign a post-dated letter of resignation from office in the event that the ticket succeeded so that ACN leader, Bola Tinubu would then step in as Vice President or appoint a replacement. Several of us objected to this and we left it for our leader to rule. True to type, Buhari would not agree to this and ruled in favour of leaving the ticket unchanged. But for good measure, he offered the ACN leadership the latitude to pick most generously from the wide array of cabinet positions that would be filled upon our joint victory. When this conclusion was communicated back to the ACN leadership, they insisted on VP or nothing and therefore had their ready excuse for calling off the alliance.

Equally underscoring the fact that their candidate, Ribadu, was indeed only a pawn in their convoluted game of cards, they likewise ignored him with little if any support on funding. We even learnt that his flamboyant and entrepreneurial running mate – Fola Adeola, was chosen partly on account of his ability to contribute funds.

Now, the elections had come and gone and we were all genuinely tired. But we knew our job was not done. After a brief period of rest, Bakare, El-Rufai and I took time out to review the events we had just come through and to decide on the best options going forward. Fortuitously, we came to the same conclusion; that those twelve million plus hard-core votes must be preserved, consolidated and built upon.

CHAPTER FIVE

Reversing A Decision

Muhammadu Buhari's announcement that he would no longer be putting himself up to contest for the office of President of the Nigerian Federation any longer at the closing run of the 2011 campaign was in our view not a thoroughly well considered position. But we fully understood the rationale and his anguish.

While it was clear that the shenanigans of the political space had been so dispiriting to the point that he, as our flag-bearer and one who had contested for office three times now, could in a sense be considered to be really tired and exhausted at this point, nevertheless, some of us were of the view that he still had a lot to give to the nation.

Also, despite the failed attempts and the incontrovertible determination of the entrenched political elite to deny him victory repeatedly, he, more than any other person was the 'leader our people could trust' and as such we resolved that everything should be done to get him to reverse this decision.

This was because we knew that if the decision stood, Nigeria would in the process also be losing its best chance to advance the larger interests of the nation in the arena of political competition. Given his performance in the previous elections where he had stood for office – despite all the odds against him – we were persuaded that all that was required for him to win was to close two critical gaps. Firstly, to increase the tally of his popular votes by about 3-4 million and secondly, to secure 25 percent of all votes cast in some five to six other states in the country.

We therefore remained determined to work on these as well as getting him to reverse his decision. But first, the election results had to be legally challenged. This is because Buhari was convinced (as with his two previous outings) that the massive incidence of manipulation and rigging that had attended the process had to be documented and filed in court for posterity to judge, even if the election results could not be reversed.

The CPC Renewal Committee

Returning from our retreat in May/June 2011, we went to Buhari and told him: "You are still the future of Nigeria. The only way we can beat the PDP is to build a formidable and all-inclusive party around you."

It was really a very simple and straightforward situation. We saw the crowds at the rallies, we saw the young guys, the *talakawa*, who would do literally anything for Buhari. We were not told, we had seen and engaged with these youth. They wouldn't even allow his vehicle to drive past. From Kano, Zamfara, all the way to Maiduguri and Bauchi, in every northern city we went to, the crowds were impossible. We couldn't just walk away from them now.

Buhari was himself to confirm this advocacy and pressure that we put on him to rescind his decision not to run again. This was in the course of the campaigns and after he had become the candidate of the All Progressives Congress. Addressing a crowd of our supporters at the formal flag-off of the campaign to elect El-Rufai as governor of Kaduna State, he admitted that indeed El-Rufai was one of the principal persuaders that had weighed in to get him to consider running again in the 2015 polls.

The CPC Chairman at this time was Prince Tony Momoh. He had a lot of confidence in us and formed a 'renewal group' of the party and made El-Rufai the Chairman and I was a member and coordinator of one of the sub-committees. As we saw it, our mandate was two-fold; we were to help revive and energise the CPC as a platform and then strategise on what to do to enhance its fortunes going forward, and notably through collaborating with other political parties.

At this time, we had gone through the now regular post-election litigation processes, all the way to the Supreme Court and lost. Ahead of this scenario, Buhari had advised Pastor Bakare as the chair of the Presidential Campaign Council to save some of the funds raised for the campaign in anticipation of the inevitable litigation. Hence, the little money we had left after the elections, some ₦45 million or so, was used to pay lawyers for the legal challenge on the conduct of the polls.

It was against this backdrop, that late in 2011, the CPC Renewal Committee was formed and we were formally given six terms of reference. They bordered on what to do to revive the party immediately as well as prepare for the future. The specific issues included how to raise money for the party, updating the membership register, developing new foundational documents and deciding on the critical question of cooperation with other opposition political expressions in the country through either the forging of political alliances or an outright merger.

Looking through the reference items, I came to an immediate conclusion which I proceeded to discuss with

El-Rufai. I said: "Mallam, we could go on to set up six sub-committees to work on these terms of reference, but as far as I am concerned, we have only one that is important, the rest are really inconsequential."

He said: "Jimi, you have always known the answer, but please don't just go there yet; let's work on all six." So we went on with the processes. We raised some money and the work of the renewal committee took off. We were meeting in the 3G office in Wuse 2 in Abuja and had called a major sponsor who believed in us and gave us some money.

I will tell a story to illustrate how we could raise some more money for the work of the renewal committee. Indeed, evidence of the fact that the electioneering process had been most tiring was that after we lost in 2011, Buhari was down and needed to go abroad for medical check-up and rest but funds were scarce.

We raised the subject with his dependable and loyal Personal Assistant, Mallam Sarki Abba, as to what could be done to get Buhari to travel abroad for much needed rest and medical check-up.

We had ourselves gone for our own post-election vacation and did not need any real persuasion to pick up the gauntlet. So, in line with Sarki's advice, we went to our leader and said to him: "Sir, you look tired and exhausted; you need to take a break and go for medical check-up and rest." His response was spontaneous: "We cannot afford it now as we need to devote the little money that is left to the election petition." We concurred but with a rider that we would try our best to raise additional funds, given that health is wealth. "Sir, but how much would be required for you to go?"

He didn't want to agree that we should fund the trip but Sarki had told us: 'About $25,000 will be required to take him and two assistants to the UK for his medicals and rest for a couple of weeks.' So, I volunteered: "I could raise the money sir, I will give you the money, and it's not a problem." But he said: "Jimi, on one condition: the luxury coach that was given to me to use for the campaign has not really been used. Sell it; take back the money you are giving me now and the balance should go to the party and the renewal committee for you guys to do a good job."

I couldn't refuse because if I did he would not take the money. Therefore, I took the coach whose book value, brand new, was about $125,000. Someone offered to buy it for $80,000. So, I gave him $25,000 and put the rest of the money as he had instructed in the work of the renewal committee.

Three or four months into 2012, we had formed sub-committees for each of the terms of reference and I remember I was both in the merger/alliance and finance committees.

However, whenever I discussed our work with El-Rufai, I would say to him: "This membership, finance, registration and other things we are doing are good but the big task really is in merger and alliance. We can't do CPC only, as CPC today cannot win the elections by itself. We need at least one other party, either ACN or APGA to make our dream come true."

I broke it further down: 'Where are our strengths? I am a Yoruba man and we have huge contacts in the South-West, the Igbos we really do not have a solid toehold in there at the moment, so let's go with ACN.'

His response: "Jimi you are right, but let's deal with membership registration first, let's raise some money and then we need to prove our strength at the time of merger." But I said: "If you do membership registration and later merge, it's useless, we need to do merger before the registration. As regards the issue of strength, our strength is already known. What is our strength? Buhari's 12 million votes. ACN's candidate got less than 2 million voters. Jonathan won the election by rigging, and at that, in truth, he got just about 16 million votes, so we just need 4 million votes. In fact, if we take 3million votes out of Jonathan's so-called 16 million votes, he's down to 13 million votes. And when you give us the 3 million votes a merger could fetch, we would be up to 15 million votes! Every other committee doesn't make sense at this point, I insisted. All we need to do first is a merger to get the 3 million votes. It is the way to go."

Even as I argued along these lines, I was well aware that there were indeed deeper issues. At this time, there was clearly no love-lost between ACN leader, Bola Tinubu, our group and the CPC because he had handed us the wrong end of the stick previously. But in the larger interest of the nation, we had to work with him.

I recall El-Rufai's reaction to this line of reasoning: "I agree with you, we can go to dinner even with the devil, we just need to ensure that we are going with the right spoon." And so we finished our work and turned over our reports to our leaders.

But we knew that it was not really going to be an easy sell. Indeed, from the time we decided that we were going to have the merger, and to work with Tinubu and the ACN, we were met with stiff resistance. A lot of initial opposition came from people who felt that there was no way we could mix the Buhari brand of no-nonsense discipline and zero tolerance for corruption with Tinubu's image and brand. They felt that it was a sign of desperation on our part. Bakare, El-Rufai and I had to meet to thoroughly re-examine the way forward.

When we met to brainstorm on the matter, fortunately for me I had done some extensive research on the subject and penned a paper for the purpose. I called it *'Puritanism versus Pragmatism.'*

What it boils down to is that in a democracy, the only way leaders emerge is by making compromises, by reaching out to the people on the other side of the aisle with compromises such that if you set out to achieve ten things, by the time you reach out to the people on the other side, those ten things may go down to six or seven because you have to take three or four of their priorities to add to your own six or seven to get a new list of ten.

In the end, only six or seven items from the original plan would have been achieved. Whereas if you say you want to be puritanical, you will never get the vote of those who you consider not to be pure; which means that out of the ten things you set out to achieve, you would do zero. But if you compromise with them, you will get six or seven out of ten. So, you are actually serving the society better by being pragmatic rather than being puritanical. I proved in my approach that puritanism is for religion, but in politics, you have to be pragmatic. After all, we were not electing a Chief Imam or the Pope!

I think that is what won the day. For example, both El-Rufai and I are liberal as Muslims such that if a friend of ours is getting married in church, we will go. Even Pastor Bakare as our leader, we used to join him in church. Most times when I am in Lagos on Sundays, I go to him, worship with him and have lunch before I return to Abuja or Kaduna. Both El-Rufai and I have done that several times and it is not an issue for us.

So, one day, after Bakare was convinced (a few members of his church felt that he couldn't possibly support the ticket if we were reaching out to Tinubu to do a merger). He gave me his platform to speak on this subject of puritanism versus pragmatism and when I had finished, they gave me a standing ovation. They were convinced. They had initially been hostile to us as we were seen to be working with Tinubu whom they were not very fond of, but at the end of the day they were largely won over.

I said: "look, Buhari had tried puritanism by not reaching out to people he could not work with and failed thrice before." I asked if they wanted him to go down as not being able to make the mark and gave a good example of what had happened with Chief Obafemi Awolowo. Awolowo was being puritanical in his approach without being pragmatic. He failed to reach out to the North, and he even ran a South-South ticket at some point because he wanted to be puritanical, but what happened? All his beautiful ideas – as Awolowo was gifted – came to zero because he didn't get the chance to implement them at the federal level. The best he did was when he was finance minister and vice-chair of the Federal Executive Council during General Gowon's regime.

So, I asked if they wanted Buhari to end up like that, because that could very well happen. Buhari could remain puritanical and say he was not going to dilute his brand but that would not get him elected. I didn't want what happened to Chief Awolowo to happen to Buhari. Both had sizable followers that were really committed to them. Awolowo's supporters in the South-West were committed; please recall "Operation wetie," they would've done anything to support him. It was the same way with Buhari in the North, and even on a larger scale at that. The followers who are practically in worship of Buhari were two times, if not three times the number of those who supported Awolowo during his days and for them he could do no wrong. So, I was therefore happy that the concept of pragmatism over puritanism in the arena of politics prevailed.

CHAPTER SIX

Science As Winner: 2014 Voters Register And The PVC

One of the conclusions that we had reached in the course of our entry into The Buhari Organisation (TBO) and which we clearly saw was a major factor in the group's failings up to that point, was the fact that they were over-milking the principal asset in the kitty – the Buhari persona – at the expense of other success factors that needed to be added in a more composite mix that would ultimately see to the actual realisation of our desired goal.

Earlier for example, we had talked about the fire brigade action we had been forced to embark upon at the time of our entry into the CPC mainstream when we found out that both the formal manifesto document as well as the structures for fund-raising were patently inadequate. The problems got to a peak in the mobilisation for the 2011 elections when we raced against time to get the best possible results that we could secure.

But even these were only a tip of the iceberg and it is our reasoning that it was our ability to identify these and other lapses and take critical action on them that encouraged Buhari to pick Pastor Bakare as his running mate, hand over the running of the 2011 campaign effort to him and was a core factor in our subsequently being nominated as anchor players in the CPC Renewal Committee.

Building on these, we then worked on other areas of TBO and CPC that required upgrading and put our findings in the consequent reports to the party which were thankfully adopted and endorsed for consequent implementation, despite the very determined move by the 'old guard' within the party to persuade the leadership to do otherwise.

Underscoring many of the conclusions in the renewal committee's report was the need to properly align our work with the under-stated reality that indeed electioneering was, all things considered, a science, and as such the deployment of scientific methods would help in making the critical difference that we so desired.

Indeed, our voting for a scientific approach in the resolution of the political challenges of Nigeria did not begin here, as we had already reported that it was the outcome of a rigorous, merit-based analysis that had in the first place set us on the path of working with Buhari, TBO and the CPC. I also recall that for the 2011 elections, we had also set up an Election Reporting Platform for the purpose of collating and monitoring feedback from the polling unit agents and supervisors in the field. But then there were larger issues of logistics and personnel that did not help its full deployment and we were now more than ever most determined to do even better in the area of scientific exploration.

The first major factor in this regard for us then was the question of ensuring a full-proof and credible Voters Register.

According to the provisional schedule of activities building up to the 2015 elections, a review of the voters' register had already been scheduled to hold in 2014. As every political observer knows, without being registered in time to vote, no citizen can lawfully participate in the process of choosing leaders during elections.

Equally, for an opposition movement that had over time continued to complain on issues of election rigging and over-voting and which wanted to also make critical inroads into certain other states where it had not done well over time, we needed to have a better handle on questions like voter demographics, spread, composition, etc.

So, we had to take monitoring the voters' registration exercise most seriously. We had to raise money to pay our army of volunteers, train agents to properly observe it, get canvassers to mobilise potential supporters to come out en masse to be captured properly during the exercise, as well as get them to return to pick up and properly secure the resultant voters' cards. It was a lot of work going forward and truth be told, this is where many an election had been won and lost in our composite political history.

Recognising the significance of this exercise, we therefore went on in the Renewal Committee to establish a framework for ensuring that when the time came, we would not be found wanting.

The next major issue that we addressed as a Committee in respect of anti-rigging was that of the Permanent Voters Card (PVC). At this time, word was already out that, upon the completion of the voters registration exercise, all eligible voters so captured would subsequently be given biometric-enhanced and relatively more secure Permanent Voters Cards.

Seeing the potential merit in the scheme for also ensuring reduced instances of malpractices, we equally bought into it as a committee and made fitting recommendations to our leaders to facilitate the success of the exercise from our point of view. These included getting agents and observers to monitor the process as well as also mobilising our people to come out en masse to pick up and properly file away their PVCs.

It is also to be underscored that the overall merger effort was as well the product of very rigorous scientific analysis. This is because, for us at that moment and with Buhari having contested fruitlessly for three consecutive times, we literally had come to properly internalise and digest the good old maxim that: "those who fail to learn from history are condemned to repeat it," and that: "someone who does the same thing the same way and expects a different result is the definition of insanity." We knew that the current effort would not work if we did the same things in the same ways as we had done it in 2011.

Indeed, our 2015 approach was heavily scientific and was all about watching the numbers. We knew that we had to get at least three million votes from outside the North-West, North-Central and North-East for us to have any chance whatsoever of Buhari emerging as President. We had to sit down and ask where the three million votes would come from: South-West, South-East or South-South? And it was from here that we zeroed in on the South-West.

We knew that apart from engaging our erstwhile leaders, we had to engage the leaders of the South-West and their governors. Very early on, we went out of our way to get Buhari to sit one-on-one with South-West governors, especially those of the former

ACN-controlled states, even when the APC merger plans had not been fully concluded. We will return to this point and notably, it's most beneficial impact, when discussing the presidential primaries in a subsequent chapter.

However, because we were very aware that voter demographics is a very important element, we had some numbers which we picked up from the analysis we did and used for this purpose. We actually did a simulation because there are two hurdles you must cross before you can become a Nigerian president. First is the number of votes, which in our case required that we bring in some additional three million votes. Then you have the requirement of securing twenty-five percent of the vote in twenty-four states. That was also quite important because one of the major problems Buhari had in previous elections was that he never had the twenty-five percent of votes in twenty-four states; the spread was simply not there for him and it was a challenge that had to be addressed.

He had always been limited to the North, which is at best nineteen states. Five more states had to come on board to give him at least twenty-five percent of their votes each. So, we did all the analysis, firstly colour-coordinating our assumptions. We painted blue for states we were sure we would win outright, yellow if winning was doable, green if we thought we could get twenty-five percent, and red if we felt we had no chance. This was to help us in taking decisions on where to focus resources and to commit to really campaigning vigorously to see if we could get at least twenty-five percent from, most notably, our target Southern states. That's what we did the moment the APC was formed before we went on to talk about creating several committees for the party as the nucleus for achieving critical milestones that were crucial.

For instance, there was a finance committee because the party had to raise money. Money is the war chest in elections and we were facing an incumbent, in the Federal Government and indeed a situation where literally, the incumbent's money supply was just limitless. Without money, we would not have stood a chance. We knew that where they would spend a billion naira, we would need to spend a hundred million naira. People were willing to vote for us but we had to spend that hundred million to match their billions. That was the job of the finance committee.

Building on this background of deep planning and the application of ideas, several more scientific input were introduced into the process later on, but these would also be outlined in subsequent chapters.

Suffice it however for us to state at this point that, for a nation of Nigeria's size, role and endowment, an even more ingrained scientific and structured commitment to leadership selection and grooming really has to be in place. In countries like Singapore and China, this is a core element in their success story and El-Rufai underscores this point most aptly in the *Accidental Public Servant*:

> It is my considered opinion that we have not developed any process of identifying, training and rewarding leadership, of putting people who are potential leaders through a crucible to determine their preparedness and worth. Instead, people just emerge out of nowhere. Sometimes we get lucky, like with Ismaila Usman, who was not on anyone's shortlist but turned out to be a fantastic finance minister. But the process from which he emerged at the point he did was mostly pure accident. Nigeria does not have the Oxford, Cambridge and LSE where the bulk of the British leadership comes

from, or a Harvard, Princeton and Yale, where a large percentage of American presidents acquired education, and were subjected to some quality control and training. This is why every Nigerian above 30 years of age believes he or she can run for governor, senator or president. The final nail in the coffin of any meritocracy or track record of governance in Nigeria as basis for leadership selection were driven in when plain-looking Umaru Yar'Adua and Goodluck Jonathan emerged as president and vice president literally out of nowhere other than being governors sympathetic to the 'Third Term' project and therefore hand-picked by Obasanjo as payback. The subsequent electoral imposition of Goodluck Jonathan as president in 2011 via military occupation and rigging has been unhelpful in raising leadership quality. Jonathan went into a presidential contest without a campaign manifesto, boasting of no experience, merit and any track record of previous performance other than wearing no shoes to school and his "good luck"! I believe that we need to work on unwinding such scripts as the routes to leadership attainment in our country.

Indeed, 'science is discovery.'

Chapter Seven

Enter The APC

Now to the big elephant in the room: the formation of the All Peoples Congress, APC.

After getting the consent of our leaders to activate exploratory discussions on the merger part of the reports of the CPC Renewal Committee, we booked an appointment to see ACN leader, Asiwaju Bola Ahmed Tinubu.

I remember very vividly the atmosphere at the first meeting that we had about our two parties attempting to work together once again. It was in Asiwaju's residence in Ikoyi, Lagos. The subject did not come as a surprise to him, given the recent botched efforts in 2011.

Anyway, El-Rufai who led our team, opened the discussions with him by drawing his attention to the formation of the CPC Renewal Committee along with the mandate for us to negotiate an alliance or preferably a merger with like-minded political parties. He emphasised that unless the opposition parties unite, we stand little or no chance of defeating the behemoth known as the PDP. It is imperative that we learn our lessons from the failure to conclude an alliance ahead of the 2011 elections and start early this time, if only to avoid last minute rush.

By that time, fortunately for us in a sense, Jonathan had also literally stabbed Asiwaju in the back. In his capacity as President, he had surreptitiously encouraged the filing of a case against Tinubu at the Code of Conduct Tribunal. So Tinubu was mad. Against his wish and the tugging of his ego, he had to go and settle issues with Jonathan and beg him vigorously, even while undertaking to be of good behaviour.

At this time also, Tinubu had equally seen the limitations of being a 'smaller player on the larger Nigerian political chessboard' and was now in a somewhat better position to do a deal with us, all the way to the top.

It made sense to him for ACN and CPC to engage in formal discussions. It was also good that we were ready to meet him here and there. We had also strategised on carrying some elder statesmen in the South-West along early enough, if only as a fall-back position. So, we went to brief Kabiyesi, the Awujale of Ijebu Land. We told him:

> The North is more or less secured, we just need the South-West. So, we need your help as a non-partisan royal father to help ensure fair play on both sides.

After this preliminary meeting with Tinubu, we returned to brief our leaders on the progress being made and it was here that we also had to continue to confront the opposition from within the CPC, that is, the legendary TBO that was led by Sule Hamma and Buba Galadima. They argued that any collaboration with the ACN should be on the basis of the traditional alliance model that largely allowed the cooperating partners to yet remain as separate and distinct parties in themselves.

But we had gone over the nuts and bolts of both options at the Renewal Committee and were therefore most prepared to take on the subject, and headlong too!

We insisted that what would deliver the expected results for us at this point was an outright merger and that indeed that was the only thing that could be guaranteed to work under the circumstances and given our history thus far. It also tallied with our knowledge of the historical facts about other similar situations in the nation's political history. "Alliance is a boyfriend and girlfriend scenario," we argued. "There are no real strings attached while merger is more definitive, like a marriage. Within a merger, we will have one party, one family and not two distinct entities."

When we got to the meeting of the Board of Trustees (BOT) of the CPC convened to decide between the options of alliance or merger, initially, the majority of members present wanted an alliance. But Pastor Bakare, notably would not budge. Between him and several others, it was a most heated debate.

On our part, El-Rufai had written one of his brilliant position papers on the subject for Buhari ahead of the meeting, who in turn had picked out the salient statement in the submission: "Given our previous experience and the state we are in today, it is either merger or political hopelessness." Buhari emphasised that position and at the end of the debate, the CPC Board voted overwhelmingly in favour of a merger.

With this victory behind us, we now went on to the ACN to get them to equally adopt the merger option and with the "God factor" on our side, the ACN Board also followed suit.

All this while, the understanding was that it was going to be a merger between the ACN and CPC. However, the moment we overcame the alliance hurdle, we were to be confronted with a new challenge. Unknown to us, the Tinubu-led ACN had entered into discussions with the All Nigeria Peoples Party, ANPP and was now insistent on ANPP coming aboard the new party as a third merging partner.

Given Buhari's history of having been disappointed by the ANPP - the reason why he had walked out to go and set up the CPC platform in 2010 – it was clear that this move was indeed a potential spoiler for the entire merger talks. And there was another concern. By bringing ANPP along, the ACN leadership very likely wanted to use them to strengthen their own hand in the resultant negotiations that were to follow given the very clear fact that CPC was bringing in, and indeed commanded, far more numerical electoral votes at the presidential election level, and as such would have a greater say on that subject.

On the ACN side however was the fact that the party had more governors under its control at the time of discussion; a total of six compared to CPC's lone star in Nasarawa.

Most notably, the role played by the Nasarawa Governor, Tanko Al-Makura, in the overall process is not to be understated. Though he flew the sole governorship flag of the CPC at this time, his loyalty and commitment was indeed most exemplary.

Tanko Al-Makura is a good man. There was no amount of pressure that PDP did not put on him to switch camp after the 2011 elections, including moves made by former President Obasanjo, but he refused. The man was so supportive and was one of those who considerably helped Buhari as well as the party all through the merger period. And within the context of the cloak-and-dagger-politics played by the PDP, he also had to continually look over his shoulder given the well-oiled attempt to impeach him at a point in time.

For the CPC as a party in the merging process, we equally knew real quite well to continue to look over our shoulders daily as, in-house saboteurs (if not outright enemies) of the merger ideal continued to throw spanners of all sorts into the works. If not one thing today, it would be another one tomorrow. While some of these as was to be expected came from the rival PDP, particularly more distressing were all kinds of shenanigans being played by some of our "leaders."

What happened as we were trying to reach the final agreements with regards to key office holders for the party was indicative of the scheming and games being played by some of the merging partners. In the Buhari camp, the CPC went into the discussions with nothing but an open mind. The style of our leader and virtually all of us is to be forthright and not play games and this was our overriding attitude and mandate.

But I can confirm that some of the other parties we had to deal with had a different agenda. At every point in time, they looked out for and capitalised on every opportunity they could find to undercut our positions in the merger.

For instance, our major partner in the merger was supposed to have been the ACN, and in spite of the fact that we were taking precautions to ensure that the ACN leadership would not play spoiler games as they had done in 2011, the antics continued.

I had already mentioned the issue of their bringing in the ANPP into the merger which had not been part of the agreement. In fact, Buhari was at first unhappy with it. Given the way he left the ANPP to form CPC, it was clearly a direct slap on his face that this was so surreptitiously thrown at him without any notice and the benefit of his input. However, we kept encouraging him to continue to put Nigeria first, if that's what will allow us to accomplish the desired goal. And he did.

Then came another point of incipient frustration: the entry of APGA. Like that of the ANPP, this was also flung at us and overall, we had to adopt the same approach we had used with the ANPP scenario. On the one hand, we were delighted that our brethren from the South-East were coming on board as a group. However, it was also a source of concern because we were afraid it might result in a damaging litigation due to the fact that if you say that APGA is part of the merging group, and yet those who have the party's registration papers are not joining us, it may be a challenge as the public may now cast the entire merger project as not being a credible exercise. And since we were ultimately building our entire brand on credibility and integrity, it was a considerable point of departure. Therefore, our conclusion then was to not recognise the APGA entrants as being synonymous with the entire APGA party itself, but rather as a faction with which we were cooperating. So, the consensus was to integrate them as a half-merging partner as the facts bore out. One more group from the Democratic People's Party, DPP was also to be admitted into the merger process and we equally applied the same principle – as with APGA – for them.

There were several of these pockets of complications but we kept working around them. The worst part of this scheming was the fact that we also knew for sure that several of the supposed new entrants –particularly some high-ranking members of the ANPP for example - were playing double games. They were informants who were working for the PDP and the Jonathan administration; and their incontrovertibly assigned role was to do everything from within to scuttle the project.

That we were able to find out the identities and mandate of the moles in our ranks is part of the "Big God" factor I keep referring to and its very clear hand in the ultimate fulfilment of the Buhari presidency project. Without our doing anything to encourage it, people who we didn't even expect to reach out to us and tell us what was going on from within their ranks were however so fed up and distraught with the workings of the Jonathan administration that they kept coming up to us with information. Indeed, access to such information was to play a major part in what we were able to achieve, particularly in the area of taking steps to counter the damage that the Jonathan informants were bringing on board our new construct.

The moment the moles go to see the president for their midnight rendezvous, before morning one of our leaders would have been debriefed. Someone there just felt that Nigeria was going down under the administration, and these were not one or two low or mid-level persons - I'm talking of senior, highly placed people and party officials. They would call and ask why we were doing deals with people who are like that. They would inform us that they came to meet with them and supply details that include dates and times of these meetings, and what exactly they discussed with Jonathan. When we held APC meetings to discuss issues in the evening, by midnight they would be with Jonathan debriefing him. Generally, our informants would then reach out to either El-Rufai, Pastor Bakare or myself, or indeed some other members of our group and give us an outlay of what the 'fifth columnists' had come to do. Armed with this information, we would then proceed to take damage control actions.

In addition to these, there was also a wide array of legal challenges that we had to confront and overcome. Equally challenging were the disputes that arose over the issue of position sharing, although this is to be expected in mergers of all kinds, however there were instances when new lines of reasoning different from what we had agreed before were introduced into the picture. But we stomached all of those things and continued with our mission, always putting Nigeria first. Eventually we filed the requisite application for registration as a new party and got the approval of INEC and the APC became a reality.

With the registration concluded, there followed several things we had to do within APC to make even greater progress. And here, it is pertinent to state some of the precautions that we took to ensure that the merger was not a stillbirth and even to guarantee that the post-approval phases of the APC's development, running up to victory at the polls, were also not derailed.

We identified the fact that beyond the very senior leadership of the ACN, which critically were Tinubu and Chief Bisi Akande, we also had to reach out to all of the merging governors directly and they consequently played very major roles in the process and with the benefit of hindsight, we were indeed very glad that we did. By the way, Chief Akande became the interim chairman of APC at this time, because what we did was to take three senior executives from each of the three major parties in the merger - namely the chairman, the treasurer and secretary from ACN, CPC and ANPP– and constitute them into the nucleus of interim officers for the APC that we put forward before INEC. Later, the commission was to insist that we must have at least twenty-five positions filled and we dutifully complied.

It was a critical part of our strategy to reach out to the governors, to get their direct buy-in and ensure that they also brought their weight to bear on the success of the entire process.

Of course, on our part, we too used one of their own, Governor Al-Makura to reach out to them and once they bought into the vision, they ultimately became a kind of counter force to ensure that if the top leadership of ACN decided not to go on with the deal, we would be able to continue without them. If the top echelon of ANPP decided to quit, we also were trying to ensure that they, the ANPP governors, would still continue with us on the project.

Part of the first fruits from this engagement came when after several sessions, the merger committee could not yet agree on a name to call the new party. Overall, we wanted something to come from CPC, something from ACN and something from ANPP. Ultimately, ACN contributed "Congress," ANPP contributed "All" and the CPC "Progressive". That's how the name All Progressives Congress eventually came to be. But we couldn't agree amongst ourselves on this at the merger committee where I was a member, until the governors met on the subject and one of them just said, look, why don't we just do this?

I can't recall the one who came up with the idea, whether it was Fashola or someone else, but one of them did and word came back to us at the merger committee, that this was the name the governors wanted and that was it. We just took it from there. It was the same thing with several of the other major decisions we had to take whenever a consensus could not be reached.

I should also mention here that even beyond the governors, one of the strategies that we adopted was to reach out to those who we called 'elders in the country' that had considerable clout and interests, to get their buy-in and to also help put pressure on our merging leaders to continue to put the country first as the process developed.

So, they were committed because of the fact that these elders continued to put pressure on them. In the North, we worked with the late Emir of Borgu and in the South, we worked with the Awujale of Ijebuland.

When we got to the point of almost concluding the merger, Tinubu called and asked for a meeting with Kabiyesi, the Awujale. All along, Kabiyesi had concerns about Tinubu because if you are not straightforward, you can't get on very well with Kabiyesi. You must be straightforward to get on with him. He is the 'what-you-see-is-what-you-get' type, as well as being one of, if not also the oldest serving first class monarch in Nigeria.

The meeting held, but because of his concerns, Kabiyesi insisted on a third party being there. And addressing Tinubu, he said: "Look, Nigeria must be saved, are you committed to this merger?" He went on to add that as far as he was concerned, the only person who could save Nigeria for now appears to be the General, that he was persuaded that if we damn the consequences and work assiduously at it, we could succeed. But he cautioned Tinubu not to bring Buhari out of retirement just to mess him up.

When Tinubu responded that he was committed, Kabiyesi then asked him what he wanted in return. He replied that he was indeed committed but that he must be on the ticket as the vice-presidential nominee.

Kabiyesi said fine and asked him whether he was also guaranteeing his support to assist Buhari in getting the presidential slot and he said yes.

Kabiyesi then promised that he would facilitate a meeting with Buhari for him to repeat his condition in person but that he would want a modification because he believed that the already circulating allegation about Buhari being an Islamic fundamentalist may hinder the prospect of having a Muslim/Muslim ticket. He explained that though he (Kabiyesi) had no problem with it, but in the event that it became a problem, Tinubu should be prepared to make a personal sacrifice of his ambition. He then suggested that in this case, Tinubu may request to reserve the right to nominate the eventual vice-presidential nominee.

Perhaps Tinubu was not quite happy with the turn of events, or perhaps for other reasons but the follow-up meeting between him, Kabiyesi and Buhari never took place.

I know this because I had been sent to deliver a message to Buhari on the outcome of the first meeting so that he could also advise on a date for the tripartite meeting. Though a date had dutifully been fixed for the meeting, Kabiyesi had to call to cancel it when there was no feedback from Tinubu. Therefore, the meeting never took place and we concluded that yes, Asiwaju may still have something else in mind, or it may be because he was not sure it was going to be a Muslim-Muslim ticket. Nonetheless it meant that we needed to intensify our other safeguard measures to ensure that we were not derailed. Indeed, we kept all our options open all through.

Back to the process of scaling all the hurdles on the way of the merger and getting the APC registered. I will keep insisting that overall, the merger succeeded because of one thing, which is the "Big G factor." The God factor was there for us all through.

So after fighting the battles in-house to get the CPC TBO to agree to a merger, and not an alliance as some of the members had wanted, we now had to formulate a combined merger committee. It had twenty-one nominees from each of the three full merging parties (ACN, CPC and ANPP) plus another twenty-one to be shared between the groups from APGA and DPP, giving a total of eighty-four members. The faction from the Democratic People's Party had also come on board and taken their place in the merger at this time and they along with the APGA group were also to be subsequently represented in the merger committee.

We then proceeded to write the constitution and manifesto for the new party. Preparatory to filing the formal application for registration, we equally did a checklist and started meeting all the conditions for INEC to get us registered and eventually, the party was registered.

Even then, the internal scheming and jostling did not let up. Because we were the two major parties and prime initiators of the merger - ACN and CPC - we had long agreed that the ACN will produce the national chairman, while the CPC will produce the national secretary.

We decided not to talk about the specific persons to be nominated at that stage but just the offices. However, on the eve of the deadline to formally nominate specific persons that would fill the positions and submit their names to INEC, we called a meeting of officers and aspirants from the merging parties to formally agree on the executives.

El-Rufai and I were in Kaduna when we learnt from General Buba Marwa rtd. that Buhari had signed off on the names for the CPC slot. We were supposed to have twenty-five members in all; that is seven each from the APC, CPC and ANPP and two each from our APGA and DPP entrants.

From the CPC side, Buhari had given out a set of names that included the chairman of the party, Prince Tony Momoh, Buba Galadima, Mustafa Salihu and so on. We knew they had simply taken the list to him for his signature. Only El-Rufai from our group was on the list. And we were told that our Leader had signed off on it and that it was thus a done deal.

Ruminating over the deep implications of this move, we called Pastor Bakare and agreed that we had to go and see Buhari immediately to reconsider the contents of the forwarded list. Our reasoning was simple; if people who were vehemently against merger - and who only wanted an alliance in all reality - are the ones we are sending to go and represent us in the merger, then the seeds for its potential failure were already unwittingly being sowed by the CPC that ought to be the prime defender of the process!

Because of the urgency involved, Pastor Bakare couldn't physically make it to the meeting but he said: "When you people get there, please call me." So we got Right Honourable Speaker, Aminu Bello Masari to go with us. We met with Buhari, sat in his private living room (the usual venue for serious discussions) and told him why we were much persuaded that the CPC may not have put itself in the best position to protect its interests through the list we learnt he had already endorsed. Pastor Bakare also weighed in by phone and in response, Buhari asked us; "Who do you want on the team?" We picked names here and there and gave him for his consideration. He personally wrote a new list and signed it. Then he said: "Jimi, you go and deliver this to Governor Al-Makura. He will lead the CPC team to the meeting to nominate the officers." I also recall that one of the things we achieved that night was to get his endorsement for El-Rufai to be our national secretary-nominee.

When we got to the meeting proper, the other CPC faction (that included Buba Galadima and the deputy national chairman – Mustafa Salihu) also had their list which they insisted Buhari had also signed. So, we had two lists but ours was the latest in time and brought by a governor, who was the leader of CPC and who affirmed to everyone at the meeting that his own list was the authentic one.

While a number of the people in the other CPC faction were kind of gentlemanly in their conduct at this point, Buba Galadima and Mustafa Salihu, insisted very bluntly that they did not recognise the list we had brought from Buhari. They said they were the authentic CPC, not us. At one point, Galadima could be heard saying: "You think you can take over what we have been building since 2002? It is not going to happen. That will only be over our dead body." We remained quiet, knowing fully well that they were not going anywhere given that the CPC National Convention had passed a resolution which gave Buhari the authority to conclude the merger as necessary. To be sure, Buba Marwa called Buhari to confirm that he had indeed authored the Al-Makura list. But even after this, Mustafa Salihu remained adamant, such that Buhari had to speak to him and tell him to go and form his own party if he had any objection to the list. It was after this that the Al-Makura list eventually triumphed and we carried the day; even as Buba Galadima's group was more or less, walked out of the meeting which was being held in Lagos House, Abuja.

Unknown to us, as we were openly fighting amongst ourselves within the CPC, ACN had done a coup against us. They had agreed with the ANPP that they will provide the national secretary. So, what were we to do? It was now about 1a.m. and we were required to submit the names to INEC early in the morning on the same day.

Underscoring the fact that the ruling PDP had planted moles within our organisation, a few days before this meeting, President Jonathan's spokesman, Doyin Okupe, had literally sworn that he was staking his life that the merger will fail. Of course, Okupe could only have been that cocksure on account of the many booby-traps that he was aware had been laid on the way, some of which were already manifesting at this very critical meeting.

So, when the ANPP now came out to insist that because they had four governors and we only had one, they should produce the National Secretary, even as they deferred to the fact that the ACN which had six governors could have the Chairmanship, we knew that we had to tread a lot more carefully in the overall interest of the merger project and the nation at large.

At this point also, the ACN which had earlier agreed with us on the sharing of the two principal positions in the executive reneged on our earlier understanding. Now, all that they were saying was that they had gotten their desired chairmanship slot, so we should go and work things out between ourselves and the ANPP. We were scandalised.

It was a shocking and most disruptive twist to the entire saga and something had to be done quickly. The CPC delegation huddled around for a quick conference at which I volunteered my opinion that the way things stood then, our making one more sacrifice was what was needed.

I addressed El-Rufai: "Mallam, they are insisting on taking the position of national secretary and give us deputy national secretary. If they give you deputy national secretary, who is the person that they will field that you will not yet dominate? This is intellectual stuff and not just a parade of titles. Let's accept." He agreed.

Immediately, we called Buhari and convinced him along the same lines and he asked: "Mallam, are you comfortable with being deputy national secretary?" El-Rufai, the team player answered: "General it's for you sir, if you want to build the country, it's not going to be about my position." That was what saved the day. They had hoped that we will not agree and the merger would collapse there and then. We went back and said: "We agree, let's go." There were shouts of disbelief in the hall! But of course, it was bad news for PDP and we submitted the names and the rest is history.

We waited for the number of days we were required to wait. INEC did their investigation and verification and eventually, APC became a party. We had met the conditions and they had no choice. The ruling party and their agents put pressure on the commission to scuttle our bid but they were unsuccessful. At a time, some two other associations – African People's Congress and All Patriotic Citizens – showed up. They said their acronym was also APC and that they had applied before us to be registered as political parties with the same acronym!

Nigerians however saw through the plot and their applications were also to be formally rejected because they did not meet all the requirements that were clearly spelt out by the Commission as conditions to be met by associations desiring to be political parties. On our part, we had met the requirements; we became APC; the party was registered.

The journey which began in February 2013, when Chief Tom Ikimi of the ACN, Senator Annie Okonkwo of APGA, Mallam Ibrahim Shekarau of the ANPP and Alhaji Garba Gadi of CPC signed the formal merger resolution, was finally completed. The new party received full and final approval from INEC on 31 July 2013 to become a political party and the operating licenses of the three predecessor parties (the ACN, CPC and ANPP) were withdrawn. Other things could then follow.

CHAPTER EIGHT

Welcoming The 'New PDP' Entrants

At this point, the continuing failure of the rival People's Democratic Party, PDP to properly institute and follow-through with the practice of internal democracy within its ranks led to an implosion at its August 21, 2013 convention which was to become a plus for our own efforts.

In the resultant brouhaha, as many as seven of its states governors were so upset with developments within the party that they and several other leaders and members walked out of the convention arena. They subsequently constituted themselves into a break-away faction, the New People's Democratic Party, 'New PDP' and chose Alhaji Kawu Baraje as their National Chairman. At first, they wanted to stand-alone as an autonomous party. But seeing their efforts being continually frustrated as well as on account of some sustained outreach from our side to them, eventually five of them subsequently crossed over, along with their supporters into the APC in November 2013.

The new entrant-governors were Chibuike Rotimi Amaechi of Rivers State, Murtala Nyako of Adamawa,

Abdul-Fatah Ahmed of Kwara, Rabiu Kwankwaso of Kano and Aliyu Wammako of Sokoto, and they generally received a very enthusiastic welcome from both the rank and file of the APC.

On the other hand, the two who were to somewhat 'chicken out' of the defection deal were Aliyu Babangida Muazu of Niger and Sule Lamido of Jigawa.

Given the constitutional imperatives for winning presidential elections in the country, the coming of these five governors signposted that we were getting closer to our desired goal. This is because before this time, the APC was only controlling twelve out of the thirty-six states in the country. On its part, the PDP had twenty-three and the non-APC faction of APGA was holding on to one, Anambra.

However, we generally reckoned Anambra to indeed be yet another PDP state, a point that was loudly demonstrated in its APGA government's continued endorsement of the PDP in successive presidential contests. Things indeed got to a head when the local PDP operatives within the state, took advantage of this and publicly expressed support to equally feather their own political nests at the expense of APGA. They quarrelled over this, which they described as 'taking the handshake too far,' even while remaining solidly in support of the PDP's bid at the presidential election level. Clearly, they had not learnt anything from the experience of the Alliance for Democracy, AD, which had lost its dominant position in the South-West on account of its similarly fraternising with the same PDP to help it win in the presidential contest of 2003. For us at the APC, the Anambra situation only helped to reinforce our position that we had to do something on the issue of state imbalance and so we had started reaching out to states and governors that we could win over.

On this, I must give particular credit to Asiwaju Bola Ahmed Tinubu. Out of all our leaders, he was one of the first that saw very early in the day that we needed to take practical control of some more states if we were to be very well positioned to realise our ultimate goal. Thus when we got word that several PDP governors, seven of them in all, were not happy and could be in a talking frame, he led the reach out to them. The estranged PDP governors on their part were led to the talks by two amongst them that we trusted most, namely, Rotimi Amaechi and Murtala Nyako.

Long before this time, Nyako in particular, had maintained a very close affinity with Buhari and we saw this as a valuable peg upon which to build at the time. As for Amaechi, he was literally being harassed by the PDP and the camp of President Jonathan. And he had made it very clear that going forward he did not want to have anything to do, politically speaking, with them.

As soon as word began to filter out that we had begun to reach out to the estranged PDP governors, there were all kinds of reactions; an unnamed South-West leader of the PDP was quoted as saying that though the leadership of the party was already alarmed over the moves but then the party yet had a definite handle on the situation. It was still early in the day. In contrast, the Chairman of PDP's Board of Trustees, Chief Tony Anenih, while addressing the Governors, Federal Lawmakers, and State Chairmen of the party from the South-South geopolitical zone in Asaba, Delta State, stated that "we must not live under the illusion that our party is invulnerable. Although, the existing opposition parties are still too small, fragile and sectional, we must not ignore the possibility that a merger of these parties may constitute a threat to our current dominance of the political terrain". How prophetic?

While our talks with those governors were generally positive, we however did all that we could to ramp up the pressure on them to ensure that their movement to the APC would be irreversible. We paid them courtesy visits and they in turn then grew bolder and openly invited us to visit them. We then went with large delegations of APC leaders to visit Adamawa and Rivers States and were very lavishly received in the open. People showed up in large numbers and we were then better assured that it was only a matter of time before a final deal would be sealed.

Anticipating the potential backlash on it of the manoeuvres that we were making, the PDP became jittery. Ahead of the visit by the national leadership of the All Progressives Congress to Rivers State for example, the party warned that the State Governor, Mr. Rotimi Amaechi, should be held responsible for any breakdown of law and order in the state!

The warning came from the Rivers State Chairman of the PDP, Mr. Felix Obuah even as he accused the governor of using state funds to organise a reception for the national leadership of the APC. He also alleged that Amaechi had sent ₦500 million belonging to the state to neighbouring states to mobilise people from such states to the airport to receive national leaders of the APC, suggesting that such an action could cause a breakdown of law and order in the state.

In his reaction, the Chief of Staff, Government House, Port Harcourt, Chief Tony Okocha, described Obuah's allegation as false and a sign of fear in the PDP. He also predicted a large turnout of Amaechi supporters at the airport and the Government House, describing the expected crowd as a storm that would show the PDP that "Amaechi remains the only politician on the ground in the state."

Similarly, leaders of the All Progressives Congress (APC) visited Governors Rabiu Musa Kwankwaso of Kano state and Sule Lamido of Jigawa State in a bid to have them dump the PDP and move over to the APC. The opposition leaders also went to Adamawa State to woo Governor Murtala Nyako.

The APC team included former Governor of Lagos, Bola Tinubu, ex-Head of State, Muhammadu Buhari and APC National Chairman, Chief Bisi Akande.

During the meeting, held at the Banquet Hall of the Government House, Yola, Chief Akande said their recruitment mission to the state was part of their drive to salvage the country from its present dilapidated state.

> Nigerians are now tired with the injustice and impunity across the land; hence their resolve to bring about change,

Chief Akande said.

> I can assure you that in APC, internal democracy will be enshrined. Please let's not make a mistake this time around. The time is ripe for change. Our discussions with other governors are very fruitful ahead of the proposed merger.'

In the same vein, General Buhari reiterated Chief Akande's statement on their mission to Yola which is to persuade Mr. Nyako to join the APC.

"All what we are trying to do is to get this country out of the current mess," he said. "In our bid to do that, Adamawa state must join us to deliver this country. That is why we are here. We need peace and prosperity in this country."

Responding, Governor Nyako said he was still in the PDP but would always identify with like minds for the progress of the country.

"What we are doing today is not politics but showing concern for our future," he said. "The fact that Buhari is here physically with other bigwigs portends hope. That leaders from various divides are meeting here gives Nigeria the hope that we are uniting for the good of the country."

Another very important plank of our discussions with the 'New PDP' governors at this point - which Tinubu also led us in reaching - was the decision to also concede the 'right of first refusal' to the incoming governors - so they could get their loyalists to take up fifty percent of the positions in the interim executive committees of the party in their states - which we had earlier approved for the governors from the 'legacy' APC-controlled states. This decision no doubt was to generate some furore from older members of the APC in those states and very notably, aggrieved former gubernatorial candidates who were the leading lights of the APC in those states before the coming of the 'New PDP' governors. I recall here that in the case of Kwara State for example, the former ACN gubernatorial candidate, Mr. Dele Belgore, SAN, a professional to the core, was so enraged that he practically dumped the party!

On the plus side however, these comfort measures helped very significantly in assuring the 'New PDP' governors that they were indeed most welcome in the APC and that they would also not really be losing any of their extant privileges despite that they were now coming into the fold after the party had been formally registered.

Then came the Big Bang, when in November 2013 the 'New PDP' governors made the public announcement of their defection and five of them formally crossed over

Welcoming The 'New PDP' Entrants

to the APC. As had been recounted, we were expecting seven in all at the beginning, but Aliyu Babangida of Niger and Sule Lamido of Jigawa had backed out (perhaps on account of threats of harassment and intimidation by the presidency) at the last minute. They had agreed all along to come on-board but were now compelled to pull out.

I recall also that one of the final things that we did then that contributed enormously in finally persuading the 'New PDP' governors to join us had to do with the unflinching solidarity and support we provided them in the 'sixteen is greater than nineteen controversy.' This had to do with the rift over the chairmanship of the Nigeria Governors Forum, NGF.

Ahead of the crucial vote on May 24, 2013, our leaders had advised all of our governors that they must support the incumbent and at this time, our friend Rotimi Amaechi, for the position and that it was not fair the way PDP were arrogantly pushing to dump and humiliate him. That massive expression of support by the APC in my view came to be the single most important reason why we got those governors to finally jump ship.

PDP were shocked as they didn't expect this outcome. They had felt that there was no way Amaechi could win in that contest because they more or less had twenty-four out of the nation's thirty-six states under their control. They had thought that, at most we would convince two or three of their estranged governors to come along with our counter-action but they didn't know that we would all vote en bloc. Very significantly here, we got the seven initially aggrieved governors from the PDP voting for Amaechi, alongside all of our twelve governors! That's how he came to score nineteen votes to the sixteen that were recorded by their candidate, and the then Governor of Plateau State, Group Captain Jonah David Jang, rtd.

So in effect, though we were practically controlling only seventeen of the thirty-six state governments in the country, the results of that vote proved that even the two that had backed out from the formal defection plan were in this sense, also not really with them! They didn't join us formally but we knew they were also not favourably disposed to the Jonathan administration. That gave us even greater confidence as we knew that this proven 'political control' of nineteen states meant that we would defeat the PDP any time, any day. We became more confident and energised with that prospect.

CHAPTER NINE

Getting A National Chairman And The Work Of The APC Strategy Committee

If anyone had thought that the registration of the APC was all that was needed to cement all of the cracks in the merger arrangement, that person would be forgiven for being unduly simplistic. This is because, rather than abate, the intrigues and jostling only exacerbated.

On our part, our singular objective was very clear; with an eye on the ball, we were committed to undertaking any sacrificial action that was required to save the day.

The first of such post-registration tests came when it was time to compose a substantive executive for the new party and the principal bone of contention had to do with filling the office of the National Chairman.

Zoned to the South-South region of the country, we looked from within the field of candidates jostling to occupy the seat and agreed to support the aspiration of former Bayelsa State Governor, Chief Timipre Sylva.

Before the decision to back Sylva was taken, we had encountered a dilemma of sort as it had to do with the aspirations of one of the leaders of the merger committee, Chief Tom Ikimi.

A political and social juggernaut who had first come to national attention during the political transition programme of the Ibrahim Babangida era where he served as National Chairman of the National Republican Convention, NRC, Ikimi, who was also a former Foreign Affairs Minister during the Sani Abacha era, had been very lavish in hosting meetings of the merger committee which took place in his Abuja home.

Determined to get the nod for the job, early in the day, he had suggested at a meeting of the merger committee that we adopt a resolution asking the leaders of the merging parties to endorse that the committee should be transformed into the substantive national executive of the party.

I recall that when this position was raised, a few of us had disagreed with the logic saying that it was really not right for, as I put it: "contractors hired to build a house to now turn around and share the rooms in the house among themselves because the owners were yet to take possession!" In my view, what was required in this instance was to "finish our work as contractors, albeit co-owners and go and handover the keys to the owners." If they subsequently elect to allow any or indeed all of us to take up lodgings within the accommodation, it was entirely up to them.

But Ikimi was too far gone in the unbridled pursuit of his ambition to listen and he then rallied several other members of the committee that were favourably disposed to this point of view and they proceeded to go and ambush Buhari to not only get his nod for their position but to also solicit his support to sell it to the other merging leaders. As I know would always happen in such situations, Buhari did not take kindly to this development and neither endorsed it, nor discussed same with the other leaders.

These limitations notwithstanding, I must here pay tribute to Ikimi, as he graciously opened his doors to the merger committee and we met in his house in Abuja countless number of times. At this point, the different merging partners were using different locations for their activities. For instance, those of us from the CPC were using the Nasarawa State Governor's lodge, the ACN were using the Lagos State Governor's lodge, while the ANPP were using the Borno State Governor's lodge. When it was time to have what we called the general sessions, we all converged in Tom Ikimi's residence, and at the end of the meeting there would be food and all sorts of refreshment.

On their part, the APC governors – we had eleven or twelve governors – are also to be strongly commended for their great contributions to the merger effort. In one instance for example, they assisted us in raising funds which we used for the filing of papers with INEC, paying all the fees, picking up all the merger expenses, constitution drafting and manifesto printing and so on. We even had some balance left. So the governors played a major role at this point, alongside Tom Ikimi who was our committee leader. The other three chairmen from the other merging parties –Alhaji Garba Gadi from CPC and Shekarau of ANPP of course did co-chair with him but he was effectively the coordinating chairman.

Brushing aside the candidacy of Ikimi, we returned to supporting for the position of National Chairman, the former Bayelsa Governor, Chief Timipre Sylva.

But there were several odds on Sylva's way. On the one hand, the ACN leadership was strongly promoting the candidacy of former Edo State Governor, Chief John Odigie Oyegun for the position and given that Oyegun and Buhari had clashed during the heady days of the ANPP, he was not our first choice, in spite of his positive antecedents and excellent credentials.

Apart from this, Sylva's opponents were loudly promoting the fact that he was at that time facing corruption charges and given the potential for this point to be trumpeted later by the PDP, it was felt that serious consideration should be given to it.

At a harmonization meeting called to resolve the impasse, ACN insisted on Oyegun while the CPC was now disposed to someone else other than Sylva. As Buhari laid it out at the meeting, the consensus should be to "let Chief Bisi Akande continue!" (Akande was also of the ACN bloc and had also been holding the position in an interim capacity since the merger process commenced).

If we recall that Akande, who as the then Deputy Governor of the old Oyo State was one of the political players that had been detained by the Buhari/Idiagbon administration between 1983 and 1985, then we will see that the period of their working together in the merger process had enabled both Akande and Buhari to re-assess their positions as it had to do with perceived animosities to the extent that they were now making dispassionate and cross-factional contributions in the overall national interest. Indeed, Chief Akande became a big fan of Buhari after he got to know him better and vice versa.

Finally however, seeing that the consensus was tilting towards Oyegun, we finally gave him our nod and he went on to be elected with the sad fall-out that Ikimi, who had really done much to help the party get started, had to angrily walk out on APC and defect to the PDP.

As if that was not bad enough, there was also to follow a very bitter exchange between him and Tinubu.

In the text of his letter dated Wednesday 27th August 2014 (see Appendix 6) in response to the outcome of the 13th June 2014 All Progressives Congress APC National Convention, Ikimi recounted the trajectory of his involvement with Nigerian politics dating from the era of the NRC and SDP between 1990 and 1993 and on to the Movement for the Restoration and Defence of Democracy (MRDD) in 2005, which transformed into the Action Congress (AC) in 2006, and the ACN in 2010, and the APC in February 2013 with the successful unification of the major opposition parties – ACN, ANPP, CPC and a part of APGA.

Insisting that Tinubu's opposition to his being national chairman was self-serving, he then announced the withdrawal of his membership of the APC.

In his response, Tinubu dismissed Ikimi's allegations (see Appendix 5) as a 'lengthy chronicle of falsehoods, cheap blackmail and abuse,' affirming that he was only being drawn out to respond so that the true facts of the matter would be on public record.

Another very critical factor that aided the eventual crystallisation of the merger and its smooth functioning going forward was the careful attention paid towards ensuring that a multi-layered platform was put in place for the emergent party.

At the apex, we had a Board of Trustees which was composed of leaders of the merging parties. Then we had the National Caucus - comprising of party elders, the Progressive Governors Forum, the Interim National Executive Committee (before substantive members of NEC were elected), the Merger Committee and several other specialised committees put in place to address critical areas. In addition, we also reached out to other notable political, traditional and religious leaders of thought from across the country from time to time to weigh in on one subject or the other or to simply help in putting pressure to bear on our leaders if only to ensure that the entire process was not derailed.

What these organs and initiatives brought to the table was most noteworthy in their own rights. For example, while the Elders were able to address issues of vaunting ambition and opportunism that crept up now and again, as is often the case in the political setting in which we found ourselves, platforms like the Governors Forum undertook to, and did contribute the funds and associated leverage needed to process the registration of the party and ensure even greater public confidence.

THE FASHOLA-LED STRATEGY COMMITTEE

Of critical note at this point also was the work of the Strategy Committee. Since the process of blending and integration of all of the merging entities was being carried out alongside other developing initiatives on the broader national political turf where we were expecting to contest and win after the process, it was considered desirable that we empanel a very strong Strategy Committee to regularly help the leadership keep an eye on the bigger picture.

More specifically outlined, the committee's 'Terms of Reference' were spelt out as follows:

1. Design and develop an internal research capability for the Party to provide data and arguments that underpin and support its platform, policies and programs at federal, state and local government levels.

2. Develop a template for gathering and analysis of political, social and economic intelligence including but not limited to voter demographics, migration, anthropological diversity and socio-economic data as input for the electoral strategies of the Party.
3. Establish national and global network of resource persons and experts in various knowledge areas that will be volunteers or paid consultants to help articulate the Party platform, manifesto, policies, programs and plans for the federal, state and local government levels.
4. Develop strategies for the establishment of the Party's think tank – The All Progressives Institute, with the support of domestic and international donors, to serve as the centre of research and policy excellence of the Party.
5. Submit monthly reports of progress, success and challenges to the National Executive Committee of the Party.
6. The Committee may wish to co-opt additional Members as it deems fit.

This committee was led by the then Governor of Lagos State, Babatunde Raji Fashola, SAN, and it worked tirelessly in ensuring that it's terms of reference were diligently pursued and faithfully executed.

For a start, we searched diligently to make sure that the people we wanted, those of like minds were the ones that got onto the committee. As luck would also have it, we not only got Fashola as chairman, El-Rufai, Oyegun (later to become the National Chairman), a couple of lawmakers such as Senators Bunmi Adetunmbi and Osita Izunaso and Honourable Parry Iriase as well as H. E. Alhaji Garba Gadi, Alhaji Nasiru Aliko Koki, Alh. Abubakar Yari and Hajia Hadiza Bala-Usman were all incorporated.

I also served as a resource person for the Committee and the secretariat, along with another hard-working young man, Terfa Tilley-Gyado. We were effectively and efficiently led and hosted by Fashola mostly in Lagos and sometimes in Abuja twice a month and in fact, it became once a week in the critical months leading up to the general elections.

After its first set of meetings, the committee approached the leadership of the party with a work plan and recommendations on how to proceed.

> 'Having regard to the current developments in the national polity, the committee has thought it fit to give priority to Items 1 and 3 of its terms of reference, in order to provide quick wins upon which Items 2 and 4, are more continuous.
>
> Some of the quick wins that the committee envisages include a clear messaging for the public about the purpose of the APC and also a clear summary of its management plan for the country.
>
> Accordingly, the committee recommends that 2 (two) documents must issue from the party in order to achieve these quick wins.
>
> The first document is a statement of commitment, in other words, the platform which helps the party present its ideology to the Nigerian public about the purpose of the APC.
>
> The second document is a revised manifesto which helps the party present its management plan for the country, when it forms a Government.
>
> In order to assist in the understanding of the need for 2 (two) documents, the committee wishes to stress that a

political party such as ours, will do well to always bear in mind that it will always be addressing at least 2 (two) broad classes of people in any society.

The first class of people will be those members of the public, who want to join a political party.

It is our committee's view that such people will make the decision whether or not to join a party because of what it stands for in terms of ideology.

Some of the members of this class are often the society's intelligentsia who need an idea to galvanise them. To this group, we believe and recommend that the APC must present a platform message.

The other class, are those who in our view do not seek to belong to any party, but are interested in knowing what the party will offer them, if it forms a Government. To these people our Manifesto must be presented.

In other words, while party members will affiliate and vote on the basis of membership and ideological commitment, non-party members will support and work on the basis of the expectation of public goods promised in our manifesto.

We intend to organise a grand launch and presentation of the ideology and platform statement, by inviting some eminent people to speak at the launch for not more than 10 minutes. Each speaker will be allotted one of the 10 items we have committed to embark upon as a springboard for the media coverage that will then follow.

It is our belief that this will provide a final and well thought out answer to those who say we either have no ideology or we are the same as other parties.

It is instructive to observe that available records do not reveal that any political party has ever done something of the scale that we plan before now.

The closest we have come was the inauguration speech of the Action Group by Chief Obafemi Awolowo in 1951.'

We then handed over the drafts we had prepared to the leadership of the party for their perusal and input.

After this, the Strategy Committee then set its sights on fine-tuning these core foundational documents with which the party would consequently prosecute its campaigns. From our experience at this point, we knew that part of the reason for the relative fluidity in Nigerian political practice was the absence of properly charted and binding statement of values that people had to subscribe to. Indeed, we had accused the PDP of doing just this! And so, the first of such documents which the Strategy Committee developed was a declaration on the founding philosophy and values of the APC. It was a list of ten cardinal principles that we spent lots of time and energy formulating. When we had finished work on it and had gotten our leaders' buy-in, we assembled all the elected APC leaders in the country to physically sign the document in a well-publicised event in Abuja. It was the first of its kind in our recent political history and helped to situate the APC as a very serious party, one that was stridently intent on raising the bar in the critical arena of national political development and conduct.

Working with AKPD

One of the other decisions we took in the committee was to engage David Axelrod's political consulting firm, AKPD to work for us, thanks to Asiwaju Tinubu who brought the firm. It was the same firm that had worked for President Obama in the 2008 election and though they come fairly expensive, being persuaded that what we were doing was for the public good, we were able to secure huge discounts on their billings.

Guided by AKPD, almost on a monthly basis, we were administering opinion polls and interpreting the polls outcome according to the colour codes of different states we had, and through this way we were seeing the states where we felt we had a chance of securing large wins, to those we felt were only possibly going to deliver as much as twenty-five percent of the total votes tally. Based on these outcomes, we were then more scientifically deploying our resources, ranging from advertising airtime to physical visits by our leaders.

The National Conference

Equally, on an account of the exigencies of political practice, the Strategy Committee was also drawn into taking a position on the National Conference which President Jonathan had surreptitiously slipped onto the political map of the nation when everyone already had their sights on the forthcoming elections! Seeing how impractical this was, our leaders almost to a man would not have anything to do with it and publicly said so. In our discussions on the subject however, we agreed with our leaders that the PDP administration was generally only playing political games with the exercise but also felt that our total non-representation at the event could subsequently be used against us!

Also, there was a moral and political risk arising from the fact that APC governors were also being expected to adopt the position of the party and distance themselves from the confab when they also doubled as leaders of federating entities where all citizens were not necessarily opposed to participating in the event! This was even more worrisome when one of the convening clauses in the confab agenda had permitted the president to nominate representatives from states where their governors had failed to do so!

Besides, given that some of the legacy parties that had now made up the APC were on record as having been the foremost advocates for a National Conference through the years, holding one without their participation would really need to be explained! Would it not be interpreted that we were being unnecessarily puritanical and self-righteous in our stand simply because we were not the ones convening it? And what about the millions of Nigerians who still believed that the country yet needed a national conference to help work out some of its structural challenges? Would they not now feel abandoned by their long-time champions and perhaps also begin to see more merit than actually was in the opportunistic posturing of the PDP conveners?

In addition to the above stated points, we also reasoned that it had over time been demonstrated in our history that engaging in boycotts was only a high-road political gesture that did not really make much practical impact on the specific points of dispute under reference. Rather than adopt that seemingly extreme measure, we added, we then suggested we could very well also use the occasion of the conference to state very clearly our positions on the issues under consideration, while firmly emphasising the point that the entire exercise was doomed to fail given its timing. So, we went back to our leaders and got their buy-in for a 'qualified appearance' by the APC at the confab.

A FEED-BACK DRIVEN MANIFESTO APPROACH

We also knew that we had to produce a befitting manifesto for the party. If the reader would recall, the absence of a well-articulated manifesto was one of the first grounds for our falling out with the CPC leadership that we had met when we joined the party ahead of the 2011 polls. And to further demonstrate that this was a general malady at that time, even President Jonathan did not campaign with a proper manifesto to win in 2011!

Again, as part of ensuring that things were now properly done in all ramifications, the APC resolved early in the day that a proper and very comprehensive manifesto document must be produced and it was the Strategy Committee that was tasked with undertaking the legwork for the crafting of the manifesto. It was a product of some of the opinion surveys that we were administering. We asked Nigerians what they wanted to see in our new party and the critical issues they would like the incoming government to address. People talked about security, healthcare and jobs. Jobs and security were consistently the highest ranked factors thus our manifesto was directed towards those. We had to go through several editions and then harmonise them.

To better understand how much work was put in the manifesto project, we should recall that initially, we had three different manifestos from the different merging parties. Of course, we submitted one for INEC's approval but that was not the same as the manifesto that was later developed for the general elections.

The manifesto for the election had to be targeted at the most burning issues of the time and as gleaned from our polls. From the onset, it was clear that the manifesto for the 2011 election could not be the same as the manifesto for the 2015 contest; that we fully understood. Just as the 2015 manifesto cannot be the same as the one to be developed for the 2019 elections as the issues would have changed by then.

In 2015 for example, people were concerned about security, and notably the combatting of the Boko Haram insurgency. In 2019, this may no longer be an issue. This is why you must have manifestos targeted towards specific elections. All those we understood and thank God that Fashola led us in that direction. He believed it, I believed it and we were able to get things done.

Now, whenever we had important deliverables from the work of our committee, we would go to the headquarters of the party and unveil what we had. We would sit our leaders down under lock and key and relay the results to them in confidence. This way we were able to get their input and buy-in as well as guide them with details of where they needed to make more appearances, the things they should be saying and what the voters wanted to hear.

Related to the work of the Strategy Committee, the crafting of the manifesto and working the opinion polls, something interesting also happened. As we had our own opinion survey firm, PDP also had its. And because these firms were operating in the same public space, they inevitably compared notes with one another. So, what we were polling, they were also polling and we found a way to get their results for comparison with ours.

Naturally their results were a flip of ours. The states that we established were prime win states for us, they saw as states where they had no chance of winning. States we saw as twenty-five percent hopeful, were the same states they were aiming to secure more than seventy-five percent of the tally (so that they would stop APC from getting the stipulated minimum of 25 percent in at least twenty-four states and the FCT).

Even more directly, we had sympathisers from within the PDP ranks who were although working with them, also giving us their polling results. I don't know if they got ours too but yes, we were able to reconfirm from what we were seeing from theirs that our polling outcomes were reliable. Both parties were getting similar results. We got to know their weaknesses and kept hammering on them. Apart from delivering our messages, we were also telling people that if you don't do something about the PDP, there would be no Nigeria left. We kept hammering on issues of insecurity, corruption, unemployment and so on.

CHAPTER TEN

National Convention, Presidential Primaries And Choice Of A Vice Presidential Candidate

Election primaries are generally not won on the day of the contest. Victory is a long process that is built upon many layers of outreach that had invariably taken place long before the D-day.

Seeing the challenges that we had witnessed in our relationship with Tinubu as well as the fact that we did not have the kind of deep pockets that a rival like former Vice President, Atiku Abubakar literally possessed, we therefore had to play more strategically.

Appreciating quite early in the day that we needed to cultivate strong layers of support from non-Northern segments of the country to make our dream of securing both the party ticket and the presidency of the federation feasible this time around, and seeing that the point of least resistance clearly was in the South-Western states and Edo, we went to work very early and long before the primaries date to ensure that the leadership of those states, one-on-one, were generally not hostile, even if they were not overtly enthusiastic and well-disposed to our cause.

So, while engaging our formal leaders and elders like Tinubu and Akande, we also went below and beyond them to engage other critical leaders of the South-West, including most notably, the governors. Here also, the engagement was varied. Beyond broad meetings with the governors under the aegis of the APC, we went out of the way to get Buhari to sit one-on-one with the governors from the region and especially those from ACN-governed states.

From the outcome of our meeting in Lagos, we were persuaded that Fashola was with us even when we were not very sure of where Tinubu was going. There was a spontaneous chemistry between him and Buhari and you could feel it. It was in a proverbial sense, a case of 'love at first sight' between them.

Underscoring this was the outcome of one of our now regular opinion polls' results which revealed that indeed, if there was going to be the likelihood of our finally having to do a Muslim-Muslim ticket at all – as had been the case with the Abiola-Kingibe slate in 1993 – the streets were more likely to go with a Buhari-Fashola pairing over and above a Buhari-Tinubu slate.

We shared this finding with Buhari as usual and he noted it but given the mood of the nation, it was also becoming quite clear at this point that we were not going to do a Muslim-Muslim ticket. But it is important to state that our opinion polls had a lot to say in terms of public appreciation of Fashola whereas from the same opinion polls and survey, Tinubu was taking away points from the ticket and had no major value addition as a prospective vice-president.

We were also lucky in the South-West that after the good news with Fashola, the governor of Ogun State,

Ibikunle Amosun was a long-time friend and almost like a junior brother to Buhari. This dated way back to their ANPP days. In fact, during the 2011 election, any time Buhari came to Lagos, he would stay either in Amosun's house or at the Sheraton Hotel. We knew for sure that we could always count on Amosun.

We also reached out to Governor Fayemi of Ekiti State as well. On his part, he asked many questions and we did the analysis for him. Eventually, he was very excited and we were sure that he had come on board. At this point, we knew that yes, even without Tinubu, these three were largely committed to us. We also approached the Oyo State Governor, Abiola Ajimobi as well and he also came on board.

The only governor in the region whose support we were not certain of at this time was Rauf Aregbesola of Osun State but we approached him all the same. Because he was the closest to Tinubu, we knew that if all else fails, he would try to convince him to see reason though he would not leave him. We nonetheless tried our best to convince him to back Buhari's candidacy but we didn't go all out as we did with the other governors.

As for Edo, we reached out to Governor Oshiomhole and he indeed was to play a very vital role in helping Buhari secure the ticket.

In fact, it is important to talk about Oshiomhole specially, because in 2011 we had quite a nasty experience with him such that when we went to Benin to campaign that year, beyond just the courtesy visit, he didn't want to associate with us. Our feelers at the time were that he was under pressure from the state of siege that the PDP had subjected the nation to then. Though he was not in PDP, he felt at the time that the PDP may come after him for being friendly with us. So, he held back from even according us the normal courtesy that would have been expected for a former head of State who came to his state to campaign. We even got feedback that we were not wanted there at all. It was that bad in 2011, so we knew that something had to be done to smoothen things this time around.

Fortunately, there is a good rapport between him and El-Rufai which started way back to his tenure as DG of BPE into 2007 when his mandate was stolen before it was restored by the courts. El-Rufai had assisted him in the process then, he remained grateful. We used that contact to reach out to him. We didn't have enough time to do that in 2011, which was part of the lessons we had learnt from that outing and it was a mistake we felt we must not repeat. We reached out to him and the moment he opened up to Buhari, we knew we could rely on him.

Overall, of the twelve governors who started the APC journey with us, most times we knew that we had at least eight to ten on our side. Of these, three of them were Buhari's staunch allies who had long been won to his side based on his character and personality. They were Ibrahim Geidam of Yobe, Kashim Shettima of Borno, and of course our own Al-Makura from Nassarawa. On his part, Governor Abdulaziz Yari of Zamfara was also supportive.

Thus, the beginning of the strategic approach that was deployed to clinch the primaries and the resultant election was to get the governors on board. That strategy really paid off and full credit for the intensification of this approach must be given to Governor Amaechi. This was one of the things we did differently from 2011, when we did not have a single sitting governor on board.

Apart from getting information on the other candidates through conducting periodic SWOT analyses (strengths, weaknesses, opportunities and threats), it was actually the critical and single most important factor that delivered the ticket to Buhari as shall be explained later.

THE NATIONAL CONVENTION AND THE PRIMARIES PROPER

We now moved on to preparations for the presidential primary election which had been scheduled to hold in Lagos on December 10 and 11, 2014. It was a very serious affair, with all kinds of advantage games being played by some of the contenders ahead of the vote.

All the time, whilst we were building the party, Buhari was most disciplined and refused to talk about his ambition. In fact, at a point, the governors were complaining because all the other candidates had started going to see them formally. Atiku had started campaigning, going round all the states not only to see Governors but also delegates with cash donations here and there ostensibly for building the "structures" in the states. But Buhari plainly refused to circumvent the process and insisted that he would do so at the right time.

We were worried at some point but we knew his style and that what he was saying made sense. We didn't have the kind of money that Atiku had and then Kwankwaso also joined the race after Kano had also defected to join us as part of the New PDP governors' train. That meant more pressure on us, yet the majority of the governors, now seventeen in all, kept saying that Buhari was the best choice to fly the party's flag, though one of them, Kwankwaso was in the race. It was difficult for them, but we all knew and kept saying that Buhari could clearly deliver more votes in the General Elections than

Kwankwaso, or indeed, anyone else at that moment, could do.

We finally agreed on 15th October, 2014 for Buhari to formally declare his ambition and it was indeed a remarkable success. In attendance were four serving governors: Fashola of Lagos, Al-Makura of Nassarawa, Oshiomhole of Edo and Amaechi of Rivers. There were also former governors Timipre Sylva, Abba Bukar Ibrahim, Ahmed Yerima, George Akume and Abdullahi Adamu. Chief Audu Ogbeh, Senator Olorunimbe Mamora, former Speaker of the House of Representatives, Aminu Bello Masari, the National Vice-Chairman of APC (North-East), Engr. B.D Lawal, Muoghalu, Sharon Ikeazor, Alhaji Mustapha Habib, Osita Okechukwu, Hajia Hadiza Bala Usman, Prince Tony Momoh, Prof. Tam David-West, Oluwatayo Oluwa and Rotimi Akeredolu, SAN were also in attendance.

At this point the media was already getting hints about where the governors were going and alluding to it as evidenced in this snippet from *Breakingtimes.com:*

> 'Buhari was driven into the arena at exactly 12.25p.m. in an open roof sports utility vehicle (SUV) from which he waved to his supporters.
>
> His frenzied supporters ran alongside the motorcade conveying him till he went into the VIP stand.
>
> As early as midnight Tuesday, all the roads leading to the Eagle Square, Abuja, venue of the declaration was swarmed with hundreds of his supporters who arrived the capital city in several convoys of buses.
>
> Security men and party officials had a hectic time controlling the enthusiastic and near-fanatical youths who took over the entry points to the covered stands, waving and displaying campaign banners. The ecstatic supporters drummed and danced around the arena endlessly till the end of the programme.'

Buhari's speech at the event was spot on as it touched on the salient issues under consideration in the election season.

Beginning with a tribute to Nigerians as a whole who are enduring all sorts of hardships and deprivations on a daily basis, he lamented that millions were "grappling with extreme poverty and barely eking out a living" and "in fear of their lives or safety for themselves and their families due to insurgency by the godless movement called Boko Haram, by marauding murderers in towns and villages, by armed robbers on the highways and kidnappers who have put whole communities to fright and sometimes to flight."

In his view also, the years of PDP rule had been a season of colossal decline for the nation. "Nigeria in my experience has never been so divided, so polarized by an unthinking government hell bent on ruling and stealing forever whatever befalls the country. Mr. Chairman, we in APC are resolved to stop them in their tracks and rescue Nigeria from the stranglehold of PDP."

Other than security, he listed some of the other casualty areas to be agriculture, commerce and manufacturing even at a time that "the Government continues to announce fantastic growth figures."

He then announced that an APC government under his watch would "put priority on the protection of lives and property, pursuing economic policies for shared prosperity and immediate attention on youth employment, quality education for development, modernity and social mobility, agricultural productivity for taking millions out of poverty and ensuring food security and reviving industry to generate employment and "make things" not just to remain hawkers of other peoples' goods.

Other areas of focus include developing solid minerals exploitation which will substantially attract employment and revenue for government, restoring honour and integrity to public service by keeping the best and attracting the best, tackling corruption which has become blatant and widespread, and respecting the constitutional separation of powers between the executive, legislature and judiciary and respecting the rights of citizens."

But where is Bola Tinubu?

Curiously however, Asiwaju Bola Tinubu was most conspicuous by his absence at Buhari's declaration of intent to run as president on the platform of the APC! We tried to reach out to him, but couldn't get him. It was only his wife that showed up. We were concerned.

Again, El-Rufai and I went to see him in his Lagos residence and he complained that we had continued to see Buhari as being 'our own candidate' and not the APC's candidate, insisting that we should let go of him. He made a big deal of that issue as a justification for his non-attendance.

We of course did not agree with him or believe that was the entire story. Just because we had moved from CPC to APC does not mean that the able lieutenants that Buhari had been relying on over time must now disappear completely from the scene. Just as we had fought over the CPC alliance bloc earlier on, you can't say you want to fight for an election and people you don't really know, who have also not demonstrated some affinity with your deeply developed lines of reasoning, would suddenly emerge to exclusively manage your electioneering process for you.

As a half-way measure, we told Tinubu to give us whomever he had in mind from his ACN group that would join in and work with those of us who were already so engaged with the Buhari campaign effort. Fortunately for us also, by then Buhari had told El-Rufai to go and run in Kaduna which lent a different picture to the entire process as it enabled us to have some vacancy within the campaign effort that needed filling, as well as the added advantage of getting almost virtual control of the majority of the voting delegates from the state.

Back to Tinubu's complaints; we told him to give us his people and he then came up with three or four people that he wanted us to hand the campaign over to, with one of them being his former Commissioner for Information and Strategy, Dele Alake. He also asked the former Lagos State Speaker and Senator, Dr. Olorunnimbe Mamora to join us. We were very happy with Mamora anyway as the gentleman had demonstrated considerable balance, maturity and creativity all through his political career as much as we knew him. Then there was also Babafemi Ojudu. Generally, we said there was no problem with his nominees and were most willing to welcome and work with them.

From experience however, we knew that there was more to it than was being discussed then and soon came to find out that Tinubu was going round to meet with Obasanjo, Ibrahim Babangida and other national leaders to sound them out on who they wanted as the presidential candidate of our new party, the APC.

As we also came to gather, initially, none of them wanted Buhari as the candidate as they were all afraid that he was going to come after them with a mission of vengeance. With this excuse, Tinubu continued to hold back from supporting us, more or less.

Indeed, things got so bad that as the scheduled national Convention of the party drew near, we weren't going to attend because we knew that the kind of people we wanted to get positions at the convention were equally being sidelined. We met as a bloc and decided to advise our principal not to go to the event.

It took the intervention of three ACN governors - Amaechi, Amosun and Fashola – who had heard about our misgivings and came to Buhari's residence where they argued that, after all we had done and still stood to do, it was not right that we were not going to be represented as the former CPC party at the convention. They assured us that the convention would be fair and that there could really not be an APC national convention when the person we have in mind to be our flag-bearer in the resultant elections would not be present. They insisted that Buhari must attend. We gave in and went to the convention.

Notably at that convention, Chief Akande stepped down from his position as Interim Chairman of the party, while our current chairman, Chief John Oyegun emerged to play the role of National Chairman in a substantive capacity.

There was however more drama to come at the convention as regards the filling of other executive positions.

You will recall the composition of the Interim Executive earlier and how, for the position of national secretary, the ANPP had imposed Tijjani Tumsa who was really no match for our nominee, El-Rufai. Though he was the national secretary of ANPP before then, he was certainly not as politically savvy as El-Rufai. Perhaps this explains why he had a chip on his shoulders, such that he was hiding virtually everything the party was doing from El-Rufai and we were literally struggling to get information.

This time around, we were determined to have our own person as the national secretary at the convention. We were not going to allow what had happened before to be repeated.

Eventually though, we again agreed to a compromise and Alhaji Mai Mala Buni of Yobe State, then became the National Secretary. Though he was from the ANPP also, he had a close rapport with Buhari. And although the ANPP were happy that they were the ones that had produced the new national secretary, in all reality, he was someone acceptable to us.

There were a few other positions we didn't agree with and we went to the convention and defeated those candidates. One of them actually became so bitter at the declared outcome that he accused Tinubu of betrayal as he (Tinubu), had promised him that position.

We did everything possible to stomach our revulsion over how things were going and at a point, when things got so heated, we appealed to the governors: "look, what about these positions that were being filled without our knowledge, let alone consent?"

Given the high stakes that were involved, we wanted to have things done generally by consensus. We didn't want to go out and fight by having any contested elections. The idea was to resolve matters by consensus so that we don't kill APC with acrimonious electoral contests for offices. It was however in the manipulation of the consensus building process by our partners that we lost confidence due to the games that were being played. We had to compromise our position, but that continued into the decision on the modalities for the primary election.

One of the problems we had on the issue of primaries was to decide whether to have direct or indirect primaries. It was a major issue. Though our Constitution allows for either of the two, the critical issue for us, as we always liked to strategise and plan in advance, was that the direct primaries option requires that all the members of APC must vote directly for their flag-bearer, whereas indirect primaries means that an elected few will be the ones to come and cast their votes. At that point in time, we had an estimated membership base of eighteen to nineteen million members; all active. We were strategising on how to do direct primaries at the state level on different days but the problem we had was that to strengthen the integrity of the vote, it was essential to conduct a biometric register of APC members. The biometric register will result in the issuance of a unique membership card that will then be validated before voting to ensure transparency, and avoid rigging. But Tinubu frustrated it by saying that we should just register members through a form he had printed by way of an automated membership list rather than conduct a biometric registration.

We were against it but he got the National Working Committee of the party divided on it. The issue was so important that we got Buhari to go and meet with Tinubu in London to iron the matter out. At that meeting, Tinubu more or less agreed and conceded to Buhari but unfortunately by the time he returned and the NWC of the party met, we still lost the vote. The ACN and ANPP connived once again to defeat the idea simply because a biometric register could not be manipulated.

Equally, two of the other aspirants, Atiku and Kwankwaso, also preferred the indirect primaries method where they hoped they could spend money to buy votes from delegates. We didn't have money for this and we knew that Buhari's strength was with the people and so the party, for a couple of months, was divided as to which way to go until we lost the vote.

Despite losing the vote, we knew that we couldn't go back on the process. We had gone too far. We were therefore still prepared to go and test Buhari's popularity by going through the approved indirect primaries method.

Indeed, the issue of direct and indirect primaries was an outcrop of the membership registration mode adopted by the party at inception. At that point the issues had to do with whether to adopt a form-based or a direct data capture approach, and the arguments for both were seriously canvassed. With the benefit of hindsight then, we had now returned to the fall-outs of that unfinished business.

As outlined then, the Direct Data Entry, 'the DDE, is a fraud-proof system that would be readily available days after the field exercise is concluded even as the logistical undertaking involved in using paper forms and the associated "total cost over program lifetime" are invariably understated and the efficacy of the forms overstated.'

Also, the printing/production, distribution, collation, audit and archiving of paper forms are huge undertakings that are almost always grossly underestimated. The risk associated with loss and/or damage to paper forms is also invariably understated. The average time it takes for data entry per form is also repeatedly underestimated, as many conditions need to be in place, which often makes it impractical.

This assertion is based on extensive experience with registrations of this nature, perhaps the most relevant glaring example being the NCC SIM Registration Front-end project, where the contracted partners deployed both models in various forms. Analysis of the feedback and results from this exercise gave a clear winning score to the deployments based on DDE as against those based on paper forms. It is the form based part of the SIM registration that has made it impossible for the exercise to be concluded well over a year after the conclusion!

In addition to the downsides outlined above, whose costs in almost all cases not only deplete the "savings" associated with avoiding the initial CapEx of DDE equipment, but actually, over the lifetime of the program significantly exceed those of DDE; the following are other demerits:

- Illegibility of form field entries; which is wholly dependent on the handwriting quality of the member and other human errors!.
- Difficulty (and in most cases inability) to enforce data entry business rules to prevent data entry errors or even deliberate errors and or fraud. This data restriction is easily automated in DDE.
- Transcription errors during data entry.
- Difficulty in implementing and enforcing an audit trail.
- Inflexibility of making changes to form design mid-stream (as printing likely to be done in bulk on off-set printers) without incurring prohibitive costs.'

On the other hand, DDE comes with 'the strategic and tactical value of using biometrics, particularly with respect to identity assurance and program integrity cannot be overstated; and the transformation of DDE's investment profile from CapEx to OpEx over the lifetime of the program is an often overlooked advantage.

The value of getting the Biometric data of members cannot be over emphasised; if only because it is the only fraud-proof mechanism that would ensure internal democracy for a major political party like APC!. This perhaps represents one of the greatest advantages of DDE as biometrics are the most rock-solid and incontestable methods of identity assurance, which lies at the core of a membership system. With respect to initial CapEx, often positioned as the soft underbelly and major weakness of the DDE approach, with the commoditisation of many of the technological components making up the solution, we can pare down the PC/netbook to bare-bones or substitute with a cheaper entry-level netbook or reduce the number of PC's to fit the budget.

Other merits worth pointing out include:

1. It is a much faster exercise and proffers the valuable opportunity for a member to verify/inspect their digital records in real-time and intercede for correction; as well as the convenience of online initiated registration!
2. Over the lifetime of the program, the incremental costs associated with future/continuous registrations is marginal as it basically becomes an OpEx, as opposed to the significant CapEx that paper forms will continue to carry.
3. Eliminates the logistical nightmare of a paper based data entry process.
4. Value Proposition for Biometric-based Identity.
5. Identity Assurance and System Integrity.
6. Value Store for Additional Revenue – many agencies are looking for verification services – can sell the data, verification service, etc.

7. Security – in various forms combined with election monitoring and prevention of rigging in sync with INEC system.'

But with the leadership concluding to go the form based route, we had to yet live with it.

Whilst still fighting for the direct primaries option, nomination forms became open for the contest proper. Buhari picked up his form and complied with the requirements.

A couple of days to the deadline for submission, we got to know that the ACN camp had arranged for Alhaji Waziri Aminu Tambuwal, the then Speaker of the House of Representatives to also pick up a form. We understood that his colleague lawmakers in the National Assembly purchased the party's nomination form on his behalf. They said they wanted a new generation of flag-bearers, not the old school of Atiku, Buhari and even Kwankwaso! We smiled and opted to wait and see how events would unfold.

It didn't stop there. At some point, Governor Aregbesola reached out to Pastor Bakare. Remember that ACN had virtually frustrated the 2011 CPC ticket and denied Pastor Bakare the opportunity of becoming vice president in our previous botched alliance. Yes, they had agreed to the alliance – everything else was settled except a disagreement over the post of vice president as they wanted to be the ones to nominate the vice president.

At that point of course, it was too late. The names had been submitted to INEC, the time for substitution had passed and besides, Buhari had stated that he would always go with someone he is comfortable with. He said nobody should tell him who to run with but the ACN and Tinubu insisted on Bakare being dropped for them to nominate the vice president. That was what they used to scuttle the alliance in 2011 and so things were really not smooth sailing between Tinubu's camp and Pastor Bakare at the personal level.

Indeed, the situation had become most complicated at that time when they had proposed that Bakare should sign a post-dated letter of resignation. We couldn't sleep the night they brought the letter and we had to run around to seek opinions on what to do. We knew it was not being fair on Bakare but to our consternation even some people in CPC were putting pressure on him, even abusing him that he should go ahead to sign and make the sacrifice for Tinubu to be happy. Meanwhile, the issue was about legality and possible exposure to blackmail. How can you be a credible candidate for vice president, one of the highest offices in the land, when you are resigning your position in advance?

It was quite a messy arrangement. Finally, we told Buhari that it was his call to make as the party was divided. Some said Bakare should resign while others objected. Fortunately, Buhari's integrity won the day. He said he would prefer to lose the resultant elections honourably than to win through forcing his vice president to resign in advance. He offered the ACN a pick of options: The Ministry of Foreign Affairs, Finance, any other cabinet positions but for his running mate to resign, he would not accept. They walked out on us. There were subsequent acrimonious public spats between Bakare and Tinubu, especially during the 2012 Ondo State gubernatorial election when the latter openly endorsed the incumbent against the ACN's candidate.

Fast forward to 2014 November, Aregbesola now approached Bakare and asked that the rift between him and Tinubu be settled. He affirmed that as Yoruba leaders, they had to be united, that Tinubu had a lot of respect for him and that there was nothing wrong with what had happened between them in the past since it was just politics. Bakare obliged him and affirmed that he did not have a problem of working with Tinubu or indeed anyone else at that, as long as it was in the national interest.

Subsequently, Bakare and Aregbesola met on a flight to London where the former asked for a meeting with Tinubu. After Aregbesola secured the appointment upon Bakare's return to Nigeria, they rode together in Aregbesola's car to the Bourdillon residence of Tinubu. The purpose of that meeting was to establish Asiwaju's personal interest in the 2015 elections if Buhari was given the APC Presidential ticket. They adjourned to meet the next Friday to harmonise Asiwaju's interest with Buhari's but that subsequent meeting never took place.

A few days to the presidential primaries in Lagos, the landmark event that we were all looking forward to, we had gone round all the states to woo the delegates. We went to states where APC had governors and states where we did not have governors. We also met all the party officials and requested their support. It was then that we received confirmation that Atiku in particular had been going around and giving them money in the name of building party offices and party structures. The word out there was about five million naira from Atiku for the Anambra and Enugu state chapters of the party for them to build party structures. We couldn't do that and yet we went to see them too. Many of them told us that Atiku had brought money and asked what we had to offer them? We told them we had brought good news and hope for Nigeria. That this man would serve them well, that he was incorruptible. And they were convinced. So, that gave us the additional confidence to continue the struggle.

Taking out Tambuwal

On the Tambuwal threat, we understood that CPC supporters from Sokoto made it known to him that should he decide to agree to be the spoiler that would run against Buhari, they would support somebody else for the governorship election in the state which they were well aware was his original desire. He called a press conference and withdrew. Yes, Tambuwal withdrew gracefully, with the following statement on November 18, 2014;

> I have carefully considered the concerns expressed by some of our leaders, whom I deeply respect, and whose support and counsel I enjoy, to the effect that my entry into the presidential race at this point, may necessitate having to rework some equations on the political chessboard of the party. Having consulted widely, taking into consideration the concerns of some elders of the party, I have decided to suspend my participation in the presidential contest for now. I havedone so as a sacrifice for the cohesion and unity of the APC. I am suspending my participation in the presidential race for now, because I do not have any inordinate ambition to occupy any office.

The pressure was so much on him. At a point when he wanted to go out to public places, people would surround him and just be saying: "Look, are you going to campaign against Baba?" He had to say publicly that he was not interested in the presidency project. He had decided he wanted to be governor, he was not going to challenge Buhari. Sai Baba!

The Ulamas' intervention

Something else also happened before the primaries. The Council of Imams and Ulama from the North, that is the Islamic spiritual leaders, came together about three weeks before the primaries and said they didn't want the North to be divided. The three main contenders for APC ticket were northerners. They were concerned that it shouldn't be that way. They called for a meeting with the three of them.

Buhari briefed us about this outreach and we encouraged him to go to the meeting. They summoned Atiku, Kwankwaso and Buhari to a meeting and said: "Look, we are praying for all of you but you people shouldn't go out there and fight amongst yourselves. Agree amongst the three of you who will be the candidate and let that person carry the other two along. After all, it is for Nigeria. If you go through an acrimonious primaries process, it would be PDP that will benefit from it."

They also went beyond that to say they had thought further about it, that the oldest and most senior one of them - who is of course General Buhari - should be the one to lead and offer positions to the other two to carry them along. They gave them one week to go and discuss about it and revert to them. Buhari came out of the meeting and we clapped and thanked God.

But the big issues now were what positions would he offer them? We said Ok; promise Atiku a big ambassadorship somewhere. We reached out to Atiku's camp but they said they did not want anything like that, that the only thing they would agree to is if Buhari would agree to do one term and endorse Atiku for 2019. Buhari's response was that it was not his personal prerogative to give anybody power or to endorse anybody and that he could not even also do that in this instance since what he was asked to do was to offer positions.

Kwankwaso's camp was more reasonable. They came back and said yes, Kwankwaso wouldn't mind stepping down provided he would be made Chief of Staff to the president. We said: "Ok, this is more sensible but the position of Chief of Staff is very personal. You don't know General Buhari other than just being political allies. You don't know him, how can you be his Chief of Staff? Take any cabinet position you want, except that. Unfortunately, you also can't be the Secretary to the Government of the Federation, SGF, because you are both from the North-West, otherwise you would have been given the position of SGF."

There is also something interesting that had happened about the Kwankwaso situation, and that interesting thing is that, if you recall before that time, the then governor of the Central Bank, Sanusi Lamido Sanusi had been removed from office illegally, because the president could not remove him without the Senate's support (and they didn't go to the Senate for that, apparently because they would not be able to push it through).

The then Emir of Kano died about that period and he, Sanusi was one of those in line to succeed him. The majority of the kingmakers in Kano voted for him to be installed as the successor, but Jonathan and the PDP were backing his rival, Prince Lamido Ado Bayero, then Ciroman Kano. They were putting all kinds of pressure on Kwankwaso that he must give it to Bayero, to the point that they actually threatened that there would be riots in Kano if he gave it to Sanusi and that the riots would lead to the federal government declaring a state of emergency in the state, which they had done in Adamawa against Nyako.

It was at this point that Buhari then got up to stand by Kwankwaso and assured him that all would be well. He sent two letters by hand to Kwankwaso, saying: "Look, if that is what you and the kingmakers want, you must give Sanusi the emirship." That's how he gave it to Sanusi.

When Kwankwaso did so, the Federal Government went on to withdraw his security details. It was that bad but there were no riots because Buhari was behind him. We knew then, that the support was there.

Atiku and Kwankwaso were supposed to call Buhari back a week after those offers but they never called and even stopped taking his calls. When this persisted, Buhari then went back to the Ulamas and briefed them that it was looking very likely that they were all going to contest and asked them to pray for them. They went to the primaries, the three Northern Muslim contestants plus two more, Rochas Okorocha from Imo State who came out to run too, along with the publisher of *Leadership* newspaper, Sam Nda-Isaiah. Consequently, there were five contestants for the primaries.

The *ThisDay* Interview

Again, another major event occurred. For the first time, we got Buhari to wear a suit and grant an interview to Nduka Obaigbena's *ThisDay* newspaper, for The Sunday Supplement where he stated his goals, his objectives, his manifesto, programmes and what he would do if he became president. We were happy that we did that and it was published on the Sunday just before the primaries. In point of fact, the cover picture for the Supplement is the same as the cover page of this book, compliments of the Publisher – Nduka Obaigbena.

D-day was December 11th 2014, on a Thursday I remember and before then, the whole of the stadium was papered with Atiku's posters. Kwankwaso also joined in the poster blitz. We didn't have money, we couldn't do that. It was Governor Fashola that called El-Rufai and asked: "What are you people doing? Have you been to the stadium? Go and see what is happening there. How can you be quiet and hope to get the ticket - when all of your co-contestants are marketing themselves very vigorously out here?" Governor Fashola then decided to single-handedly arrange for posters to be printed and pasted by his Deputy Governor and his aides on the Friday night before the convention on Saturday morning.

By this time, some of the delegates had started arriving from all the states of the country. When we got there and saw the posters, we were very impressed, but decided we had to do more. It was then that I recalled that the contents of the *ThisDay* Sunday supplement were so good. I called Obaigbena and asked if he could get us ten thousand copies which would cover our nine thousand delegates. He said he could get us five hundred free and the cost of the rest would be a thousand naira per copy. That was to come to about ten million naira including transportation, which we also didn't have any budget for; it was that bad.

I went and picked up the five hundred copies from him. And guess what? They were going like hot cake, with delegates struggling among themselves to grab copies! When we had like ten copies left, we stopped and a good Samaritan proceeded to make photocopies for less than thirty naira per copy. He made close to five thousand copies and paid cash for it. It was as if we were distributing very rare trophies or even US dollars! It was indeed a rare memento, as before then, it was almost impossible to see Buhari wearing a suit and a bow tie. They didn't expect it and he was really looking good.

Even when we got the information the night before the primaries that money was going around, delegates were being promised as much as three thousand dollars by one of the contestants – something like fifty percent now with the balance paid later - and all we could give them were mere copies of the *ThisDay* supplement. Yet they were asking whether they could get more. We were a little bit convinced that there was yet hope for us.

It was at this point that it was also becoming obvious to Tinubu and other political watchers that Buhari was going to be the very likely winner of the primaries.

We went through with the contest and it was a whole-day affair. The entire proceedings were televised live and there was real-time live voting and counting, and of course, we had pushed for a credible person to be chairman at the convention and the responsibility had fallen on Ekiti State Governor, Dr. Kayode Fayemi. If you remember we reached out to him, amongst many others before now, we were assured of fairness if nothing else. We didn't want anyone to rig for us, but we also did not want anyone to rig against us. We were happy that we had spoken to the governors and one of them was to chair the convention. And once we were sure of fair play, we knew that we would have no problem.

The candidates were given a few minutes each to address the delegates and the moment Buhari finished with his address, we knew that the game was over because I remember the lines in the address where he said:

> "I am sorry, I don't have any company, I don't have any money to give you but I have one hundred percent of me and I will work day and night if you give me this mandate to make sure that Nigeria is changed for the better."

They clapped and clapped and clapped, and wouldn't stop clapping.

Again, we remained all night at the convention ground and Buhari refused to move. All the other contestants were going and coming. We took a room there at the stadium; the VIP room at the back. I ordered food, we had dinner and breakfast there and we were dozing off on the chairs.

I also started doing my usual stuff at this point. I like to be scientific in my approach. We started polling the delegates and by 2a.m. I had the projected results though the official results had not come in. I went to Buhari and told him he had won. I gave him the results, the projections I had made and he said: "I see; let's go and pray." We prayed. The votes were being counted and when it was finally released at about 10.00a.m., what I didn't get from the projection was that I had reported that Atiku would be second but by the time the results came out, Atiku was third. Kwankwaso beat him to the third position. It was unbelievable. Money had failed, the delegates had voted their conscience!

From the final tally of results declared by the Kayode Fayemi committee, General Muhammadu Buhari recorded 3, 430 votes to emerge as winner of the APC primaries, Kwankwaso polled 974 votes, Atiku Abubakar 954 votes, Owelle Rochas Okorocha 624 votes and Mr. Sam Nda-Isaiah 10 votes.

A total of 7,214 delegates had been accredited to vote at the convention and following this victory Buhari, was then scheduled to run against incumbent President Goodluck Jonathan, whose adoption was ratified by the People's Democratic Party, PDP, at its special convention held within the same week that the APC was picking its flag-bearer for the 2015 presidential election.

VICE PRESIDENTIAL ISSUES

In the process of putting the party together and going forward, the question of a running mate for Buhari in the event of his being elected APC flagbearer had been a very sticky point in the relations between our group and Bola Tinubu.

While we generally wanted the best slate that would ultimately deliver the presidency to the party and nation, Tinubu for a very long time continued to insist that he had to be on the ticket, no matter the circumstance.

The issue came up again on this night of reckoning.

When the results were about to be declared, it became obvious that Buhari had won the primaries and like I said earlier, we had done a poll by 2a.m. and seen it actually, so we knew that we had won, the only thing that we got wrong was that Kwankwaso came second rather than Atiku. We then decided to go ahead and edit the customary acceptance speech, which had been prepared in advance for Buhari to vet and approve.

In the morning, Tinubu and the rest of our leaders joined in when the official counting started. A very important thing occurred at that point in time. Once it became obvious that Buhari had won, Tinubu came to him and gave him an acceptance speech that his staff had drafted. Buhari read it and said that it would not be necessary, that he already had one done.

Tinubu then asked if he could see the one that Buhari had written but Buhari said: "There is no time sir," and Tinubu pretended as if he did not hear him. That really was the first major public point of friction that was forcing its way out of the pressure cooker.

At that point in time, I think that if Tinubu had been more perceptive, he would have seen the handwriting on the wall. Buhari was not and could never have been someone anybody could control and just dictate to. It was not once, not twice, that he had said that he would rather go back to Daura than do what he was not prepared to do. So, he was not prepared to read a speech that someone had prepared for him without his knowledge and input.

It is also important to mention that Buhari had, in October, granted an interview to *The Cable News*, just as he did with *ThisDay*. In that interview a question was posed to him as to whether he would consider running on a Muslim-Muslim ticket. I think the General's response was not a categorical no.

> "I have not absolutely closed my mind to picking a Christian or Muslim as running mate if I get the ticket. Because I firmly believe that Nigerians, having gone through what they have gone through, realise it is not a matter of religion, but a matter of Nigeria. And the main religions, Christianity and Islam, they know and they believe in the almighty God. The question of stealing and short-changing people in the name of religion should stop."

Underscoring his point, he made allusion to his previous three attempts when he had run with Christian running mates, the success of the Abiola-Kingibe ticket in 1993 and the 1961 fielding of Imam, a Kanuri Muslim by Joseph Tarka's United Middle Belt Congress in Christian-dominated Tivland. He also made reference to the attempt on his life by Boko Haram after he had denounced the sect as ungodly, wondering what more he needed to do to personally demonstrate to Nigerians that he was not a religious fundamentalist?

But the moment he won the primaries, all hell broke loose on this subject.

The Conference of Catholic Bishops started demanding for a meeting with him. We scheduled the meeting and they went straight to the point: "Look, you have emerged now, we thank God for your emergence and maybe you are indeed going to make it this time around, but please do not force us to campaign against you by coming up with a Muslim-Muslim ticket. We are going to give you the benefit of the doubt that you are not the Islamic fundamentalist you are being portrayed to be but certainly there is no way we will accept that out of one hundred and eighty million Nigerians, you cannot get a Christian to run with you and then go on to pick a Muslim."

Back to the primaries; we left the venue with Tinubu not being quite happy but with the rest of us elated and in a celebration mood. We returned to Abuja and continued strategising.

Then came another epoch-making event. A couple of days after the emergence of Buhari as the flag-bearer of APC, the pressure on him to announce a running mate became very strong indeed. We did an evaluation as usual by having job descriptions and personnel specifications to match the leading candidates with what is expected of a running mate and awarded marks for each important quality.

I remember that we had at least four candidates shortlisted. We had Tinubu, Fashola, Fayemi and Rotimi Amaechi. We had Oshiomhole also but I'm not sure we had Osinbajo. We conducted a straw poll on them and came out with two outcomes. Firstly, that if Buhari was inevitably to do a Muslim-Muslim ticket, we would be better off with Fashola. Secondly, if not, the outcome was in favour of Fayemi. We went outside the governors and also included several other hopefuls in the list as well. We did all that and shared our findings with Buhari who thanked us for being most analytical as usual.

We had used a scientific approach that was not subjective. We could see that a Christian candidate was going to add value, we could also see that in terms of experience and value to the ticket, Fashola got more scores than Fayemi. Fayemi got more marks on the Christian and Muslim factor but in terms of performance, Fashola got more. Thereafter, we rated them together overall and Fashola came first but we knew there was a very clear political risk in that. As for Tinubu, I think he came a distant fourth, if not fifth in the evaluation.

Then there came a request one afternoon that Tinubu would like to see Buhari. We were with him in his residence in Abuja when the message came.

By the way, it is worth mentioning that both in the 2011 and 2015 contests, Buhari had no personal home in Abuja, despite the fact of his having been a former head of State and with all the positions he had held. Therefore, he always had to rent a house during the electioneering seasons. The house he rented for the 2011 election campaign was in Queen Elizabeth Drive, Asokoro. For the 2015 race, he rented a different house in Maitama. It was paid for by a long-standing Good Samaritan who had unflinching confidence in him.

We were there when we got the message that Tinubu wanted to see him in the company of Chief Bisi Akande. Buhari said on this occasion that they should not bother to come, that he would go to them instead. The meeting was fixed for 8p.m. and El-Rufai, I, and a few others went along to drop him off in Lagos House where the meeting was to hold.

When we got there, we saw that it wasn't just Tinubu and Akande that he would be discussing with. Rauf Aregbesola was also there and Governor Adams

Oshiomhole too. We whispered to Buhari whether we should get someone to join him but he said no; that since they had wanted to come and see him but he had offered to go to them instead, it would not be right for him to have a second person in attendance. He also asserted that just because they were four on their side does not mean that he could not hold his own. Nonetheless, Sarki Abba, his dependable aide stayed with him even though he did not go into the meeting room. The rest of us departed.

We knew they were going to stay for a couple of hours and probably run into midnight, so we couldn't see Buhari again that night. The following morning, of course, we were more than anxious to see him and to get the feedback from the meeting. And the feedback was that they had an inconclusive meeting. Tinubu had insisted that he had to be the running mate; that the South-West people had met and chosen him for that role and given the way the primaries went and the support that the South-West gave Buhari, they believed they should be the ones to produce the VP.

Buhari said he had no objection to heeding the call of the South-West as it concerned offering the zone the position of running mate, but that it would not be a Muslim-Muslim ticket. He told them about the meeting with the Conference of Catholic Bishops and said that apart from that, he just believed that it was not fair.

He also told them that he greatly appreciated Tinubu and his contributions and that what he was going to do as a compromise was that Tinubu should give him three alternative names of people he wanted to endorse for the position from the South-West which he would then choose one from. But Tinubu, Chief Akande and the rest supported him saying that those who were saying they did not want a Muslim-Muslim ticket would not vote for him anyway but that the Yoruba did not care, and will yet vote for him irrespective of the religious slant of the ticket.

Aregbesola, a Muslim, gave himself as an example, asserting that most people in Osun would vote for a Buhari-Tinubu slate. But it was an inconclusive meeting because Buhari refused to budge and insisted that Tinubu should come with three names and that he was willing to give one of them the ticket. We were kind of pleased but also concerned. Pleased because we knew that once he had made up his mind, it would not be Tinubu and that would be it. We were however afraid that they may yet push vigorously for him to reconsider this position, although this was not to be.

Another point of concern was that we were already suspicious even then, of who else would be in Tinubu's mind at this time because we were aware that Tinubu had gotten Professor Yemi Osinbajo to meet with Buhari one-on-one. It was then that it clicked for us that he had been preparing a back-up, just in case and we grew to have no doubt in our minds about this. We were however hoping that because Buhari had said three names, Tinubu would yet put in Fayemi, Mamora or Adams Oshiomhole as options.

I guess somehow, Tinubu didn't want to take a chance with any other names, and we couldn't go with Fashola because the same Muslim-Muslim issue would knock him off. Tinubu returned and gave only Osinbajo's name and not three names. Buhari was surprised as to why only one name instead of three that was requested. Nonetheless, we were pleased with the choice of Osinbajo; given his competence and intellectual capacity as the former Attorney General of Lagos State.

Buhari subsequently had a meeting with Osinbajo, to find out his plans, goals, and accepted him. It was then that the announcement was made that Buhari had chosen a running mate. I remember that by this time it was the Thursday after the primaries - a whole week's time - and it had dragged on for that long because of Tinubu's reluctance, if not refusal to accept that he would not be on the ticket. But now however, the "God factor" had come to play once again and the impasse had been resolved.

That's how the issue of Buhari's running mate was eventually sorted out. It was indeed a most interesting development. Since then, there have been several versions of this story, including one where Tinubu denied that he actually wanted to be on the ticket but those of us who were there know that was not a correct record of what had transpired. Besides the moves made while the merger was being arranged, we have the activities at the convention ground where the primaries were conducted, up to the meeting a couple of days later in Lagos House where his team of four met and decided to put pressure on Buhari, but Buhari stood his ground.

There was also an issue where Vice President Osinbajo was asked if he was nominated by Tinubu. At first, he seemingly didn't want to inflame the fires, but there was so much pressure and he had to say that somebody has to nominate somebody! We know of course that he was handpicked and endorsed by Tinubu. Thank God that Osinbajo has his merits and we knew even then that he was a gentleman we were happy though the poll had favoured Fayemi, chiefly because of the fact that Fayemi had won an election – a strong factor in electoral contests - and was also a Christian. It was this democratic deficit that really robbed Osinbajo of higher consideration in our ranking in the first place until Tinubu weighed in on his behalf and Buhari accepted.

CHAPTER ELEVEN

Election Planning And Monitoring Directorate And The Campaign Trail

FRAMING THE CAMPAIGN MESSAGE

As we approached the actual election season, the feedback we were getting from the continuing work of our pollsters and other related indicators were reaffirming our earlier projections on the nature of the Nigerian crisis. And it was chiefly, three-fold. Firstly, we did not – in the real sense of the word – have a country anymore as the physical space in which we lived and cohabited was generally not safe. Not only was there an insurgency that was ravaging significant sections of the north, the word out there was that we had at least two Boko Haram bands on the field!

For one, we had the original Boko Haram sect that had been founded by Mohammed Yusuf but in addition to this it was also being rumoured that there was a 'military Boko Haram.' We got this information from intelligence sources both within and outside Nigeria and were aghast. You will recall here for example, the revelations of the Australian, Stephen Davies, who had spoken out publicly about this at the time. From all that was coming to the public domain, it was in our view a fact that some high-level officials in the Jonathan administration – but perhaps unknown to him personally – were in some way engaged in fuelling the continuation of the insurgency because a lot of money was being appropriated to combat it as long as the crisis persisted.

However, this money was not being spent on our military and that was why our soldiers were fleeing from the battlefields or defecting and consequently being court-martialled. How do you send men to go and fight without adequate weapon and munitions cover? Like a bad script, they were being set-up for the Boko Haram fighters to come out, engage them, take their weapons and kill them. They felt that they then had no other option left to them as rational human beings other than to run.

They were being given antiquated and ramshackle weapons while a lot of money was being taken out of the system in the name of buying weapons. Nigeria's existence was grossly endangered and we were about to lose our country, and we knew that.

Now we have witnessed some change and indeed no right-thinking Nigerian will say the situation in the country has not improved presently, at least as far as the Boko Haram insurgency is concerned. Even the international community will not come out and say Nigeria has not done something about Boko Haram. They cannot say that and even if they do, with the information at everyone's disposal, such a statement would be highly suspicious and questionable. There are a few hundred US military personnel in Nigeria as I write that are assisting the country in the fight against Boko Haram. They know that we now have a leader with the appropriate experience and trust quotient required to address the crisis.

Indeed, some reason that a major problem Nigeria has faced over the years is this issue of trust deficit within the leadership. Without that level of desired trust, nothing really can be done to save the country.

The second major problem that the polls outcome reconfirmed for us was the endemic level of corruption. Corruption was so pervasive in the country that we knew that there couldn't be any real governance because we could not get value for money. If you wanted to build a road, it would cost you ten times the actual cost and you could also end up not having the desired quality of construction at the end of the day or no road at all.

When the PDP administration wanted to do a power project, they reportedly spent a humongous sum of seven to eight billion dollars with nothing to show for it because corruption had gone viral. Indeed, corruption was largely responsible for the Boko Haram insurgency, for when loosely translated, Boko Haram simply means Western education is ungodly. The sect was indeed justifying its carnage on account of the corrupt practices of our western educated leaders. So, within this scenario, societal problems could not be solved quickly in that no government programme would succeed under this atmosphere, hence the need to have somebody of Buhari's stature, who had long demonstrated an avowed penchant for good governance, along with an innate passion to fight corruption and rescue the country.

On the third plank, namely the economy, the country was in shambles with what had been aptly described as "jobless growth"; an economic phenomenon in which our GDP was reported to be one of the fastest growing just as we were also experiencing high level of unemployment. Nigeria even overtook South Africa to become the biggest economy in Africa at some point in 2014, as a result of statistical GDP rebasing, yet jobs were nowhere to be found.

The high level of unemployment was so bad that, in one very regrettable instance, hundreds of thousands of job seekers turned up to contend for four thousand places in a job interview with the Nigeria Immigration Service (NIS). Not only had they been made to part with non-customary interview processing fees, when the logistics, crowd control, welfare, emergency and security arrangements put in place to cater for the unbelievable number of job seekers failed, as many as sixteen lives were lost and scores injured in the ensuing stampede. Thus, it was against this backdrop that we formally entered into the 2015 Presidential Elections Campaign season.

We however had our doubts over our candidate's economic management abilities. Buhari had been our leader and I had worked with him for many years and knew him. But as we saw things, we would not be able to have a good economy without enhanced security and, without Boko Haram being eliminated.

Anybody that criticises Buhari on the premise of his handling of the economy is not really saying much that is new. This is because we know why we wanted him to run, why we begged him to do so, worked for him and helped to ensure that he won. We saw him as the leader of a Nigeria that is stable in terms of the security of lives and properties and in terms of minimising or eliminating corruption. When this foundation is made, it is hoped that whoever emerges as the Vice President would focus on the economy. Thus, the goals of securing our country, combating corruption and developing the economy will be achieved.

Too many cooks will not spoil this broth

As outlined above, we had a straightforward 3-point manifesto message for the 2015 presidential elections. But it was not arrived at just like that as given the nature and history of our merger, there were still 'quasi-factional challenges' that had to be addressed even as they showed up at this point.

It had to do with which team would prepare the campaign message by way of a manifesto. While the Strategy Committee under the leadership of Governor Fashola had produced a draft manifesto which drew from the work of our pollsters, consultants and the survey outcomes that had been conducted since the inception of the APC, we later discovered the existence of an 'economic team' that included Professor Pat Utomi, Mr. Wale Edun and Professor Yemi Osinbajo which was directed by Tinubu to also produce a draft manifesto. We therefore ended up with two documents.

But given our resolve to do everything to ensure a seamless process leading to eventual victory for our candidate as well as the benefit of our experience in the CPC of 2010/2011, we formed a committee which then went to work, harmonising both drafts from which the final approved economic plan in the manifesto document was distilled. Patience had paid off once again and we crossed yet another seemingly difficult hurdle.

Amaechi as Campaign Director-General

Given his courage to stand up against the Jonathan administration, the stellar role that he had played in rallying the 'New PDP' governors to join the APC and his subsequent full identification with the political aspirations of the APC flag-bearer, General Muhammadu Buhari, the appointment of Rotimi Amaechi as the Director-General of the Buhari-Osinbajo campaign effort was a most fitting choice.

Underscoring the excellent support that Amaechi provided for the campaign effort was the fact that he threw in all the goodwill he could muster into his assignment and indeed spared no effort towards ensuring that the campaign did not lack in any conceptual, material or logistical way.

Amaechi and his team at the Presidential Campaign Council (where I served as a member of the Election Monitoring Directorate) went to work on these and other issues most ebulliently, courting all manner of groups and interests and joining in with our long-running effort to maximise the intellectual, technocratic and scientific elements of the process.

In addition to the work done by AKPD - the firm established by the former Obama campaign manager, there were also local consulting agencies that were to come along in the Amaechi era and they brought with them a panoply of youth groups and a very strong youth-oriented flair that fitted in most aptly within the nation's demographics.

Something else worthy of mention here is the fact that up until the time the 'New PDP' governors joined us, we were generally dependent on Tinubu and our own limited resources, and I tell you, it is important to acknowledge that the situation changed the moment the New PDP came on board. It changed because Rotimi Amaechi stood out. Of all the New PDP governors, he stood out. Maybe Nyako would have been just as supportive also but he had his problems. Of the remaining New PDP governors, of course, they were divided, with Kwankwaso also coming out. But one New PDP governor that joined APC and made a difference was Rotimi Amaechi. Therefore, this section would not be complete without my paying tribute to him.

I remember a couple of occasions before this time when Buhari was to travel with Tinubu and we would be at the airport in Abuja or Kaduna waiting for him to pick us up. Buhari was and remains a stickler for time. If the flight is supposed to be at 9a.m., by 8:30a.m., he was ready. He would get to the airport five minutes to 9a.m., not at 9a.m. To him, we had to arrive on time if not before, that was how he worked. And on many occasions, we would arrive at 9a.m. and by 9:30a.m., we would be calling to find out where the plane was. But Sunday Dare, Tinubu's able Lieutenant, was always available to ameliorate the situation with explanations.

During such moments, we had to live with the situation as we did not have much of a choice. But the moment Amaechi arrived, we now had a choice. Whenever we needed him, he was there. Remarkably also, Amaechi was the one that brought in the main youth media group – Adebola Williams and his team at Red Media Africa, when it got to a point when we needed to reach out to the youths and therefore needed people who can reach out to them. We wanted the young guys – who would speak the language of the youths – and that's what we got. And they were fantastic. They did very well. So it was part of our strategic approach to reach out to that sector of the electorate and Amaechi indeed made the difference, even as he was ably supported by the amiable Deputy DG - Senator Olorunnibe Mamora and the hard-working Secretary to the Campaign Council - Hajia Hadiza Bala Usman.

The Election Management Committee

Now we were done with the primaries and running mate issues and the nationwide electioneering campaign started in earnest. Every hand was on deck and for us in the Election Management Committee; it was a lot of work that had to be done, and in very little time too!

We developed the APC Election Winning Management System and went to work. It involved tracking all of the phases of the process until victory was eventually determined in our favour. A science-based application, it involved an Election Monitoring Analysis and Reporting System that enabled us to conduct real time election monitoring.

Overall there were three objectives, namely, the delivery of winning messages, mobilising voters to the polls and monitoring the polls with a view to calling the outcome within minutes of the close of voting.

Specifically, it saw us developing campaign messages, arranging for the training of our polling agents and supervisors, the filing, documentation and transmission of incident reports, polling units' information and indeed the entire string of polling events.

It also involved monitoring the actual elements of voting on D-day, including the recording, transmitting and following up on when voting materials were delivered, when accreditation and voting started and closed, when results were declared and whether all the stipulated procedures were complied with by every actor in the process.

In terms of actual expected votes in the polls, our projections were between 15 and 22.5m in all and in appreciation of the critical need to adopt a bottom-up approach if we were eventually going to meet this target we went to work on developing a composite training manual which we then proceeded to administer in all the states of the federation.

The manual spelt out that the roles of party agents in the process were essentially three-fold:

1. **CANVASSER:** To get registered voters to come out on election day and vote for APC candidates and enlighten them on the correct method of thumb printing so as not to void the ballot paper.

2. **REPORTER**: To report information – conduct of INEC and security officials, timing and number of accredited voters; incidence – card reader malfunction, PVC, malpractices, security threats; and results via SMS.

3. **FRAUD PREVENTION**: To ensure that only voters with valid PVCs are allowed to accredit and vote; no undue influence or buying of voters and results are not inflated or manipulated before signing the Result Sheet – Form EC8A.'

Determined not to leave any small detail to chance, we then went ahead to break it down into detailed 'Specific Duties of the Party Agents on the day of Election:'

i. All Party Agents must report to their appropriate polling units by 6.30a.m.

ii. All Party Agents must send report to the control centre the exact time the Electoral Officers report in their various Polling Units.

iii. All Polling Agents must verify the materials brought by the INEC officials and send a report to the control centre.

iv. All Polling Agents must ensure that Form EC8A is available in all their polling units before the commencement of election and report to the control centre where it is not available.

v. Ensure that only those who registered are allowed to do accreditation in their unit.

vi. Take note of the numbers of the accredited voters and send same to the control centre.

vii. Ensure that only one ballot paper is given to each voter, which must be signed and stamped in the presence of everybody.

viii. Ensure that the sorting and counting are done in a transparent manner.

ix. Ensure that the original and duplicate of the result sheet Form EC8A is stamped and signed by the Presiding Officer.

x. All Polling Agents should sign the result sheets and collect the duplicate copy even if their party lost in their polling units.

xi. All the polling Agents must send the result of the Polling Units immediately it is announced. Where an agent is in possession of a camera phone, he/she should take the picture of the result sheet and send it to the control centre.

xii. All Polling Agents must accompany the result and the INEC officials to the Ward Collation Centre where the result of various polling units comprising the ward must first be added up by the ward collation agent before the real collation.

Atop the party agents' level, were the ward collation agents and we equally outlined their specific roles:

i. The Ward Collation Agent must ensure that what is contained in the Form EC8A of the various units is what is recorded in the Form EC8B.
ii. The Ward Collation Agent must send the result as collated from the Ward Collation Centre to the control centre.
iii. The Ward Collation Agent must ensure that original and duplicate of Form EC8B is signed and stamped by the INEC Collation Officer.
iv. The Ward Collation Agent must ensure that he/she signed Form EC8B and get a duplicate copy of the result duly signed and stamped by the Collation Officer.
v. The Ward Collation Agent must accompany the result as collated from the Ward Collation Centre to the Local Government Collation Centre.

Moving on we equally spelt out the duties of the next level in the process, the Local Government Collation Agents:

i. The Local Government Collation Agents must ensure accuracy of the figures recorded in Form EC8B to be transferred to Form EC8C which is the Form for the collated result in the Local Government.
ii. The Local Government Collation Agents must send the result as collated from the Local Government Collation Centre to the control centre.
iii. The Local Government Collation Agents must ensure that original and duplicate of Form EC8C is signed and stamped by the INEC Collation Officer.

iv. The Local Government Collation Agents must ensure that he/she signed Form EC8C and gets a duplicate copy of the result duly signed and stamped by the Local Government Collation Officer.

v. The Local Government Collation Agents must accompany the result as collated from the Local Government Collation Centre to the State Collation Centre.

And capping the chain were the state collation agents for whom we equally spelt out their duties and trained them accordingly to carry same out:

i. The State Collation Agents must ensure accuracy of the figures recorded in Form EC8C to be transferred to Form EC8D which is the Form for the collated result in the State Level.

ii. The State Collation Agents must send the result as collated from the State Collation Centre to the Control Centre.

iii. The State Collation Agents must ensure that original and duplicate of Form EC8D is signed and stamped by the INEC Collation Officer.

iv. The State Collation Agents must ensure that he/she signs Form EC8D and gets a duplicate copy of the result duly signed and stamped by the State Collation Officer.

v. The State Collation Agent must ensure he transmits the result as collated from the State Collation Centre to the National Collation Centre.

All of these were taking place between late December 2014 and early January 2015. As the reader will recall, the presidential election was to take place on the 14th of February, which precisely is St. Valentine's Day.

Let me again bring up the 'God factor' because there were a couple of things we were praying and hoping for which were outside our control. Those things happened without us having orchestrated them. I will give a couple of examples of those critical success factors that we had evaluated and said that if they were to happen, we stood a very good chance of ultimately emerging victorious at the polls.

One of them had to do with the sequential order of the elections. In 2011, it was the presidential election first, followed by the National Assembly and those for the gubernatorial and state houses of assembly seats. At this point however, the PDP wanted to change the sequence to start with the National Assembly, proceed to the gubernatorial and state houses of assembly and then conclude with the presidential contest.

We knew that this proposition was not in our best interest because for us, our most critical asset was our presidential flag-bearer, General Buhari. If we could get him to make a strong showing in the first election in the series and with a big bang at that, we knew that the outcome would invariably propel us as a party to get more state administrations under our control and as well secure even more seats in the legislative houses at the state level and the National Assembly. So, we wanted the presidential contest to come first.

However, the argument of the PDP was that they were afraid that after the presidential election, there may be so much destruction and violence as was the case in 2011, so they wanted to change the order so that the presidential contest would be the last. That was the debate that was going on then but as luck would have it, after much debate on the subject, it was finally resolved to have the presidential contest first. This was really not in their best interest but they failed to see it. It was rather in our interest because we would benefit from the consequential bandwagon effect!

As the facts stood, voters would indeed be rooting for General Buhari and not for the less popular APC assemblymen and women, representatives, senators, and governors. It was only if Buhari won that it would become an almost automatic victory for most of the APC candidates, hence the bandwagon effect.

The smarter strategists within the PDP kept pushing for the presidential election to come last. If Jonathan had agreed to this and pushed hard for it, I think it would have been a little more difficult for us but he did not really put out his hand and so we got our head-start.

The national brand was 'Buhari for us.' And the people coined all manner of supporting texts. In the Yoruba heartland, the election for 14th of February became 'FeBuhari...Love Buhari.' The electorate coined these themselves and we dutifully adopted them in our own official advertising messages. The buzz was electric and the South-West grassroots was fully with us!

Evidence of this even dated somewhat further back. Indeed, on the day after we had held our presidential primaries in Lagos, I remember I had to return to Abuja quickly. It was a late afternoon on the second day of the primaries and the traffic was really bad. I couldn't find my driver. In fact, when I finally found him, he was blocked where he had parked and I had booked a flight for 5p.m.

It was already about 2p.m. at this time and I knew that there was no way I would catch that flight if I waited for him to free the car from where it was trapped. I walked out from the stadium to Ojuelegba and tried to get a taxi there. It was impossible to move; the traffic was so bad. Loads of people were dancing in the streets, I am talking about mainly Yoruba folks (who would have passed for "area boys") dancing enthusiastically because Buhari had won the primaries and intoning: "May God not allow our efforts to end up in vain ...the next challenge is to defeat Jonathan." They were jubilating as if they were the ones that had presented the candidate! And I was walking in their midst.

I had on me some loud APC trappings which I had to remove; I didn't want to be identified because I was walking to find a taxi. And so I mingled with the crowd like the normal average guy. If it were the "talakawas" in the North, jubilating so unabashedly over the Buhari win, I would not have batted an eyelid as it was standard fare. But we were in Lagos and it was largely Yoruba folks that were giving themselves 'high-fives' that Buhari had won the primaries. They were speaking Yoruba to themselves and were very elated. I knew there and then that we were up to something.

Rebranding Buhari and the APC

Then came the issue of rebranding the party and the candidate. We had formed a formidable media group and purposely chose young brands and image consultants because we knew that the demography was youth-friendly. We couldn't get them in 2011, so we targeted them now. We got the people who could speak their language and had to literally rebrand Buhari as it were. He had to be wearing more suits, even T-shirts! He was now going for all kinds of youth events like talents shows and stuff like that. All those we did in Lagos and Ibadan just to get the youth to buy into our platform and to our delight, they came on board.

We also established a Facebook account and a Twitter handle for Buhari and they were being effectively managed. Brand Buhari was really now bonding most powerfully with the youths and the age and cultural gaps were bridged in effect.

TO DEBATE OR NOT TO DEBATE

One other issue which came to the fore at about this time also had to do with plans by a battery of media-related players to convene a debate involving candidates for the office of President. Though it was led by *ThisDay* publisher, Nduka Obaigbena, this Presidential Debate organising Committee had a lot of its members drawn from the leadership of public sector media agencies that had been appointed by the incumbent president who was running for a second term in office. Sensing the danger involved in such a set-up for our candidate, we proceeded to request that the committee be reconstituted. At first this would not be done, but later on, they obliged us.

There was also the issue of President Jonathan having shunned a similar debate in 2011, leaving Buhari, Shekarau and Ribadu to debate amongst themselves then. And finally, there also arose the issue of whether the debate in itself had any real electoral value for our ticket given that all of the polls at this time were placing us already ahead of the other candidates. At this time, the point was made that winning candidates do not really benefit much from participating in debates and could in fact lose points from participating in them. Nevertheless, we went on to prepare our candidate for the debate which however was not to be held.

CHAPTER TWELVE

Technology As A Game Changer: The Card Reader

Sometime in late 2014, INEC called a meeting of all the political parties and their leaders and demonstrated a machine known as the card reader which they informed us they wanted to use for the polls because it would help in reducing the incidence of rigging and ballot paper stuffing.

They explained that the way the card reader worked was quite simple. Using an embedded chip, it would be able to identify if the voters card being presented by all would-be voters at the polling stations had been authentically issued by INEC and also record the total number of such cards that were correctly screened and cleared before the voting period.

Through this method, fake voters cards would not only be detected but in addition, the record of the total number of cards screened and cleared per polling booth would be setting the verifiable upper limit on the total number of votes that could emanate from that polling booth, irrespective of how many supposed voters were listed on the nominal voters roll.

As our history had borne out over the years, without a smart technological gadget like the card reader, there had been massive instances of ballot box stuffing and a lot of lives had been lost with people trying to snatch ballot boxes to stuff them illegally and equally those struggling to protect their votes.

Because the gadget being displayed was seemingly transparent and obviously a very good addition to the mass of efforts that had been developed over the years to help ensure greater credibility of the elections, representatives of notably the big parties tested it with their PVCs and confirmed it was good. And since nobody really could admit that he or she wanted to rig and was therefore against it, there was no definite disavowal of the machine. So we signed on as APC. PDP also signed on and indeed all the major parties signed on, so it was adopted.

INEC then went ahead and placed the orders for them. With a hundred and ten thousand or so polling units nationwide, what they did was to double this figure to effectively have two of the machines per unit. In all, the estimates were for about two hundred and fifty thousand machines. They then proceeded to get the necessary appropriation for its funding to be approved by the National Assembly. The money was then paid and that was it. Contracts were signed for the card readers to be manufactured abroad and then brought into the country early enough for testing, training, distribution and voters education ahead of the general elections.

By the time the PDP realised the impact of what they had signed up to, they started saying: "Wait a minute, this thing we signed on to may not really be in our best interest!" This was clearly because they were the ones that wanted to rig and snatch ballot boxes. They started looking for ways to kill the card reader project but they did not succeed.

There was also another critical related development at this time which was important for us to strategise on. Because of their complementary nature, we knew that the moment the card reader was adopted, the other key game changer, combined with the card reader would be the collection of Permanent Voters Cards, PVCs, which we have talked about in an earlier section. We started looking most intently at the rate of PVC collection, especially in our must win states, because without a PVC, you could not vote. We knew that we had to get our people to go out there and get their PVCs.

We were not going to wait on INEC to carry out all of the statutory voters awareness drives on the exercise and on our own, we started mobilising all of our grassroots leaders at the ward levels, months before the D-day to monitor the rate of collection of the PVCs. Interestingly, there was no evidence that PDP were doing the same thing.

In all the states that we knew we had to win, we got our people out into the field to persuade potential voters to come out for the exercise in order that they would functionally bring the PVCs in. We provided transportation for our agents to ensure total coverage, we were putting pressure on INEC to get the cards ready and we were monitoring distribution. Whatever it took to ensure that we achieved our target ninety percent collection rate in our strongholds, we did. Again, we had to raise money for that and once more, the director-general of the overall campaign effort, Rotimi Amaechi was the master strategist who coordinated the effort to get this job done. He got the point when we explained it in detail to him and he fully supported the efforts so we were able to accomplish the task.

What was the PDP's response when they realised that they couldn't stop the card reader? We were having a meeting one afternoon when we got a very important call from a security operative, and El-Rufai and I went out to get the details. Our informant told us that the PDP, having now realised that they could not stop the card reader scheme, had placed orders for a card reader jamming device to ensure that the card readers would not work on election day.

If you remember, both the APC and the PDP had been conducting regular polls and surveys to gauge the mood of potential voters and with just a couple of weeks to the elections, it was obvious that APC was leading with fifty-five percent to the PDP's possible best effort of forty-five percent. And this indeed was our own worst case scenario!

In all our stronghold states, the polls showed us leading by seventy-five to eighty percent and that they were at risk of not getting even the minimum threshold of twenty-five percent in several of the states. In states like Kaduna, Kano and Katsina for example – all states where they had been able to secure over forty percent of the votes in previous contests – they were now projected to win less than twenty-five percent a-piece! In the nineteen states in the North overall, we polled and saw that they could only get some fairly substantial votes in two states and the statutory twenty-five percent and above in at most, five states in all!

With twenty-five percent in five northern states plus votes from the seventeen remaining states in the South, we knew that there was no way Jonathan could win the election, because he would not have secured twenty-five percent in the mandatory twenty-four states plus FCT. We were getting these projections from our opinion polls and they were also getting the same results, so they became desperate and felt the only way to stop us was to deploy the card reader jamming machines. The machine functions in the same way as a similar one that is used to jam mobile phones and obstruct their capacity to continue to receive transmission signals. This is because the card readers operate with about the same SIM technology that mobile phones use, so they had spoken to some security experts to help them get the jamming machines in.

Our informant thereafter came and took us to a location in Maitama, Abuja where samples of the jamming machine were being tested and we also found out that the PDP's plan was to buy one hundred and ten thousand units thereof – one for each polling unit in the country – to be used to jam the card readers, discredit the polls and in the process, frustrate the electorate. We relayed all of our findings to the press and even arranged for the house where the samples were lodged to be 'invaded.' But once they knew that they had been found out, they panicked and relocated the machines.

We also got their financial estimates for the project and saw that they had planned to spend over two hundred million dollars to buy the card reader jamming machines, and because they were seriously committed to the plan, they had already paid some five million dollars in advance payment for the samples! Again, somehow because we got to know all of these reports and went public with the information, they could no longer go ahead with it. They abandoned the scheme. Their next course of action was to arrest and detain the local agent of the manufacturer of the Card Reader on the flimsy excuse that he was an

APC sympathiser who had programmed the machine to favour us!

With all of these manoeuvres from the PDP side, we were compelled to fight very hard against the negative campaigns and efforts to undermine the card reader and the voter cards.

Seeing that defeat was staring them plainly in the face, the PDP high command hastily convened a review meeting two weeks to the election, when it had become very obvious that things were not going in their favour. Jonathan had become upset and was complaining that people were just taking money and the money was not getting down to those who were going to vote for them. He then personally took over the distribution of money. He moved to Lagos for several days and campaigned furiously for an extended period, throwing enormous amounts of money into the campaign. He visited several traditional rulers including the Awujale with specific requests for endorsements. Some did but Awujale characteristically declined and this made headline news.

By this time, they very well knew that the battle ground was the South-West, but they were too late in the day. We had known from day one and that was what had primarily informed the merger for us. Precisely, we knew two years before this time what they were now finding out two weeks to the election. It was too late. Whilst for the PDP's gross panic had set in, for us grew a realisation that we were on the cusp of an historic moment.

It is important to point out that at this time, there were strong rumours that Jonathan was determined to organise an in-house coup as he would rather hand over power to the Military, specifically his kinsman, General

Minimah, the Chief of Army Staff, to take over as Head of State than handover to Buhari.

When we had fully reviewed the development, the consensus was for us to adopt a wait and see approach, even as we took several steps to address the situation.

We however relayed the message to the American ambassador and the British High Commissioner and later learnt that a message was sent back to Jonathan that "American drones can fish him out, even in Otuoke!"

Not done, within two days, the Americans publicly responded with a terse statement that whoever disrupted the elections would definitely pay a price.

It is also instructive to mention that, at this point we almost had a face-off with Pastor Bakare on account of these manipulations by the PDP, although we never for once doubted his loyalty to Buhari. For the first time in about five years of our having and sharing very close political, personal and family relationships, the PDP games, we discerned, were beginning to eat away at his sterling resolve to stand and fight alongside us in the 'National Rescue Mission' that we had been mutually engaged in.

Over the years of our engagement, El-Rufai and I had started calling him "Egbomi atata" (Yoruba for 'my dearest brother'), and he in return also called us "Aburomi atata."

We had become very close and there was no way we would come to Lagos without going to his house. He would insist we meet before leaving for wherever we were going to sleep. He even gave us an apartment, from a block of flats he had at GRA Ikeja to use each time we were in town, but we did not want to labour his hospitality and therefore continued with the practice of staying at our own place or somewhere else.

Now, Bakare said: "Look, we have always put the country first," and for him then, the way to put the country first was to come together as leaders of the country and tell Jonathan to step aside, so we would have an interim government that would run the country for six months and then conduct fresh elections. That way there would be no issue of winner or loser in the unfolding scenario.

But then this line of reasoning synchronised exactly with one of the decoy gambits of the Jonathan camp! By this time, they had started flying this particular kite, publicly, as a reasonable option to be considered in the public interest, since Jonathan had said he was not going to hand over anyway. For good measure, they also threw in the line that the Federal Government was so powerful and that nothing would happen even if Jonathan insisted on remaining in power! Going back to borrow some details from our national history, they threw in the fact that even when Babangida annulled the June 12 elections, nothing had really happened and that the rest was already history. People can shout and scream but it would not make Buhari president, so to avert bloodshed, according to Bakare, it was better to have a middle-of-the-road solution.

As we saw it, we were being given a message to see if we could persuade Buhari to accept this compromise option, with the sweetener that, in six months' time, he could still win. But we insisted that this would not fly, particularly when the polls were telling us that this was the best time to win outright! We were not going to budge so we increased the pressure on PDP and the presidency by getting world leaders to continue to insist that the electoral calendar should no longer be interrupted.

Mallam asked me to verify from the then Attorney General, Mohammed Bello Adoke, about the veracity of the Government's position on Interim National Government; to which he assured me that there was no such thing and that in any event if there was such a plan, he as the AGF who is a constitutional purist would not be a party to such a scheme and that he was going to confront the President on it. He did and Jonathan denied any knowledge of it and agreed as suggested by Adoke that a public statement denouncing the subject be issued and to assure the nation that such a scheme was unknown to our Constitution. He issued the statement and that put an end to the matter.

On the sidelines also, one of the notable opinion moulders on Africa in America at this time, and former Ambassador to Nigeria, Mr. John Campbell had published a prediction that Nigeria could break-up in 2015 if the electoral processes were mishandled. So, that prediction, along with the threat from Jonathan, got Pastor Bakare very troubled as reflected in a "State of the Nation" broadcast he delivered on January 4, 2015 in church.

The address which was on the theme, 'The Gathering Storm and Avoidable Shipwreck: How to avoid Catastrophic Euroclydon' advocated an immediate suspension of the ongoing electoral calendar and the declaration of a state of emergency in the country. And he argued thus:

> "In the year 2015, a crucial year in the unfolding history of our nation, the Four Winds of the Earth are about to hit the nation in one combined storm that will not leave her the same. The purpose of this broadcast is to give a timely warning before the storm arrives…as well as to proffer an alternative pathway even if the warnings and the proposals are rejected…."

He continued:

"It is clear that a great storm lies ahead as we are approaching elections without addressing the fundamental flaws in the polity. These flaws include:

i. The awkward geopolitical structure that has the form, but lacks the substance, of federalism.
ii. The consequent lopsided economic structure in which a single product from one region of the country contributes the bulk of the revenue of the entire nation despite the abundant resources spread across the nation.
iii. A Constitution that lays claim to the phrase "we the people" but to which the people made no input.
iv. Contentious population figures that have been the harbinger of election disputes since the pre-independence era.
v. An electoral body that wears the label 'independent' but is practically under the control of the presidency.

These factors have directly and indirectly contributed to the current economic crisis, the political instability, and the security situation."

Building on this background, he then requested as follows:

"1. **Activate the constitutional provisions for the suspension of elections**
Section 135(3) of the 1999 Constitution provides as follows:
If the Federation is at war in which the territory of Nigeria is physically involved and the President considers that it is not practicable to hold elections, the National Assembly may by resolution extend the period of four years mentioned in subsection (2) of this section from time to time; but no such extension shall exceed a period of six months at any one time.

2. **Create a Transitional Government**
   In suspending the elections, to gain the support of all stakeholders, the president must not act with the intention to seek re-election. Rather, he should, within the period, commit himself to building a non-partisan coalition comprised of major stakeholders and competent statesmen from each geopolitical zone. This coalition, headed by the president, will constitute a combined force that will tackle terrorism and address what I have earlier referred to as the fundamentals, within a time frame of two years or less.

3. **Address the Fundamentals**
   Addressing the fundamentals calls for immediate implementation of the report, or part thereof, of the 2014 National Conference especially as it relates to:

   A. Restructuring with a view to achieving true federalism under Zonal Commissions as well as fiscal federalism ensuring, as proposed by the report of the National Conference, that adequate allocation is given to a Solid Minerals Development Fund in addition to other recommendations geared towards economic diversification.

   B. Achieving national reconciliation and integration by adopting, constitutionalising and propagating the National Charter for Reconciliation and Integration.

4. **Conduct accurate census**
   Aside facilitating development planning, an accurate census will lay the foundation for a sound identity management scheme, facilitate effective and efficient local government administration, provide the basis for proper constituency delineation and enable the conduct of well-organised voter-registration exercises.

5. **Establish a truly independent electoral body**
    A truly independent electoral body whose head will no longer be appointed by the president and whose funding will be drawn from first line charge on the federation account will guarantee the conduct of free, fair and credible elections.

6. **Create a true people's constitution that will reflect the aforementioned features**
    A true people's constitution, rather than being preambled by a military decree, as in the case of the 1999 Constitution, will be preceded by the people's expressed interest to co-exist as a nation and be governed under agreed principles as espoused in the Charter for National Reconciliation and Integration adopted at the 2014 National Conference.

7. **Conduct free, fair and credible elections in the consensually accepted constitutional arrangement**
    In the end, as an integrated rather than regionally and religiously divided nation, we will arrive at the same juncture we are currently but, at that time, better prepared with the fundamentals in place and with the nation set for the leadership of the best of the north and the best of the south while the federating units, truly federal, are constitutionally empowered for collaborative and competitive development."

Another flank of emphasis in the message was the sceptre of looming violence as it contained the hint of imminent violence when a wind from the North-East would blow in and collide with another wind from the South-South and that may lead to the disintegration of Nigeria.

We interpreted this to mean that if Jonathan won, the violence that had been witnessed in the North in the aftermath of the 2011 polls would be child's play. On the other hand, if Buhari won, the Niger Delta people would revolt, such that Boko Haram would be child's play. Thus, as far as he was concerned, there could really be no victor and nobody would win the elections, so it would be better for us to save Nigeria and not have the elections at that moment.

We were agitated and El-Rufai and I had to embark on a special trip to Lagos to "demand" for an explanation from our *Egbon,* given that we had specifically agreed that at least two out of the three of us must agree on any major issue before its implementation.

We vigorously disagreed with him. For the first time, I looked him in the eye and said: "No Pastor, we are not going to give this up. We will fight and ensure that there is an election."

For the first time in our relationship, we could not arrive at a resolution as Pastor remained convinced about the spiritual nature of his message. To his credit however, we did not leave empty handed as he offered to pray and fast some more for spiritual guidance. On our part, we reached out to Awujale for his intervention as he had also called to express concern and surprise about the sermon. Kabiyesi spoke to Pastor and we agreed to wait and see!

But it was not only us who were bothered by the effect that the PDP's win-at-all-costs game was having on the nation. In the last week of January, 2015, and with just three weeks to the scheduled February 14 date for the presidential elections, the United States Secretary of State, Senator John Kerry came to Nigeria and advised the PDP and Jonathan not to contemplate derailing the process because they were seeing the same thing we were seeing and knew that indeed all roads were pointing to the likelihood of an electoral upset.

They had a meeting with President Jonathan and made it clear at that event that the American Government had an interest in the peaceful conclusion of the election, that they would not sit idly by if any fraudulent games were played at this stage and that the process must be completed.

Chapter Thirteen

Dealing With The Postponement

When all else had failed and the PDP realised that they didn't have enough time to reach out to the electorate to attempt to influence them to change their mind and vote for Jonathan – even with all of the money they were now frantically throwing all around – they released a bombshell. The then National Security Adviser, Col. Sambo Dasuki during a lecture delivered at Chatham House in London on the 22nd January, 2015, announced that the nation was not ready for the elections and as such it would have to be postponed!

He used the principal excuse of the ongoing campaign against the Boko Haram insurgency as a prime factor in arriving at this conclusion but in this, he conveniently forgot to add that only a couple of days before then, the government which he was a part of and indeed the PDP, had been strongly advertising their security achievements and claiming victory over Boko Haram!

At that point they didn't want to accept that they had failed as a government by losing vast portions of Nigerian territory to the insurgents, so they said they were pushing Boko Haram back, but when it became obvious that they were losing the election, they had to use the enormity of the same Boko Haram challenge, as the reason for the postponement of the polls!

We fought back, launched a counter-attack and campaigned vigorously against the postponement. Indeed, there was so much pressure that the moment they formally announced the postponement plan, the whole world rallied against it. Jonathan was then forced to announce that it was not his decision, but INEC's.

Meanwhile, INEC chairman, Attahiru Jega was also publicly insisting that the commission was fully ready to conduct the elections, starting with the critical presidential contest on the scheduled date of February 14. His hands were however forced by the announcement made by Dasuki and the lack of cooperation from other agencies that had supportive roles to play in the exercise.

Eventually, he had no choice and had to publicly affirm that if the agencies that were supposed to give security cover for the exercise were saying that they were not ready, there was nothing he could do. He knew he was ready but he couldn't have allowed them to go and kill people and then turn around to say: "But we told you so!"

Being the only ones with coercive power and formal control of the nation's security agencies, and whipping up the elements of fear and apprehension, they could railroad everyone – the political parties, INEC and the public – into 'tolerating' the postponement and went on with it despite an overwhelming avalanche of criticism – national and international. With just one week to the scheduled February 14 date of voting and with international election observers and monitors already in the country to witness the process, INEC then made the announcement postponing the polls until March and April, 2015.

Seeing that the postponement had become *fait accompli*, we also went to Chatham House and equally arranged for Buhari to speak with the British Government and the world press, explaining at every turn, that in truth, the reason why the elections had been postponed was because the PDP knew they were going to lose!

We went on further to share the outcomes of our various polls with those who matter in the British Government and the House of Commons, and they actually knew the people who conducted the polls for us first-hand, and had faith in their sense of professionalism and integrity. It was becoming very clear to all that indeed an APC and Buhari victory was set to happen.

Following the postponement also, the US and the rest of the world equally restated their calls on the Jonathan administration to ensure a seamless electoral process, notwithstanding.

At this point, Jonathan became upset with the entirety of the Western establishment and this was also corroborated to us by the then British High Commissioner who had asked for a meeting with Jonathan but the seriously embattled President refused, saying that they "were all APC sympathisers!"

Having met Kerry ahead of the postponement and gotten the stern message from President Obama, he didn't want to listen anymore to the UK or the EU because he knew it would be the same message they were bringing and this was what he did not want to hear.

Keep in mind that Buhari's erstwhile spokesman in 2011, Yinka Odumakin had since defected to PDP and was more or less sharing whatever information he had gleaned from working closely with us, with Diezani and the rest of the Jonathan camp.

Odumakin, a former journalist, also happened to be one of the first persons who had, shortly after Umaru Yar' Adua was incapacitated in 2009, urged us to form the G54 group which later merged with the Save Nigeria Group. He therefore deserved credit for being our first formal link with Pastor Bakare in that sense.

Subsequently, Bakare took Odumakin as part of our team to Buhari who accepted for him to serve as his spokesperson and was going everywhere with him. So it was a major loss when he defected; indeed it was a virtual act of betrayal. We had done nothing wrong to him but he premised his action on the fact that we were working on a merger with Tinubu and that he wanted nothing to do with Tinubu as they were sworn enemies. He alleged that Tinubu was about to take his life over a disagreement in the past when he was Lagos State Governor. I however saw through him and we had a very heated verbal exchange, indeed a near physical fight one day at the premises of The Latter Rain Assembly in Pastor's dining room after a Sunday service.

I had said to him: "Look, you are not a principled person, it is money that you worship." He abused me in return, using the problems I had in my earlier banking career against me (more on this in the 'About the Author' section). His response was not novel or unusual. I have become accustomed to Odumakin resorting to such lows and making claims such as: "We know how you made your money, you stole money from the bank." Claims that were largely unsubstantiated to begin with and have been effectively debunked.

However, this time, I was not going to let him get away with that antic and decided to take him head-on, because not long before then he had been stranded in

China, needed money and called me to urgently send money to him. I said: "Yinka, even if I stole money, it shouldn't come from your mouth because you took some money from me!" He said he had only borrowed it (and to be fair to him, he did repay at some point), to which I reminded him tongue-in-cheek, that since I lent it to him upon his request, if I were a thief, he was worse having knowingly received a part of the stolen money.

All these incidents were going on and we had all kinds of betrayals but fortunately we were winning more than we were losing. More people were showing more confidence in Buhari than those who were going over to the PDP because of money. Those who were going to Jonathan were going for money, those who were coming to Buhari were coming mainly on principle, not money.

Ultimately, we knew that cash would lose its value and that ideology would trump cash, and that was the outcome of the election. People who had principles supported principles. Some even took the money that was being offered but still voted on their conscience. In fact, at a point, we got Buhari to adopt the phrase: "If PDP gives you money, take it, but vote on your conscience for a better Nigeria." APC became a movement rather than a political party and we built on this. We also adopted another saying that: "You don't need to join the party, just join the movement. No payment required; the only payment is your PVC!"

We likewise learned that they also tried to clone the PVC when the card reader jammer scheme had been abandoned on account of it being detected and our consequent alert to the public. Again, we got to know about this new disruption, stepped in and made a public outcry about their latest antic, forcing them once again to back off. Then they tried to buy PVCs from registered voters, sending out word that they were ready to pay as much as ₦5,000 per card! Again, we encouraged the voters to take the money but not part with their cards and on the day of the elections, to yet vote on their conscience. We reacted literally on a day-to-day basis as each challenge arose.

Their campaigns were by and large extremely negative on their part. Partly also because they had very little achievements and were immensely under pressure to win at all costs, so they employed all kinds of tricks and schemes they could think up but we managed to consistently beat them at their games and stay one step if not several ahead. There were all kinds of negative attacks aired on the African Independent Television, AIT in particular which aired a a false and libellous documentary on Buhari a couple of weeks before the election.

As if that was not enough, they also tried to persuade Tinubu to jump ship and cross over to their side and when he would not budge, they viciously attacked him with another equally damaging documentary that was again broadcast on AIT.

Incensed, we wrote a petition against AIT to the Advertising Practitioners Council of Nigeria, APCON, one of the regulators in the media industry; which ruled in our favour in respect of the offensive content in one of the adverts. We were also going to sue because the documentaries were actually defamatory and we had evidence of defamation of character.

On the contrary, we at the APC, had long decided that we were going to keep our own sound-bites clean and positive and to just stay on the main issues. We advised our leader that his campaign should be focused on the three main issues that the electorate was most concerned about.

The first was that he would secure Nigeria. We were divided, we were insecure, we had a destructive insurgency, we were losing our territories and Nigeria was no longer the country we had grown to know with the way things were going and certainly not one we could wholeheartedly bequeath to the next generation, so security came first.

The second campaign thrust had to do with the war against corruption. We were determined to fight corruption to a standstill. People knew of Buhari as a no-nonsense General with a reputation for standing resiliently on the path of courage, patriotism and integrity. So, Nigerians believed that he could do something decisive when push came to shove and in this instance, they particularly believed he could tackle the insurgents and fight corruption.

The third campaign issue was the economy. The imperative of creating jobs was of top concern for us. Even then, we knew that the way to structure the country when it came to management was to get the president to remain focused on issues of security and corruption while the vice president would manage the economy.

That's the way it should be anyway as the Constitution makes the vice president the chairman of the National Economic Council, NEC, which has oversight on the overall economic management of the country. There is also a statutory provision for the vice president to be the chairman of the National Council on Privatisation, NCP. These are two major economic organs for driving the economic blueprint of the country. This was one of the reasons why all along we were keen to have a VP that is economically savvy, knowing fully well that Buhari's strength will be on the first two out of the three planks of our campaign thrust while the VP would focus on the third segment.

That's why, post-election, when people criticise Buhari over the economy, I know better because he has delegated the monitoring of the economy to the VP. If the economy is not working as well as it should, though he is the president, but really and truly for me, it is the VP that needs to do more because the president actually doesn't interfere in what you are doing. As stated earlier, once he gives you a mandate, he trusts you to handle it until you let him down.

So, we remained on our campaign message and would not accept to be pushed.

RUNNING OUT OF CASH

At this point also, we had almost exhausted our 'war chest' because it was like a week or two before voting was to take place. We had done all the campaigns and all the adverts we had scheduled to do, as well as our share of going round the country and our funds were almost exhausted.

For the PDP however, the postponement offered them a strategic advantage to deal with their state of disadvantage, as the polls were so clear that if elections were to have held on the 14th of February, they would have lost. They had bought more time.

Jonathan once again relocated to Lagos and from there started making trips across the South-West, visiting traditional rulers, mosques, churches and other assorted places of religious worship, to the point of even kneeling down at different points for them to do all kinds of 'voodoo stuff' on his head and so on.

We also had no option but to strategically fill out the waiting time and so we continued campaigning. Before now, we had budgeted that we needed to pay polling unit agents in the one hundred and twenty thousand polling units throughout the country. Given their critical gate-keepers role in the entire exercise, that money had been reserved *ab initio* from the funds we had raised before now. But we were now forced to spend part of it for the extended five to six weeks of additional campaigning.

As things stood then, we had to pragmatically consider what we were going to do about our polling agents' fees. This was because without polling unit agents, any result could be declared! Therefore, every unit had to be manned. In 2011 for example, we couldn't man all of them. And in most of South-East and South-South states where we could not man the polling units, those were the critical points where outrageous results emanated from and the elections were very heavily rigged. Overall, false and inflated figures were declared and we lost.

In the current scenario, though we also knew from our polling outcomes that we were not going to win in the South-East and South-South, we however insisted on yet having our agents in place there, at every polling unit and subsequently at the collation centres to stop the PDP from dangerously inflating the resultant figures. So to now have to spend that money was a major blow for us.

However, we kept going on and a week before the election, what we called The Lagos Group, came in to assist us with fresh funds.

The group was composed of big business people in Lagos who now believed that it was possible to have an upset. Interestingly, many of them had bought into 'the Change agenda' only after the Jonathan government had panicked and postponed the election in the first place. Thus, while the postponement had forced us to use up the funds we had reserved for our polling agents, it however also brought into our fold the Lagos elite who started making calls to ask us what we needed!

They didn't want to go down with PDP. They had been giving money to PDP over the years and in particular, were big supporters of the PDP in 2011. Now they were coming to us!

When we began to get the calls from them, we knew that something more had given in; that the elite saw what was about to happen and were now calling to come along with us. The elites had finally decided to join the area boys and the *talakawas*! This did not happen in the three previous elections, so change was truly in the air!

We had trained all our polling unit agents on election monitoring, I personally had been to about seven states for this because apart from serving in the strategy committee of the party, I also served in the Election Campaign Council and was in the election monitoring department. So we had to compile a computerised database of all the agents, with their names and phone numbers so we could reach them directly. We even had automated robot calls to agents and electorates with special pre-recorded messages (text and voice) from Buhari.

We went around the states to train the agents with manuals, working with the International Republican Institute, IRI and the National Democratic Institute, NDI, to teach them what was required of them as regards the elections. These included how to ensure that the votes were properly counted, how to ensure that the card readers worked, that the total votes declared did not exceed the number of accredited voters and so on.

Additionally, we operated from the campaign office located in the Central Business District, Abuja. It was a big building and here again, money wasn't a problem as we were able to raise the money for it in December after Buhari's emergence as the APC flag-bearer. We had it renovated and fully furnished. By January when we opened for the campaigns, we had a place where we were meeting, strategising and doing whatever we needed to do. All the different groups were now meeting here.

Very importantly also, one of the things that we did in the extra weeks of campaigning that had been forced on us was to review our operational capacities in the critical area of election management and monitoring. It afforded us extra time to hold one more very crucial session with our monitors from all over the country. I recall that among others, our elections adviser, Dr. Hakeem Baba Ahmed, addressed the session, and called our attention to the need to deepen the synergy between the campaign efforts of local contestants at the states and constituency levels with what we were doing with respect to clinching the presidential ticket, as this would surely have a positive and complementary effect overall. That's how we fought the election.

After the postponement therefore, we returned to the streets, campaigning vigorously once again. We visited a couple of the states for the second time, especially the battle ground states to make sure we got the required twenty-five percent. We did what we had to do and the rest is history.

The periodic polls outcome also never went down right up to just before the voting day in March. In fact we were going up to fifty-six, fifty-seven and on to sixty-three and sixty-four percent of the votes.

For example, on March 12, 2015, the Eurasia Group, the world's leading global political risk research and consulting firm, tipped All Progressives Congress (APC) candidate, Gen. Muhammadu Buhari (rtd.), as Nigeria's next President. Interestingly, Eurasia had been previously more disposed to a Jonathan win.

However, given recent developments, the group's Africa practice head and Analyst Philippe de Pontet in a write-up said that there is a 60% probability that Buhari could beat President Goodluck Jonathan in the March 28 election.

Pontet wrote:

> "The election will still be difficult to call, but our expectation of a narrow Jonathan win was predicated on several factors that are losing some saliency late in the campaign.
>
> "Chief among them is the incumbency and financial advantages of the ruling People's Democratic Party (PDP). While this still helps Jonathan, its impact is blunted by the intensity of support for Buhari, lacklustre grassroots campaigning by the PDP, and new anti-rigging measures by the electoral commission. New permanent voting cards and card readers will sharply reduce the level of rigging seen in 2011, when Jonathan beat Buhari in a landslide...
>
> "While we expected the electoral map to favour Jonathan, current trends suggest that the swing regions may side with Buhari, including the Christian-majority and heavily-populated southwest around Lagos. That could be the decisive demographic factor in the election."

Eurasia Group put Jonathan's approval rating at below the 40% threshold under which incumbents have a hard time getting re-elected.

According to the organisation,

> "Despite some important military gains against (the Islamic terror group) Boko Haram in the North-East, and a partial exoneration of its oil revenue management in a recent PWC audit, (Jonathan's) People's Democratic Party is starting to look desperate. ... (But) it is not clear ... that Buhari has a strong economic policy orientation. This uncertainty is a chief risk for investors."

Thus rather than the PDP gaining points at our expense and closing the gap, we gained more points even with all the money being spent by them. We knew money was not going to work in this election. And so the nation went out to vote.

Hours after the close of polling, the final tally of results started trickling in. Again, our election monitoring centre was automated and the agents that we had trained were told to text the results to us from each of the hundred and ten thousand polling units. We had received enough results by about 3a.m. on March 29th, which was early Sunday morning. And with these figures, again, I was able to do a projection and confirm that we had won. I called Buhari early in the morning as he had gone to his country home in Daura to vote and await the results and said: "Ranka dede sir, we have some preliminary results, this is the projection of the results." Like I had done in the primaries but this time through the phone, I told him he had finally won the presidential election; irreversibly so. He asked if I was sure and I said: "Yes Sir, by the grace of God. Congratulations Sir." He replied: "Thank you Jimi, keep it to yourself until you are absolutely sure."

From the projections, we were leading with about 5.2 million votes. We had gotten the accreditation figures for the South-East and South-South, where results had not been fully declared publicly at this time and surmised that even if they rigged there, inflating the figures by two million votes, they still could not catch up on us. In fact, they delayed the results in those PDP states for about two days but we were already home and dry as we had enough margins to wipe out any surprises. We waited.

CHAPTER FOURTEEN

Drama At The National Collation Centre

Tense anticipation had gripped the nation at this time. The elections had been concluded by Saturday and vote counting done on the same day. Thereafter the collation of results had commenced, first at the ward and then the local government and later the state level before coming to peak at the National Collation Centre in Abuja.

These had taken the rest of the weekend and it was Monday, March 30. Official results from several of the states had already been declared and there was keen anticipation at the National Conference Centre and indeed across the nation and globally. The outstanding results were already in and shortly, the Chairman of the Independent National Electoral Commission and Chief Returning Officer for the presidential elections, Professor Attahiru Jega, was to announce the final tally of results, and in the process formally declare the winner of the election.

When it became obvious that things were going on very well for the APC and that the PDP had lost, several diehards from the PDP led by the former Minister for Niger-Delta Affairs, Elder Godsday Orubebe decided to invade the International Conference Centre, venue of the collation, to stop Jega from announcing the results from the remaining states and as a result stop Buhari being declared as the President-elect. They claimed that they were there to re-enact the annulment of the election of June 12, 1993; saying that Babangida, who had done that was still alive and well, so why should Jonathan not do the same?

All this while, with all of the camps having gotten details of the results collated by their respective agents at all levels and from the states whose results had already been certified by INEC, there was really no doubt as to who had carried the day. It was Buhari. The challenge of the moment however lay in how to respond to the outcome.

On this score, Jonathan's camp was severely divided. This we do know because we were getting feedback from those who were inside the thick of it all. I will mention one example that I was directly privy to. It had to do with a high-level meeting held on the 30th of March, at Aso Villa.

The then Attorney General, Mohammed Bello Adoke, who I must here compliment quite warmly, called me and was sounding very distressed. He wanted to see me immediately and I went over.

The man was weeping. He was all emotions at this point and sobbing quite profusely. The source of his agitation had taken place about an hour before I saw him, but he was still so badly shaken by it. He kept crying. I had to spend a lot of time in calming him down before he was able to speak.

He relayed that he had gone to see President Jonathan, to approve the appointment of the Chief Judge of FCT who had just been confirmed by the Senate. While waiting for Mr. President to come down, the First Lady, Madam Patience Jonathan, came into the sitting room and those present included Dr. Ahmadu Ali - the DG of the President's campaign, the Permanent Secretary, Ministry of Power, himself and a few others. They stood up to greet her. While she responded to others she totally ignored him so he repeated the greeting. There and then she launched an attack on him saying that he and a few others had betrayed her husband. She claimed that while Mike Aondoakaa used the same office of the Honourable Attorney General of the Federation to "make a dead man rule Nigeria from Saudi Arabia", he (Adoke) used the office to scare her husband with legal advice and thus contributed to his losing the election. She proceeded to pour all kind of tirades on him. He was prevailed upon to keep quiet and await the arrival of the President.

When the President came down, he was briefed about what had happened and he appealed to Adoke to please ignore her and told him what she did to some other persons. Adoke subsequently left the Villa distraught knowing that he had faithfully served the President to the best of his ability whilst also ensuring that the spirit and letters of the Constitution he swore to uphold were not undermined.

When Adoke recovered and he was finally able to put in a word, he asked me: "What have I done to deserve this? What kind of job is this? I told the president the truth, and I meant it because he is my boss, I don't want him destroyed. Where did I go wrong?" I again consoled and reassured him that he had done his best in the circumstances, and that I was disappointed that Jonathan did not call his wife to order there and then, let alone get her to apologise. This was once again confirming our earlier conclusion that we had a weakling as president. He was indeed a weakling, and that's why we didn't work with him. If I were in his shoes, I would never allow my wife to speak to the Attorney General of the Federation and Minister of Justice like that; particularly when in fact the advice he gave was a sincere and honourable advice being given in the fulfilment of his duty to the President and citizens of the country. I would register my displeasure at her conduct there and then in the presence of all others.

From another angle however, the incident reveals how much panic and confusion was in their camp over what to do. This would also explain why they couldn't restrain Orubebe. It was so bad they had reportedly told the SSS operatives guarding the ICC to withdraw. And they actually withdrew!

We had people monitoring the place who called us on this and from whom we learnt early in the morning that they had been withdrawn. There was also talk of plans to bomb the place and stop Jega from concluding the announcement of the results. We called Jega to warn him, but we didn't get him personally. We got his assistant and said this is what was going to happen. He said they were also aware.

Apparently, that morning before he left his office, the PDP people had also gone to court to obtain an injunction to stop Jega from announcing the results, but he refused to accept service of the injunction, directing them instead to the Commission's Secretary/Legal Adviser. They had first also wanted the Attorney General to file the injunction, but he had refused because he did not believe in it and it was contrary to the professional advice he had given. They now paid someone else to go and get a judge to do it.

But when they brought it, Jega told them to go and serve it on the INEC legal adviser, and not him as the chairman of INEC. If he had been served, he could have been held in contempt of the court for carrying on with the process thereafter. This was how he was able to get to the venue and finish his work.

Jega was also very brave and heroic. Despite all of the tension, he was calm and generally remained composed and fearless. And he did so most commendably. His reaction to the attack by Orubebe for example was most notable. He took it all calmly in his stride. He had been warned, and was prepared. He had seen it coming. They had first tried to use the courts. And now there was this physical abuse. And that was taking place on national and international television. It was shocking.

At this point, about the whole world started calling Jonathan. "Don't allow this to happen." It was indeed a very tense period in the annals of the country with many people believing that it was really divine intervention that saved the day.

Before now, several non-partisan elders within the polity had, in anticipation of a very tough and challenging electoral season, and also amidst the backdrop of the predictions by Ambassador John Campbell and a US research think tank, waded into the arena with a political mediation team designed to ensure that no matter how charged the electioneering process would be, all issues must eventually be resolved at the table.

Dubbed the National Peace Committee, it had been voluntarily set-up to help the nation get through the most critical crisis resolution aspects of the elections and it was headed by former Head of State, General Abdulsalami Abubakar. Following the signing of 'The Abuja Accord' on the 14th January, 2015 in which participants and stakeholders in the 2015 elections committed to prevent violence, refrain from negative campaigning, ensure credibility at the polls and also had former External Affairs Minister, Professor Bolaji Akinyemi, the billionaire businessman, Alhaji Aliko Dangote, former President of the Nigeria Bar Association, Mrs. Priscilla Kuye and the Catholic Archbishop of Sokoto Diocese, Bishop Matthew Hassan Kukah as some of its other members.

Others were Commodore Ebitu Ukiwe, rtd, Catholic Bishop of Abuja Diocese, Cardinal John Onaiyekan; Sultan of Sokoto, His Eminence, Sa'ad Abubakar; Alhaji Muhammad Musdafa; Primate of Anglican Church, Most Rev. Nicholas Okoh; President of Christian Association of Nigeria, Pastor Ayo Oritsejafor and Justice Rose Ukeje.

The roll call of elder statesmen included Prof. Ibrahim Gambari, Prof. Ameze Guobadia, Prof. Zainab Alkali, and Publisher of *Vanguard* Newspapers, Mr. Sam Pemu-Amuka.

Indeed the emergence of the National Peace Committee in itself is traceable to the Goodluck Jonathan administration.

> 'Concerned by the potential violence that could emerge from the hotly contested 2015 General Elections, the Office of the Special Adviser was asked to convene a committee of eminent Nigerians and elder statesmen to the President on Inter-party Affairs under the leadership of Senator Ben Obi in collaboration with the Office of the National Security Adviser (ONSA) on January 14, 2015 facilitated the signing of the 'The Abuja Accord' on the prevention of violence and acceptance of results by parties contesting the elections.
>
> In signing the Accord, the presidential candidates and chairpersons of the parties contesting the election committed themselves and their parties to the following:

i. To run issue-based campaigns at national, state and local government levels – In this, we pledge to refrain from campaigns that will involve religious incitement, ethnic or tribal profiling both by ourselves and by all agents acting in our names;

ii. To refrain from making or causing to make in our names or that of our party, any public statements, pronouncements, declarations or speeches that have the capacity to incite any form of violence, before, during and after the elections;

iii. All institutions of government including INEC and security agencies must act and be seen to act with impartiality;

iv. To forcefully and publicly speak out against provocative utterances and oppose all acts of electoral violence whether perpetrated by our supporters and/or opponents.

The signatories also committed themselves to the monitoring of the adherence to the Accord by a National Peace Committee made up of respected statesmen and women, traditional and religious leaders.'

After the signing ceremony, it was felt that there was a need to take the move a step further and Bishop Matthew Hassan Kukah, the founder and Board Chair of The Kukah Centre then took up the challenge 'to help convene such an eminent body of highly respected Nigerians with former Head of State, General Abdulsalam A. Abubakar, rtd. (GCFR) emerging as its Chairman.'

Instructively, the committee's very clearly expressed terms of reference were: 'to observe and monitor compliance with The Abuja Accord signed by the political parties on January 14, 2015; to provide advice to the Government and INEC on resolution of political disputes and issues or conflict arising from issues of compliance with The Abuja Accord; and to make itself available for national mediation and conciliation in the event of post-electoral disputes or crises.'

With the state of affairs in the country at the time, this Peace Committee stepped into the fray to reiterate the need for all parties to honour the outcome of the process that the nation had just laboured through and ensure that it was brought to a fitting close.

It would be recalled that in line with this mandate, the committee had early in January, 2015 organised a session to which all the contenders in the presidential race had been invited to come and publicly affirm their commitment and resolve towards working for a rancour-free electoral process. They signed a pledge to that effect and took the added step of publicly embracing each other.

For Jonathan in particular, the pressure to accept the ensuing outcome of the polls was therefore most phenomenal and he could not easily stare it down despite the desires of the hardliners within his team. Another critical part of the challenge for him at this point was the growing rumbling from within his own party. In one such instance, the then Chairman of the PDP and former Governor of Bauchi State, Adamu Ahmed Muazu had sent word to Jonathan that he would not be part of any shenanigan and that he was prepared to step out even then to concede defeat on behalf of the party if the President would not do so. Thus, President Jonathan was boxed in from many angles and something had to give.

He then called Orubebe and his associates who were at that moment holding the nation to ransom at the INEC Collation Centre and told them to withdraw. For once, he insisted! And they withdrew. It was that call that saved Nigeria from going down the precipice.

Besides this, we also knew that the nation not only had less than hundred thousand soldiers anyway, but that indeed, some of the soldiers were actually saying quite loudly that they would not come out to truncate democracy if they were to be called against the people. It was that bad. Some of the soldiers were calling us to say that their bosses had called them and told them to get ready for possible deployment onto the streets but that they would not come out; that they themselves had voted in support of change.

'All is well that ends well'; all of the pressure ultimately worked out for good. Common sense ultimately prevailed and Jega was left alone to announce the final tally of votes and to now formally declare General Muhammadu Buhari (rtd) as the President-Elect of the Federal Republic of Nigeria.

ANALYSIS OF THE 2015 PRESIDENTIAL ELECTION RESULTS

Please recall we had in Chapter 12 declared technology as a game changer through the use of Card Reader. The evidence to this effect which is known in legal parlance as *res ipso loquitur* (the thing speaks for itself), is to be seen in the table below.

TABLE 1
COMPARISON OF RESULTS FOR 2011 & 2015 PRESIDENTIAL GENERAL ELECTIONS

		2011	2015	Difference
1.	No. of Valid Votes	38,209,978	28,587,564	-9,622,414
2.	No. of Rejected Votes	1,259,506	844,519	-414,987
3.	No. of Votes Cast	39,469,484	29,432,083	-10,037,401
4.	No. of Accredited Voters	39,469,484	31,746,490	-7,722,994
5.	No. of Registered Voters	73,528,040	67,422,005	-6,106,035
6.	Muhammadu Buhari	12,214,853	15,424,921	+3,210,068
7.	Goodluck Jonathan	22,495,187	12,853,162	-9,642,025
8.	Others	3,499,938	309,481	-3,190,457

Source: INEC Website:- inecnigeria.org

Inference:

1. Reduction by Card Reader
2. Normal
3. Reduction by Card Reader
4. Reduction by Card Reader
5. Reduction by Card Reader
6. Mainly Southwest votes
7. Reduction by Card Reader
8. Product of Merger

As can be depicted from the table and the inferences to be drawn therefrom, the following conclusions are incontrovertible:

(a) General Buhari's result is the only positive difference with an extra of about 3.2million votes in 2015 over and above the 2011 figures;

(b) conversely, the total votes cast for President Goodluck Jonathan dropped dramatically by 9.6 million votes between what he was purported to have received in 2011 and 2015;

(c) the loss of 9.6million votes by President Jonathan in 2015 is almost identical (with insignificant statistical difference) with a 9.6million reduction in the number of total valid votes cast as in '1' in the table above. It can therefore be concluded that the card reader eliminated 9.6million ghost votes between 2011 and 2015, which entirely came from Goodluck Jonathan's votes; and finally

(d) the incremental figure of 3.2million voters in Buhari's votes between 2011 and 2015 is almost identical with the difference in the figure for all the other voters in 2011 and 2015; from which it can be concluded is the benefit of the merger being nearly equivalent to the votes that were received by ACN and other parties.

Lesson

In concluding this critical chapter, it is important to emphasise the lessons learnt in order to ensure credible, free and fair elections and achieve peaceful transitions in the future, devoid of violent outcomes such as those experienced in the aftermath of the 2011 elections.

We must not only continue to deploy Card Readers for all elections, we must also eliminate collation centres from ward, to local government, to state levels. Thus, election results should be automatically and electronically transmitted, immediately after closing and counting at polling units; to a central election results database which is open and accessible to all citizens, at state and national levels via a digital platform. This solution may also involve the adoption of an electronic voting system in the near future.

CHAPTER FIFTEEN

Transition Matters

The General Abdulsalami Abubakar Committee which had before now met at least three times with both Jonathan and Buhari, now went into overdrive.

It is really to the credit of the assembled statesmen and women in that august body that they continued to play a critical role in mediating between President Jonathan and General Buhari in their bid to douse tension, calm inflamed political tempers and ultimately ensure that whatever the case, the eventual outcome of the elections would be respected by all the contending sides. Thus, they also played a most commendable role which must be very explicitly stated in the course of this chronicle on 'The Making of a President.'

Their efforts were finally to be complemented by the patriotic advice of some senior cabinet ministers in the Jonathan administration, who defied all odds to make it very clear to President Jonathan that the mood of the nation at the moment was in favour of his taking the path of nobility by conceding defeat and not dragging the country through any post-election problems. These pressures came to bear very heavily on the then president, setting the stage for what was to follow.

About a couple of hours before the announcement by Professor Jega declaring Buhari as the winner of the presidential election, we got a call from one of our informants in the then government that President Buhari should expect a call; a congratulatory message from Jonathan and that I should please have the president-elect ready to receive the call.

I remember that I immediately rushed over to Buhari's office and he was in a meeting. I interrupted him to deliver the message, and as I was there delivering the message, the call came. President Jonathan made the concession statement, congratulated President-elect Buhari and arranged for them to meet and begin the transition process. Indeed, the two gladiators are to be seriously commended because they saved the country from unimaginable calamity that could have befallen the nation, had they respectively opted for a more belligerent line of action in the alternative.

Following this and the formal declaration of the results by the INEC Chairman, Attahiru Jega which revealed that Buhari had defeated President Goodluck Jonathan in the presidential elections, scoring 15,424,921 votes to Jonathan's 12, 853,162 votes; thereby confirming Buhari as President-elect, the Federal Government of Nigeria now formally provided transition offices for Buhari and his team at the old Defence House in Abuja.

In turn, the President-elect set up a transition committee under the leadership of the indefatigable, retired civil servant, Alhaji Ahmed Joda, even as he approached the outgoing President to request names of his nominees that his own team would be working with to facilitate the hand-over process and enable him hit the ground running.

This was not to be a smooth engagement as hardliners within the Jonathan camp interpreted this normal transitory arrangement as 'the establishment and running of a parallel government.' Sadly, the outgoing President sided with them, leading to a scenario where the Buhari administration was sworn in without a clue as to the exact state of affairs in the country.

Indeed, the intendment of Buhari in disclosing his transition team and announcing his readiness to govern and to move the country forward was a basic preparatory activity as should be expected. However, the hawks in Jonathan's cabinet met and made it clear that they were not willing to cooperate with President-elect Buhari through volunteering information on the workings of government. They even went as far as pushing President Jonathan to adopt a somewhat stern, if not hostile posture, and he came out to say that there could only be one president at a time in the country and that he was still the president, as if it was in doubt that he remained president until May 29.

That pronouncement doused the jubilation that had attended his initial concession statement. We were summarily turned back and the programme was disrupted. Relations were so severely strained that by the time the President-elect formed his transition committee and they proceeded to meet and receive data from the transition committee of the President Jonathan administration, virtually no information of substance was offered. If any information was made available, it was just publicly accessible information. So inside details of the precarious financial and security situation of the country for example was not known until after the handover on May 29. It was impossible to get information officially at this time and Jonathan's administration had become very hostile. The hawks had their way once more, but again we thank God they didn't go as far as to truncate democracy, but they had their way in making sure that it was not going to be an easy ride for Buhari and his team.

We however continued to do the best we could under the circumstances and, without any attempt at sounding defensive, that singular act which spanned from the time of the election in March and the inauguration on May 29, cost the incoming administration some two and a half months in critical planning time and was partly responsible for the inability of Buhari to form a cabinet quickly enough when he took over from the Jonathan administration.

It was after the departure of Jonathan and after Buhari was sworn in, that he could get briefings from the permanent secretaries, and the information that would be critical to forming the next government then became available. The transition committee was therefore forced to work for weeks into the tenure of the new government, to collate the said information, and make them available to guide the president on what to do and what would, as a result, be the immediate focus of his administration.

Another point worth mentioning is the fact that even after his inauguration, President Buhari could not immediately move into the official residence, the Aso Villa. Shortly after his victory at the election, he had relocated to Aguda House and though on the night before the inauguration, he had met with President Jonathan to formally take charge of the Villa, he couldn't move in until a month or two afterwards.

All kinds of cleaning, both physical and spiritual had to take place and, in fact, a couple of months before then, many concerned people were sending warning messages to us that the next plan was to have Buhari poisoned such that he would not be the one inaugurated on May 29th. All we could do was to pray and hope that the doomsday prediction would pass. And once again, it passed. However, the president did not move into the Villa until sometime in July 2015.

All things considered then, everything finally came to a head on May 29, 2015. The new dawn that we had joined others in conceiving and executing had arrived in Nigeria.

We will not conclude this session without making reference to the various moves that were made by different leaders and interest groups within and around the party to recommend persons who they deemed fit to serve in the Buhari administration. However, following his long-stated insistence to pick his team by himself, several of these lobby activities did not yield fruit. For example, former president Olusegun Obasanjo, whom Buhari has very high respect for, did send in several names, including that of former Osun State Governor, Olagunsoye Oyinlola, that were not to be honoured. Also Bola Tinubu equally sent names that also could not be honoured.

In Tinubu's case in particular, a number of convergences did indeed come to play in arriving at what was clearly a very difficult decision for the incoming administration.

One such convergence had to do with the ministerial nominee to be chosen from Lagos State. While Tinubu was rooting for the slot to be given to his former Commissioner of Finance, Wale Edun, Buhari had long decided to have former Lagos Governor, Babatunde Fashola, play a most active role in the incoming administration on account of his sterling performance as governor; and track record of performance and loyalty in all the party assignments that had been handed to him since the formation of the APC, including very notably, the agenda-setting Strategy Committee. So Fashola was chosen over Edun.

It was the same logic that was to play out in Ekiti State where the choice eventually fell to former Governor Kayode Fayemi. Like Fashola, he had also served the party in several meritorious capacities this far, including his unblemished role as Chairman of the Presidential Primaries Organising Committee and Returning Officer at the event that validated Buhari as the flagbearer of the APC.

Another nominee that got the President's preference on account of his sterling contributions to the party was our spokesman, Alhaji Lai Mohammed. As the President saw it, it was most inconceivable that one who had given literally everything to the cause and was, in the public eye, literally synonymous with our party should be dropped. Indeed, his absence would have been 'headline news!'

In the instance of Ogun State, it was Governor Ibikunle Amosun's nominee, Mrs. Kemi Adeosun that was adopted by the President.

Indeed, when it became clear that Tinubu was not having his way with some of his nominations, he was most unhappy and was even credited with saying that he would be quitting partisan politics altogether. On hearing this, El-Rufai, I and several others went over to see him in London and pleaded with him to reconsider: he had done so much for our mutual effort and still had yet more to offer.

Another party leader that weighed in strongly on the subject was Chief Bisi Akande. Indeed for him, his intervention was to even come much earlier than ours, and precisely at the point where it was becoming evident that Buhari was determined to appoint some of these nominees as ministers.

He approached Tinubu and pleaded with him to give in and let the President have his way. He also made the point that though some of the nominees under contention were not the ones on Tinubu's original slate, they were still his own people given their close association over the years. He then urged him not to go on record as being seen as opposing the President's nominations, such as to indicate that the President was nominating Tinubu's people without Tinubu's consent.

Eventually, good sense prevailed. Tinubu returned to Nigeria and a fence-mending meeting was arranged for him to work out those and other issues with Buhari. The APC had weathered yet another storm.

Epilogue

Beyond Buhari: How Nigeria is governed; significance of the Buhari presidency and the future of Nigeria

The significance of the Buhari Presidency is one that in our view must not be under-stated. For one, it is the first successful example of a party-to-party transition in Nigerian political history. But it is also more than this.

In the First and Second Republics, the populist Kano politician, Mallam Aminu Kano, tried unsuccessfully to be president of Nigeria. An advocate of the views and interests of the *talakawa*, he no doubt commanded a huge following amongst them, but was unable to push this further beyond the confines of Kano, Kaduna, Katsina and Jigawa States. In Buhari's emergence, the *talakawa* had finally gotten their day in the sun.

Then there are issues of the Buhari programme and particularly as it has to do with the National Rescue Mission; the point where our group in itself, was compelled to make the critical beeline unto his direction.

Two of the elements of the programme are foundational and this far, Buhari continues to give his best on them. These are the issues of securing the country and fighting corruption. We expect this to continue and over time to get more institutional deepening that will ultimately guarantee that they are not easily reversed in the post-Buhari years as had been the case with gains recorded in the earlier phase of his military presidency and the PTF era.

On the equally critical issues of economic growth and job creation, the hope is that over the months and years ahead, some of the initial seeds presently being sowed will begin to germinate and mature in such a way that Nigerians from all walks of life will also be able to reap dividends of economic progress and a sustainable rise in their standards of living.

Yet another critical footnote of the Buhari emergence goes even deeper. It cuts to the essential premise of how Nigeria is governed.

In a rather interesting sense, several personalities have tended to dominate the Nigerian political space in the past forty years. They are Obasanjo, Babangida, Danjuma, Abacha, Buhari, Aliyu Gusau and Shehu Musa Yar'Adua. While the trajectory of this development goes back to the civil war years, it was however to find its firm crystallisation in the immediate aftermath of the coup that ended the nine-year rule of General Yakubu Gowon and ushered in the short-lived tenure of the ebullient and mercurial General Murtala Ramat Muhammed. But as we can clearly see now, about the youngest of that group that remains alive is at the least today a septuagenarian. And this raises issues of leadership succession planning for the country.

Indeed, all of these came to play out during the election of Buhari and particularly so when President Jonathan had made his statement to Pastor Bakare that the powers that be will not accept Buhari as president.

And this was to put an extra burden on our campaign structure to ensure that we took even more heightened damage control measures.

The first of such outreaches that we undertook had to do with former President Obasanjo. And it is instructive that he was also one of the 'national leaders' that Tinubu had consulted to enquire whom he would want the APC to field, shortly before the primaries of the party in December of 2014, and was then being seen as one of the proponents of the 'generational shift' argument of that period.

One source, which we tapped to reach out to Obasanjo was his step-daughter, Dr. Adedunni Adegbenro. We had known her for some time and she had been close to El-Rufai during Obasanjo's tenure as president. Just before the primaries in December, Adedunni came up to us and became extremely active as part of President Buhari's campaign. She even made a substantial donation and I was forced to ask her why she was doing it and whether we could take that as a hint that Obasanjo himself was also well-disposed to Buhari's aspiration. I knew they were very close and that she won't have gone that far just like that. She laughed and said: "Well, Uncle Jimi you are always very pre-emptive."

She then confirmed that initially, President Obasanjo was not going to support President Buhari though he admires him. Then, his attitude on the subject was like, 'don't waste your time with Buhari.' But at some point later, he (Obasanjo) dropped his opposition and more or less encouraged her to go ahead and support him.

We knew the timeline when this change took place was sometimes in December 2014 because El-Rufai and I took Adedunni to Buhari and she made the already stated contribution to the campaign. She went with us virtually everywhere. When we were flying to most of the states, if she was available she will fly with us and campaign with us. She was more than just a financial contributor. Thus, we had more or less a part of Obasanjo in the team eventually. That credit should be given to him.

Again, if you recall, before then, there had also been a spat between Jonathan and Obasanjo, wherein Obasanjo published a public letter, so we knew then that certainly Obasanjo was not going to support Jonathan. Jonathan's team had reached out and tried all kinds of stuff to get him back but Obasanjo was adamant. Nonetheless, that in itself did not translate into supporting Buhari until much later after everything else had failed.

At the time of the APC primary, we heard the rumour that Obasanjo's preference was Kwankwaso but he did not make it. All these were the pertinent issues as to where Obasanjo stood, and where he was coming from before we finally arranged a meeting between the two generals.

I remember the first meeting took place at the Murtala Muhammed Airport in Ikeja. Adedunni had called me and said that Baba (Obasanjo) was travelling and since she also knew that we were coming into Lagos to campaign, she could get him to do a VIP lounge meeting with Buhari. We confirmed the meeting, they had their discussion and at that point of course, the issue of support had been cemented and it was a case of what next can be done to ensure that democracy would not be truncated. Former President Obasanjo then came on board fully.

Our damage control measures also took us to former President Ibrahim Babangida. On this, we went to Kabiyesi, the Awujale to request his help, but he sent us back to Buhari for him to reach out directly to Babangida for a meeting. Again, the meeting took place in the course of one of our campaign sessions in Minna. After the public campaign event, Buhari went to Babangida's house. He hosted us and after the meal and public reception, a one-on-one discussion took place and whatever fences needed to be mended were mended and a public position taken to show that there was no acrimony between them.

We also reached out to former National Security Adviser, General Aliyu Gusau, rtd. Here, it was El-Rufai and I that met with him, and he was more or less assured that with the roles we were playing in The Buhari Organisation, the campaign and the APC, if he could not reach Buhari directly at any time, his friend El-Rufai could always be reached to pass on the requisite message and bring feedback for him.

As for T. Y. Danjuma, the facts of the matter readily confirm that, just like the late Shehu Musa Yar 'Adua, he was very close, and indeed has been a most supportive benefactor to Buhari. Accordingly therefore, he could not be one of the proverbial 'owners of Nigeria' that would now be standing in the way of a Buhari presidency.

Evidence of his respect for Buhari's capacities and support for the current president can be seen for example in two historic interventions he had made. One, he had nominated him to go to the US War College in 1978 and also warned him about the impending Babangida coup when he got to hear about it in 1985.

Given the severity of the issues that had transpired between Buhari and some of his erstwhile colleagues, we had to approach him on them. At that meeting, he made it clear to us that he has moved on, and couldn't thank God enough that he is alive and well and in a position of being able to contest elections. He affirmed that he had no interest whatsoever in looking into issues of the past. So we went to represent this outcome either directly to President Babangida and General Aliyu Gusau for example or those who were close to them to be sure that this was his frame of mind. And as God would have it, all of the fabled opposition from a section of the elites — 'owners of Nigeria' thinned out.

But the determination of the direction that a country would take usually involves much more than the work that is done by one generation of leaders. And going forward then, this is going to be the challenge. After the Buhari years in power – which will effectively signal the close of an era - what other tendencies would come to the fore in the continuing drive to right size and properly shape and administer the sleeping continental giant that Nigeria has all along been destined to be? That indeed is the trillion-dollar question that will be answered over the years.

Suffice it to say however that in the Buhari Presidency today, the nation may very well have its best chance yet to begin that process. And we can set the tone for that most fittingly through our commitment to continually support him towards ensuring we get the best that he has to give today.

APPENDIXES

Appendix 1

CPC Renewal Committee – Interim Report

1. Background

The Congress for Progressive Change (CPC) was registered in December 2009 and had to organise and put up structures in time for general elections in April 2011. With barely a year to register members, conduct congresses, primaries and conventions at various levels throughout the thirty-six states of the federation and FCT, teething challenges as well as self-inflicted problems were experienced.

In the end, and as a result of some of these challenges, militarised occupation of some parts of the country and the blatant electoral manipulations of the federal government and its agencies, there is some unanimity that the CPC's overall performance in the elections was inconsistent with the high expectations and levels of hope that it generated in the Nigerian political landscape.

After dutifully going through the tribunal processes at state and federal levels, and sequel to the receipt of many position papers and memoranda on the future of the Party, the leadership of the CPC decided to establish a renewal committee under the chairmanship of Nasir Ahmad El-Rufai (NAE) to design and implement a far-reaching and nationwide program of rebuilding the party.

2. THE CPC RENEWAL COMMITTEE

The Renewal Committee (RC) was inaugurated by the chairman of the Board of Trustees and presidential candidate of the party, General Muhammadu Buhari (GMB) on 13th December 2011.

In attendance at the inauguration were his running mate, Pastor Tunde Bakare (PTB), Party Chairman Prince Tony Momoh (PTM) and several other party leaders from across the country.

The Renewal Committee was given organisational latitude, broad terms of reference and no specified time limit for its assigned mandate. And the RC chairman was free to appoint members of the Committee. The letter of appointment is appended to this report as Annex 1.

A long list of proposed members was developed in consultation with the National Executive Committee of the party, various party leaders and state branches. The final list of the Renewal Committee members is attached as Annex 2.

The Committee immediately constituted a core group to design an initial work plan and presentation for its maiden meeting. This was presented to the Committee membership, the National Executive Committee of the party and key leaders between the 14th of December and 16th of December, 2011. This preliminary work plan presented is attached as Annex 3.

The RC faced many challenges from inception. Older members of the party viewed with suspicion, the decision to hand over such an important assignment to a relatively new member and inexperienced politician like NAE. Some of the party leaders who claim connections to GMB from the early days of TBO, and therefore the creators and protectors of 'the Buhari Brand' felt that the decision was a ploy to hijack the party and take away their meal.

Many people were therefore nominated into the RC not because they had any value to add, but to be gatekeepers in case the assignment turned out to be a threat to their privileges. Others struggled to be in the RC because they thought it would replace the current party leadership at various levels, or recommend such. Such persons lost interest once they realised that the RC was not mandated to do either. Yet some other members thought the RC was synonymous with the Investigation, Discipline and Reconciliation Committee set-up by the party, whose White Paper is being awaited.

3. Approach to the Renewal Assignment – Organisation, Funding and Challenges

The RC constituted a Central Working Group (CWG) to steer the affairs of the Committee in the delivery of the Party's mandate. The members are Dr. Larry Esin, Hadiza Bala Usman, Mrs. Salome Jankada, Jimi Lawal, Dr. Hassan Lawal, Adamu Mohammed Aliero, Otunba Basirat Nahibi, Ms. Sharon Ikeazor, Yinka Odumakin, Yusuf Tuggar and Osita Okechukwu.

Each CWG member took charge of one of the mandate areas either as Task Team leader or head of an operational and administrative aspect of the RC assignment as follows:

- Membership Mobilisation — Ms. Sharon Ikeazor
- Membership Registration & IT Platforms — Jimi Lawal
- Finance and Fund-raising — Otunba Basirat Nahibi
- Policy Development/ Think Tank — Dr. Hassan Lawal/ Yusuf Tuggar
- Media & Communications — Yinka Odumakin

- Forthcoming Elections — Osita Okechukwu
- Alliances and Merger — Adamu Mohammed Aliero
- Joint Secretaries — Mrs. Salome Jankada/ Dr. Larry Esin
- Head of Secretariat/ Administration — Mrs. Hadiza Bala Usman

The RC held regular CWG meetings and circulated Actions Points arising from the meetings with copies to GMB, PTB and PTM. A weekly brief which is a summary of RC activities in not more than two pages is also circulated to selected party leaders. These will be collated and included in the Final Report of the Renewal Committee to the Party on completion of the assignment.

The RC was conceived to be self-funding committee of the party and has remained so. Every member paid his or her way to attend meetings, undertake tours and other assignments. The RC raised its initial funds by taxing CWG members and soliciting donations from friends and sympathisers. The RC could therefore only work as fast as it is able to raise monies for its operations, without any need for the support of the Party. It was the operational and financial burden the RC had to bear in respect of gubernatorial elections in Kogi and Adamawa (where the RC raised ₦10 million and ₦15.6 million respectively for the candidates) that largely diverted it from making progress in its core mandate areas until after February 2012.

The RC faced difficulties getting key documents from the Party – guidelines for congresses, primaries and convention. Even getting the authentic version of the CPC Constitution took some time as it appeared there were versions in circulation. There appeared to be zero institutional memory and records of the attempted alliance with the ACN for the RC to review and proceed with steps to progress it. The RC also lost two key members of the CWG to defections to the PDP. The Joint Secretary, Mrs. Salome Jankada from Taraba State and Task Team Leader in charge of Alliances, Adamu Mohammed Aliero from Kebbi State unceremoniously left the party and membership of the Committee.

These destabilising developments along with funding challenges discouraged the RC from setting up the two secretariats planned for Lagos and Abuja. Instead, all the RC meetings were variously hosted in the homes of Dr. Hassan Lawal in Asokoro and the offices of the Good Governance Group in Wuse 2. The chairman of the Renewal Committee regularly updated the party leadership of the status of the assignment.

Membership Registration:

Shortly after the inauguration of the Renewal Committee and subsequent composition of the Membership Registration Task Team, we discovered there is a subsisting agreement between our party and an IT consulting firm – SW Global Ltd ("SWG"), for the provisioning of services similar to those with which the Team has been charged.

It was therefore deemed apt to obtain a copy of the agreement with a view to ensuring its suitability and fitness for the specific purpose of accomplishing the Renewal Committee's mandate in this regard. In the process, we discovered that even though the draft agreement was not executed, (please see attached document, marked Annex 4) a deposit of ₦22.5 million was nonetheless paid by CPC to SWG since early 2011 on account of the membership registration exercise.

As a result, even though we sought and obtained a competitive proposal from another IT consultant – Bedazzle & Associate Ltd, the strategy was to use the alternative proposal as a negotiating tool to secure more favourable terms from SWG. This approach culminates in a revised draft agreement from SWG, a copy of which is attached and marked Annex 5.

In essence, the following points are the major improvement we have been able to secure.

1. *Technology* – the initial agreement calls for membership cards with basic bio-data and passport photograph being provided by SWG for sale to CPC; which cards shall thereafter be given to members upon registration. This essentially means that the underlying technology is neither a bio-metric based identity card system (better tamper and fraud proof) nor is it a web-based platform that can facilitate seamless online initiated registration. Worst still, the old agreement was founded on the premise that CPC and or its chieftains would collect cards from SWG for onward "sale" to its members; thereby creating room for bulk purchase by wealthy chieftains, rather than the establishment of a genuine direct membership registration system.

2. *Cost* – the cost per-member under the initial agreement is a flat fee of ₦225 each, which makes a total of ₦450 million for the envisaged minimum of 2 million members and ₦1.125 billion for up to 5 million members. Whereas, for a better technology biometric web-based, fraud and tamper-proof registration system, we succeeded in securing a total cost of ₦185.5 million and ₦427 million for 2 million and 5 million members respectively, thereby resulting in significant saving of at least ₦264 million and up to about ₦700 million if up to 5 million members registered in the next 10years. Better still, CPC would enjoy the benefit of having 10 members of staff/volunteers and up to 30 stakeholders trained on how to use the technology along with ownership of data capture machines worth about ₦80 million that will boost its balance sheet under the revised agreement as opposed to no training and ownership under the initial agreement; where all the assets would have been owned by SWG.

3. Obligation - in accordance with clause 2.2.1 of the initial agreement (Annex 4), CPC was obliged to "ensure the participation of a minimum of 5 million CPC members in the registration exercise, and the payment thereof for their identity cards". This commitment has been reduced to a realistic minimum of 2 million members (clause 4.1.2 of Annex 5) with the option to increase to and beyond 5 million members at CPC's sole and absolute discretion.

4. Merger – express provision has been made in the revised agreement for it to survive any merger or consolidation by either party as per clause 8.2.1

The Way Forward

I. Consideration, approval and execution of Agreement as per Annex 5 with SWG.

II. Raising of funds to cover total cost of ₦185.5 million: (a) Hardware Purchase of about ₦80 million; (b) Software, Data Centre, Support back office, Management and Training

₦105.5 million, with total net cash required being ₦163 million; being ₦185.5 million less initial deposit of ₦22.5 million payable to SWG within 10 business days of executing agreement; (c) Annual recurrent cost from year 2 to 10 of between ₦19 million and ₦25.4 million and (d) Incremental cost beyond 2 million members of ₦16 million per 1 million additional members.

III. Approval of ₦200 flat registration fee per member, thereby generating a total revenue of ₦400 million for the first 2 million registered members with a net surplus of a little over ₦100 million and over ₦500 million if up to 5 million members are registered.

IV. Establishment of a steering committee of up to 10 members for implementation - to include a project manager that would serve as the contact person with SWG.

V. Nomination of up to 30 participants for training as stakeholders, other than the steering committee members; may be drawn from membership registration task team and volunteers.

4. POLICY DEVELOPMENT

The Policy development task decided to split into two sub-groups. One focused on the internal documents of the Party – the Constitution, the guidelines for congresses, primaries and conventions, chaired by Yusuf Tuggar. The second sub-group is working on the Party's manifesto in light of the developments in the political economy, internal security and the militarisation of parts of the country where the CPC is politically-dominant, chaired by Dr. Hassan Lawal.

The Internal Party Documents sub-task team submitted a work plan which was approved by CWG, and entailed engaging consultants to provide technical support, undertake research into global best practices, include Nigerian experiences and then make recommendations to improve the Party Constitution, and its processes for the conduct of Congresses, Primaries and Conventions.

The technical consultants to the Tuggar Task Team – Festus Okoye and Emma Ezeazu have submitted draft reports which are being considered by the Task Team. The output of the task team will be studied by the CWG and debated at a Renewal Committee Conference tentatively scheduled for 9th June, 2012. The revised and updated versions will then be presented to party leadership and membership during RC field visits to all the states of the federation.

The sub-group working on revising and updating the CPC manifesto is pursuing a similar track but has chosen to use resource persons within the RC and has not engaged any consultants so far. The output of the team would be subjected to review by CWG, debate in the RC conference, further debate during RC field visits before presentation to the NEC and BOT of the Party.

5. Membership Mobilisation

This task team will achieve the objective of mobilising the party rank and file for registration and party activities using State Renewal Teams (SRTs). The RC membership mobilisation task team is chaired by the National Woman Leader of the CPC, Ms. Sharon Ikeazor with 17 members. The team will deliver on its mandate through the SRTs, consultations with Party rank and file, and field visits to each state of the federation. The tentative schedule of field visits and states' tours is appended hereto as Annex 6.

It is vital that GMB, PTB and PTM make themselves available to support the task team by scheduling to join the field visits. Other principal officers of the Party will also be invited to join the mobilisation task team. The membership registration team intends to utilise the opportunities of GMB's crowd-pulling capacities during such field visits to undertake biometric registration of party members.

The CWG also debated and approved the constitution of SRTs to include the following membership:

- State Chairman of the Party who will chair the SRT unless there are factions in the state. In the cases of Bauchi, Kano and Katsina States for instance, a neutral and renowned party elder will chair the SRT,
- State Vice Chairman,
- State Secretary,
- State Woman Leader,
- State Youth Leader,
- Representatives of each senatorial zone,
- Selected technocrats, professionals and grassroots politicians in the state, and
- Renewal Committee members that are residents of the State.

In the course of the renewal assignment, we have received party delegations and stakeholders from Bauchi, Taraba, Ondo and FCT. We have also visited CPC leadership and stakeholders in Anambra State and engaged in consultations with several past and present party stakeholders like Chief Mike Ahamba, Senator Rufai Hanga and Chief Nwankwo Nwabuchi.

6. Alliances and Mergers

This task team lost its initial chairman, Adamu Mohammed Aliero to the PDP, but made some progress in initiating discussions on electoral cooperation in Adamawa and Kebbi States' governorship elections. In the circumstances, the RC chair NAE has taken temporary lead of the alliances and mergers effort.

Discussions have begun with leadership of the ACN and ANPP with a view to consummating initially electoral cooperation as and when the need presents itself, and ultimately a merger of the parties into a single formidable nationwide opposition platform. These discussions are ongoing at various levels, and the party leadership kept abreast of the developments.

It is hoped that before the end of the year, a framework for the merger along with consequential actions to be taken by all the parties to enable unity of the opposition would have been approved by the NEC and BOT of the CPC.

7. Forthcoming Elections

The forthcoming elections task team is led by Osita Ikechukwu and participated in the organisation, mobilisation and fundraising for the gubernatorial elections in Kogi, Adamawa and Kebbi States. The CWG also reviewed the campaign strategy and request for logistic and financial support for the Sokoto, Cross River and Bayelsa gubernatorial elections and was unable to intervene in any significant way.

The Task Team is now studying the forthcoming local government and area council elections with a view to recommending interventions from alliances with other progressive parties against the PDP to logistic and financial support. The schedule of forthcoming local government and area council elections is appended hereto as Annex 7.

8. Finance

As previously stated, most of the expenses incurred by the RC to-date have been raised through voluntary taxation of the CWG members; through which a total of ₦15 million was pledged and about half thereof at ₦7.5 million has been redeemed. The RC has raised an additional ₦160 million, and working on raising more to fund the timely implementation of the party's membership registration platform.

The finance committee chair, Otunba Basirat Nahibi has been away to Senegal and Canada for medical reasons and vacation, and this has affected our overall fund-raising efforts. She is now back and recuperating, so we expect this to be ramped up and improved immediately. Our expectation is to raise enough funding to cover the membership registration costs and renew the tenancies of some of our party offices particularly in states where our prospective alliance partners have limited presence.

9. Media and Communications

The RC has relied mostly on GMB's spokesman, Yinka Odumakin and National Publicity Secretary Rotimi

Fashakin to take the lead in engaging the media. Going forward, we intend to co-opt electronic media experts like Yusuf Mamman and other correspondents of international media organisations active in Nigeria to propagate the party's message and the Renewal Committee's activities; when so authorised.

10. NEXT STEPS

The RC hopes to complete the assignment before the end of the year 2012, and submit its final Report and recommendations for the consideration and approval of the NEC and BOT. Implementation would then commence in earnest.

Respectfully submitted,

Nasir Ahmad El-Rufai
Chairman CPC Renewal Committee.

Appendix 2

CONGRESS FOR PROGRESSIVE CHANGE
RENEWAL COMMITTEE SECRETARIAT

Final Report of the CPC Renewal Committee May 2013

PART 1: PRELIMINARY MATTERS

Background

THE CONGRESS for Progressive Change (CPC) was registered in December 2009 and had to organise and put up structures in time for general elections in April 2011. With barely a year to register members, conduct congresses, primaries and conventions at various levels throughout the 36 states of the federation and FCT, teething challenges as well as self-inflicted problems were experienced.

In the end, and as a result of some of these challenges, militarised occupation of some parts of the country and the blatant electoral manipulations of the Federal Government and its agencies, there is some unanimity that the CPC's overall performance in the elections is inconsistent with the high expectations and levels of hope that it generated in the Nigerian political landscape.

After dutifully going through the tribunal processes at State and Federal levels, and sequel to the receipt of many position papers and memoranda on the future of the Party, the leadership of the CPC decided to establish a renewal committee under the chairmanship of Nasir Ahmad El-Rufai (NAE) to design and implement a far-reaching and nationwide program of rebuilding the party.

The CPC Renewal Committee

The Renewal Committee (RC) was inaugurated by the Chairman of the Board of Trustees and presidential candidate of the party, General Muhammadu Buhari (GMB) on 13th December 2011.

In attendance at the inauguration were his running mate, Pastor Tunde Bakare (PTB), Party Chairman Prince Tony Momoh (PTM) and several other party leaders from across the country.

The Renewal Committee was given organisational latitude, broad terms of reference and no specified time limit for its assigned mandate. And the RC chairman is free to appoint members of the Committee. The letter of appointment is appended to this report as Annex 1.

A long list of proposed members was developed in consultation with the National Executive Committee of the party, various party leaders and state branches. The final list of the Renewal Committee members is attached as Annex 2.

The Committee immediately constituted a core group to design an initial work plan and presentation for its maiden meeting. This was presented to the Committee membership, the National Executive Committee of the party and key leaders between the 14th of December and

16th of December, 2011. The preliminary work plan as presented is attached as Annex 3.

APPROACH TO THE RENEWAL ASSIGNMENT

The RC constituted a Central Working Group (CWG) to steer the affairs of the Committee in the accomplishment of its terms of reference. The members are:

1. Nasir Ahmad El - Rufai
2. Larry Esin
3. Hadiza Bala Usman
4. Salome Jankada
5. Jimi Lawal
6. Dr. Hassan Lawal
7. Adamu Mohammed Aliero
8. Otunba Basirat Nahibi
9. Sharon Ikeazor
10. Yinka Odumakin
11. Yusuf Tuggar
12. Osita Okechukwu

Each CWG member took charge of one of the mandate areas either as Task Team leader or head of an operational and administrative aspect of the RC assignment as follows:

- Membership Mobilisation — Sharon Ikeazor
- Membership Registration & IT Platforms — Jimi Lawal
- Finance and Fundraising — Otunba Basirat Nahibi
- Policy Development/ Think Tank — Hassan Lawal/Yusuf Tuggar

- Media & Communications   Yinka Odumakin
- Forthcoming Elections   Osita Okechukwu
- Alliances and Merger   Adamu Mohammed Aliero
- Joint Secretaries   Salome Jankada/Larry Esin
- Head of Secretariat/ Administration   Hadiza Bala Usman

The RC held regular CWG meetings and circulated Actions Points arising from the meetings with copies to GMB, PTB and PTM. A weekly brief which is a summary of RC activities in not more than two pages was also circulated to selected party leaders.

The RC was conceived to be a self-funding committee of the party and has remained so. Every member paid his or her way to attend meetings, undertake tours and other assignments. The RC raised its initial funds by taxing CWG members and soliciting donations from friends and sympathisers. The RC could therefore only work as fast as it is able to raise monies for its operations, without any need for the support of the Party. It is the operational and financial burden the RC had to bear in respect of gubernatorial elections in Kogi and Adamawa (where the RC raised ₦10 million and ₦15.6 million respectively for the candidates) that largely diverted it from making progress in its core mandate areas until after February 2012.

The RC also lost two key members of the CWG to defections to the PDP. The Joint Secretary, Mrs. Salome Jankada from Taraba State and Task Team Leader in charge of Alliances, Adamu Mohammed Aliero from Kebbi State unceremoniously left the party and membership of the Committee.

These destabilising developments along with funding challenges discouraged the RC from setting up the two secretariats planned for in Lagos and Abuja. Instead, all the RC meetings were variously hosted in the homes of Dr. Hassan Lawal in Asokoro and the offices of the Good Governance Group in Wuse 2.

PART 2 : TASK TEAM REPORTS

1. Membership Mobilisation Task Team

This task team was to achieve the objective of mobilising the party rank and file for registration and party activities using State Renewal Teams (SRTs). The RC membership mobilisation task team is chaired by the National Woman Leader of the CPC, Ms. Sharon Ikeazor. The team is to deliver on its mandate through the SRTs' consultations with Party rank and file. This will be done during the proposed field visits to each state of the federation by the RC

The CWG also debated and approved the constitution of SRTs to include the following membership:

- State Chairman of the Party who will chair the SRT unless there are factions in the state. In the cases of Bauchi, Kano and Katsina States for instance, a neutral and renowned party elder will chair the SRT,
- State Vice Chairman,
- State Secretary,
- State Woman Leader,
- State Youth Leader,
- Representatives of each senatorial zone,
- Selected technocrats, professionals and grassroots politicians in the state, and

- Renewal Committee members that are residents of the State.

In the course of the renewal assignment, we have received party delegations and stakeholders from Bauchi, Taraba, Ondo and FCT. We have also visited CPC leadership and stakeholders in Anambra State and engaged in consultations with several past and present party stakeholders like Chief Mike Ahamba, Senator Rufai Hanga and Chief Nwankwo Nwabuchi

2. Membership Registration Task Team

Shortly after the inauguration of the Renewal Committee and subsequent composition of the Membership Registration Task Team which was Chaired by Jimi Lawal, we discovered that there is a subsisting agreement between our party and an IT consulting firm - SW Global Ltd ("SWG"), for the provisioning of services similar to those with which the Team has been charged.

It is therefore deemed apt to obtain a copy of the agreement with a view to ensuring its suitability and fitness for the specific purpose of accomplishing the Renewal Committee's mandate in this regard. In the process, we discovered that even though the draft agreement was not executed, a deposit of ₦22.5 million was nonetheless paid by CPC to SWG early 2011 on account of the membership registration exercise.

As a result, even though we sought and obtained a competitive proposal from another IT consultant – Bedazzle & Associate Ltd, the strategy was to use the alternative proposal as a negotiating tool to secure more favourable terms from SWG. In essence, the following points are the major improvement we have been able to secure.

1. *Technology* – the initial agreement calls for membership cards with basic bio-data and passport photograph being provided by SWG for sale to CPC; which cards shall thereafter be given to members upon registration. This essentially means that the underlying technology is neither a bio-metric based identity card system (better tamper and fraud proof) nor is it a web-based platform that can facilitate seamless online initiated registration. Worst still, the old agreement is founded on the premise that CPC and or its chieftains would collect cards from SWG for onward "sale" to its members; thereby creating room for bulk purchase by wealthy chieftains, rather than the establishment of a genuine direct membership registration system.

2. *Cost* – the cost per member under the initial agreement was a flat fee of ₦225 each, which makes a total of ₦450 million for the envisaged minimum of 2 million members and ₦1.125 billion for up to 5 million members. Whereas, for a better biometric web-based technology with fraud and tamper-proof registration system, we succeeded in securing a total cost of ₦185.5 million and ₦427 million for 2 million and 5 million members respectively, thereby resulting in significant saving of at least ₦264 million and up to about ₦700 million if up to 5 million members registered in the next 10 years. Better still, CPC would enjoy the benefit of having 10 members of staff/volunteers and up to 30 stakeholders trained on how to use the technology along with ownership of data capture machines worth about ₦80 million that will boost its balance sheet under the revised agreement as opposed to no training and ownership under the

initial agreement; where all the assets would have been owned by SWG.

3. *Obligation-* in accordance with clause 2.2.1 of the initial agreement CPC is obliged to "ensure the participation of a minimum of 5 million CPC members in the registration exercise, and the payment thereof for their identity cards." This commitment has been reduced to a realistic minimum of 2 million members with the option to increase to and beyond 5 million members at CPC's sole and absolute discretion.

4. *Merger* – express provision has been made in the revised agreement for it to survive any merger or consolidation by either party as we anticipate the utilisation of this membership registration platform by the merged party. We propose that key parties to the merger are intimated of this project with a view to adopting it for the merged party.

5. *Implementation Challenges* - Following the BOTs approval to proceed with the project, taking into account the revised provision, the NEC endorsed the contract agreement but we were unable to commence implementation as we were frustrated by bureaucratic bottles necks engineered by some members of the NEC and BOT. We currently in default of some of the terms of the agreement. Attached as Annex....is the letter from the Service Provider.

3. Policy Development Task Team

The Policy development Task Team decided to split into two sub-groups. One focused on the internal documents of the Party – the Constitution, the Guidelines for

Congresses, Primaries and Conventions, chaired by Yusuf Tuggar. The second sub-group chaired by Dr. Hassan Lawal worked on the Party's Manifesto. This Manifesto document has been adopted by the Merger Committee for the Merged Party.

The Internal Party Documents sub-task team submitted a work plan which was approved by CWG, and entailed engaging consultants to provide technical support, undertake research into global best practices, include Nigerian experiences and then make recommendations to improve the Party Constitution, and its processes for the conduct of Congresses, Primaries and Conventions.

The technical consultants to the Tuggar Task Team – Festus Okoye and Emma Ezeazu in consultation with the members of the Task Team submitted draft documents which were presented to the members of the party leadership, RC members and key party faithfuls at a Stakeholders Forum held on 16th June 2012. Notable contributions and comments on the draft documents were made at the Forum. These were noted down for further consultation with grass root stakeholders at the intended field visit to the States following which the final document will be submitted to the NEC and BOT of the party for consideration and approval.

4. Alliances and Mergers Task Team

This task team lost its initial chairman, Adamu Mohammed Aliero to the PDP, the RC chair NAE took temporary lead of the alliances and mergers effort. This resulted in the CWG presenting a position paper to GMB in which the need for the party to constitute a Merger Committee was articulated. The Merger Committee is consequently constituted and their assignment has culminated in the party voting unanimously to merge with 3 other political parties at a convention held on 12th May 2013.

5. Forthcoming Elections Task Team

The forthcoming elections task team is led by Osita Ikechukwu and participated in the organisation, mobilisation and fund-raising for the gubernatorial elections in Kogi, Adamawa and Kebbi States. The CWG also reviewed the campaign strategy and request for logistic and financial support for the Sokoto, Cross River, Bayelsa and Edo gubernatorial elections and is unable to intervene in any significant way.

6. Finance Task Team

The finance committee is chaired by Otunba Basirat Nahibi. As previously stated, most of the expenses incurred by the RC to-date have been raised through voluntary taxation of the CWG members; through which a total of ₦7.5 million raised. The RC has also raised an additional ₦160 million. The monies raised were utilized for the activities of the Committee.

7. Media and Communications Task Team

The RC has relied mostly on GMB's spokesman, Yinka Odumakin and National Publicity Secretary Rotimi Fashakin to take the lead in engaging the media. Funds were provided to fund for such. The RC also funded an electronic news media platform – Nigeria Intels. The news media platform is geared towards providing us with an avenue to put out our own news and information as the majority of the Nigerian electronic news media platforms are funded by the ruling party. The platform is currently operational but we are working on expanding it to take on board experienced electronic media personalities who will provide us with a leverage that will increase our daily hits.

PART 3: RECOMMENDATIONS

The Renewal Committee wishes to recommend the following;

1. That the Membership Registration project as conceived by CPC is adopted by the merged party for implementation and the Contract agreement with the Service Provider is consequently transferred;
2. That the Media and Communications electronic news media platform - Nigeria Intels is sustained;
3. That the details of actualising the merger through submission of the required documentations to INEC are prioritised and concluded in a timely manner;

While thanking you for the opportunity afforded us to serve our great party, we wish to assure you of our continued loyalty and support.

Respectfully submitted,

Nasir Ahmad El-Rufai, OFR
Chairman, CPC Renewal Committee

APPENDIX 3

Puritanism vs Pragmatism

From: JIMI LAWAL <jimilawal@hotmail.com>
Sent: Friday, April 5, 2013 6:47 PM
To: Adebayo Adejuwon
Subject: Fw: Purist v Pragmatism

------Original Message------
To: Pastor Tunde Bakare
Subject: Purist v Pragmatism
Sent: 20 Oct 2012 11:47

My dearest Egbon,

A very good morning to you sir. Just a note to share what I consider words of wisdom on the above subject that I just re-read in my Harvard Business School notes that makes more sense to me now!

In essence, the thesis is that to be a good believer and a good politician, one's approach to religion must be markedly different from that of politics.

Thus, a good believer must be a purist on the issue of faith in the Creator; whilst for a good politician, the emphasis must be on pragmatism by way of reasonable compromise across the political divide. For, to adopt an uncompromising approach in politics would no doubt keep one pure; but in the final analysis won't get anything done! And the society shall be the worse for it! Whereas, a pragmatic politician would compromise as necessary not only to get into office but to also get things done; even if not all! And the greater public good would have thereby been served!

I hope this makes sense to you as it does to me!

Have a good day and stay blessed sir.

Peerless respect sir.

JAL.

Re: Puritanism v Pragmatism: A Must-Read: An Open Letter to General Muhammadu Buhari - Dr. Dokun Adedeji

From: JIMI LAWAL <jimilawal@hotmail.com>
Sent: Friday, April 5, 2013 7:11 PM
To: Sarki Abba
Subject: Fw: A Must-Read: An Open Letter To General Muhammadu Buhari - Dr. Dokun Adedeji

Salaam alaikum Sarkin Galadimawa,

Grateful if you can please bring the three emails exchanged below to General's attention; at your earliest convenience.

Trust all is well and many thanks for your continued kind assistance.

With best wishes.

Jimi

Sent from my BlackBerry wireless device from MTN
-----Original Message-----
From: jimilawal@hotmail.com
Date: Fri, 5 Apr 2013 23:03:34
To: Adebayo Adejuwon<adeadejuwon@yahoo.com>
Reply-To: jimilawal@hotmail.com

Subject: Re: A Must-Read: An Open Letter To General Muhammadu Buhari - Dr. Dokun Adedeji

Dear Mr. Adejuwon,

We still do not know each other well, but I have interacted with you long enough, albeit from a distance; to know you are an eminently good man!

Thus, I had to depart from a fundamental principle by sharing a personal email I sent to Pastor Bakare last year on this subject; for your perusal.

To be sure, there is nothing wrong with the approach advocated by your good-self and Dr. Adedeji; so it is just a question of tilting the balance and trying another approach.

The new approach is do-able largely because GMB is a strong character that would not compromise his integrity for anyone and anything! In which circumstance, our nation would be better off if pragmatism is adopted over puritanism; having adopted the latter with our late sage - Chief Awolowo, why not try the former with our current saint - GMB?

In closing, I hope this submission makes sense; even if you are not fully persuaded! May the Almighty God continue to guide and guard us aright.

With best wishes.

Jimi

Sent from my BlackBerry wireless device from MTN
-----Original Message-----
From: Adebayo Adejuwon<adeadejuwon@yahoo.com>
Date: Fri, 5 Apr 2013 22:04:57
To: <jimilawal@hotmail.com>
Subject: A Must-Read: An Open Letter To General Muhammadu Buhari - Dr Dokun Adedeji

Dear Mr. Lawal:

How are you? This is for your attention. I hope we will have time to revisit this issue once again. I am persuaded that you and Nasir have good intention but I have some serious concerns that you may be disappointed along the line. Please read my comment on Dr. Dokun Adedeji's letter. I do not know Dr. Adedeji from Adam but I share his views.

................Dr. Dokun Adedeji. May the good Lord bless you. I will have to talk to you privately on this open letter. You made my day with this letter. I am a strong and passionate admirer of General Muhammed Buhari. I supported him in 2011 and I will support him again. Just like you I am strongly opposed to the APC merger and I have expressed my opinion directly to some CPC members behind the merger. What I have not done, unlike you, is to write an open letter to General Muhammed Buhari . Once again, thank you for this letter and may God bless you. For some reason I remain hopeful that God will be merciful to General Muhammed Buhari so much so that even if at the eleventh hour something will happen that will take him out of the muddled waters of APC. This is my hope and I have an assurance that God will hear my prayers concerning the good genera.....

Adebayo Adeneye-Adejuwon

A Must-Read: An Open Letter To General Muhammadu Buhari - Dr Dokun Adedeji

Posted April 5, 2013 by newsbytesnow in News <http://newsbytesnow.com/category/news/>, Articles <http://newsbytesnow.com/category/articles/>.Tagged:politics <http://newsbytesnow.com/tag/politics/>,Nigeria< http://newsbytesnow.com/tag/nigeria/>,elections <http://newsbytesnow.com/tag/elections/>,party <http://newsbytesnow.com/tag/party/>,governance <http://newsbytesnow.com/tag/governance/>,Letter <http://newsbytesnow.com/tag/letter/>,CPC<http://newsbytesnow.com/tag/cpc/>,Merger<http://newsbytesnow.com/tag/merger/>,GeneralBuhari<http://newsbytesnow.com/tag/general-buhari/>.1Comment <http://newsbytesnow.com/2013/04/05/a-must-read-an-open-letter-to-general-muhammadu-buhari-dr-dokun-adedeji/#comments>

My Dear General,

I have tried to get to meet with you on many occasions as I have tried to write you but it has been difficult. I am sufficiently disturbed by all the happenings in CPC as well as the merger intentions with some other parties, to push my interest to seek some form of interaction. In order for you to appreciate my efforts, I spoke to Mallam El-Rufai and sent him a few texts and also sent a mail to Mr. Rotimi Fasakin - all in a bid to reach you.

You may wonder what my locus standi is to go to this extent. If you do ask this question, you will be right.

I am a Nigerian professional who has followed the trajectory of our nation and also, your track along our nation space - these many years. I must confess my adulation for you for many reasons - I consider you a good man that our nation needs to put her acts right and so help us occupy our rightful place in the comity of nations.

Let me assure you that many Nigerians who truly love this country feel the same about you. But, it will be foolish to think that those who have brought us to this humiliating pass will root for you. No, they will wish that this bazaar continues to enable them make a billing enough to give them succour and protection to their offspring.

In all the 'elections' we claim to have had, I had always voted for you even when my friends think I was wasting my vote! I preferred to waste my vote than contribute to the 'victory' of those who have stolen us blind and brought our development to a grinding halt.

Nigerians have chosen to direct an unfair scrutiny at you, your past period of stewardship and poured innuendos on what you stand for without affording the same scrutiny to the Lilliputians that have placed a stranglehold on our national destiny.

General, I thought CPC was ready to put its house in order to present a formidable front to tackle these termites in power but events since then have shown the short-sightedness of the men who surround you. Alas, 2015 is almost upon us and it will take a tsunami of sort to dislodge these vultures in power.

It is now the new song in town that CPC and you are working in tandem with some other parties to arrange a merger to capture power from PDP! And this is the kernel of my open letter to you Sir.

I would rather you do not become a President holding a poisoned chalice. I am struggling to see how you can work with many of these men for the reason of becoming President. I will rather retain a memory of who you are and what you stand for even in defeats than see you as President in the midst of these gang of power-grabbers and looters of our commonwealth.

I wish you stand above the crowd and retain your respect and integrity than become a President who presides over a brood of vipers. The men who surround you today are plastic and replicas of those you wish to dislodge. Pray,

General, what is the difference between six and half a dozen?

Sir, please, let them not dismiss this my appeal to you with the wave of a hand that I am an emissary of the ruling PDP. No! Nothing can be farther from the truth, I am an independent who love our nation with passion and hates PDP and her friends with coats of many colours with equal passion. I simply desire the best for my country which cannot come through PDP or the band of vampires trying to climb upon your integrity and name.

Would have wished CPC had begun to work since 2011 and be not a part of this bandwagon of political termites. In the muddied pool are men who once bestrode the length of our nation with impunity as if tomorrow - which is today! - will never come. Their antecedents do not speak to a better future for Nigeria.

I do not envisage a party of angels; neither would I pride myself in the collection of these vermins who merely seek another opportunity to rape our unfortunate nation.

My dear General, your place is not amongst these men. I would rather you remain the epitome of integrity that you are and watch this drama play out.

This is my wish for you as I am willing to add that my advice is both unsolicited and so, open to dismissal. I will not be surprised but it will pain me to see you sacrifice your hard-earned reputation and diminish your stature with your engagement with many of these men who brought us this low.

You have fought gallantly but Nigerians in our foolishness have cast you aside. Let us rue the day we forsook you and chose the present band of carpet-baggers and marauders who are alien to honour and dignity. Our experience since they 'won' has been like giving gold to swine!

I assure you Sir, that soon and very soon, Nigerians will re-claim their nation from the clasping hands of these thieves and locusts.

I therefore plead that you remain on the right side of history and play no part in the unfolding drama of comedy and the shameful orchestra of opportunists euphemistically referred to as merger. Many of these men want to ride on your back to stardom and the opportunity to partake of the national bazaar on another platform. They miss power and its attendant spoils and appurtenances.

Please, General, stand aloof and retain your courage and untainted platform to speak for ordinary Nigerians who ask for nothing more than to be treated with respect and consideration in a nation that they call their own.

Do you not wonder why Pastor Tunde Bakare cries to high heavens about this unholy marriage of convenience and opportunism? You should worry sir, moreso, he was your running mate!

Nigeria and Nigerians deserve more than these men and women will offer.

Chief Awolowo was never permitted the opportunity to be President but his memory speaks of respect, adoration and adulation of a grateful people. I wish same for you General.

I can understand if this letter or this medium of presentation riles you, I have no other choice.

May Allah guide you right as you make a decision for this country. Thank you and please, do have a great day.

Your friend and Compatriot, Dokun Adedeji

- Dr. Dokun Adedeji is an Human Resources Management practitioner and a Social Worker. He writes from Lagos, Nigeria (www.dokunadedeji.com(@dokunadedeji on Twitter) __._,_.___

Reply via web post <http://groupsyahoo.com/group/NaijaPolitics/post;_com?subject=Re%3A%20A%20Must-Read%3A%20An%20Open%20Letter%20To%20General%20Muhammadu%20Buhari%20%E2%80%93%20Dr%20Dokun%20Adedeji>Reply togroup<mailto:NaijaPolitics@yahoogroups.com?subject=Re%3A%20A%20Must-Read%3A%20

An%20Open%20Letter%20To%20General%20Muhammadu%20Buhari%20%E2%80%93%20Dr%20Dokun%20Adedeji> Start a New Topic<http://groups.yahoo.com/group/NaijaPolitics/post;_UwODEEc2VjA2Z0cgRzbGsDcnBseQRzdGltZQMxMzY1MTk4NTgy?act=reply&messageNum=415081> Reply to sender<mailto:adeadejuwon@yahoo.

Recent Activity:

* New Members <http://groups.yahoo.com/group/NaijaPolitics/members;_Visit Your Group <http://groups.yahoo.com/group/NaijaPolitics;_

Disclaimer:

Forum members are reminded that NaijaPolitics is established to be a moderated forum for gavel-to-gavel discussion of political developments in Nigeria, Africa's largest democracy. Freedom of opinion/expression is inherent in NaijaPolitics. Views and opposing views expressed in NaijaPolitics forum are the rights of individual contributors. Mutual respect for people's views is the corner stone of our forum. Freedom of speech applied responsibly within the guiding parameters of Yahoo! Inc (our hosts) and NaijaPolitics Rules and Guidelines (broadcast monthly and accessible to all subscribers in our archives) is our guiding principle. Everyone posting to this Forum bears the sole responsibility for any legal consequences of his or her postings, and hence statements and facts must be presented responsibly. Your continued membership signifies that you agree to this disclaimer and pledge to abide by our Rules and Guidelines.

NaijaPolitics is division of Afrik Network Groups.

Latest Version of Disclaimer released (December 15, 2005) <http://groups.yahoo.com/;_

APPENDIX 4

CONGRESS FOR PROGRESSIVE CHANGE (CPC)
Motto: EQUITY, PEACE & PROSPERITY

9th December, 2011
Jimi Lawal
Ogun State

Dear Jimi,

NOMINATION TO CPC RENEWAL COMMITTEE

The National Executive Committee of our great Party, the Congress for Progressive Change (CPC) has set up the CPC Renewal Committee to renew and reposition the Party.

In view of your avowed commitment to CPC's ideals and stand for social justice, it is my pleasure to formally convey to you the Party's approval of your nomination to serve on the Committee as a member. We thank you and look forward to your active participation.

Yours sincerely,

Prince Tony Momoh
National Chairman

CONGRESS FOR PROGRESSIVE CHANGE (CPC)

GEN. *Muhammadu Buhari*, GCFR
CHAIRMAN, BOARD OF TRUSTEES

February 5, 2013

Barr. Jimi Lawal

Dear Sir,

I am pleased to inform you that you have been selected and appointed by the Board of Trustees to serve as a member of the **Fund Rising Committee** of the Congress for Progressive Change, CPC.

The Fund Raising Committee is one of the committees set up and charged with reorganising and repositioning of CPC. As its name says, the committee will be responsible for raising the funds required for the day-to-day running of the operations of the party, and for financing and effective management of the party's campaign. The committee's terms of reference and other details that will be supplied by the chairman will guide your proceedings.

This assignment will be demanding and will require substantial investment of your time and resources, and may involve some travelling; and, accordingly, I urge you to consider it carefully and respond accordingly. You may wish to indicate your acceptance of the offer by signing and returning the enclosed copy of this letter to the chairman of the committee.

While thanking you for your support and continuing confidence in us, please accept the assurances of my highest esteem.

Thank you very much.

Yours sincerely,

General Muhammadu Buhari, GCFR

CPC: EQUITY, PEACE & PROSPERITY

NATIONAL SECRETARIAT
Plot 1132 Festus Okotie Ebo Crescent, Utako District, Abuja P.O. Box 17312, Garki, Abuja.
E-mail: gmb2@gmail.com

Appendix 5

Presidential Election Results for 2003, 2007, 2011 and Projections for 2015

DaMina Advisors LLP
FRONTIER MARKETS SPECIALISTS

1/19/2015

DaMina Advisors Special Report I: NIGERIA's Elections Forecast & Analysis

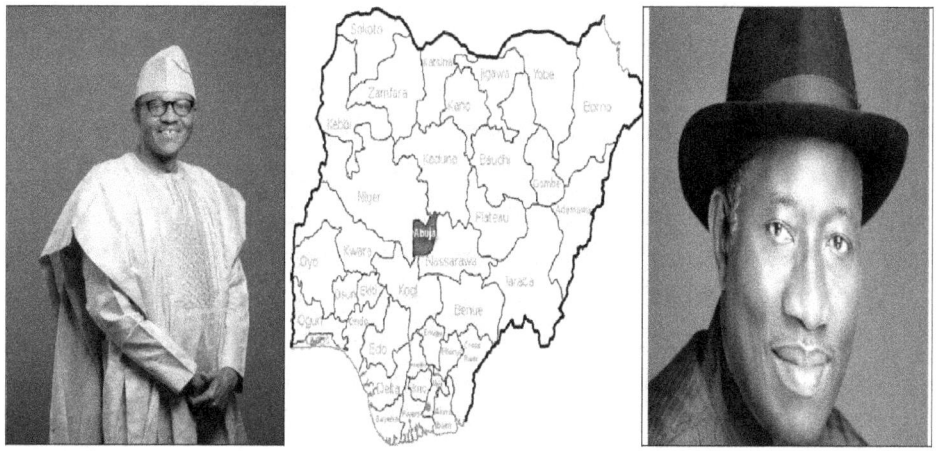

Retired General Muhammadu Buhari poised to narrowly unseat incumbent President Goodluck Jonathan

On Saint Valentine's Day February 14 2015 Nigeria, Africa's most populous country and largest economy is poised to likely witness a major revolution in its two-decade democratic politics. According to DaMina Advisors's proprietary 'VERITAS Frontier Markets

Electoral Forecast Statistical Model,' (reproduced in full below) the opposition candidate Retired General Muhammadu Buhari will narrowly unseat incumbent President Goodluck Jonathan in an unprecedented electoral upset. Nigeria, since 1999 predominantly a one party state, is poised for change.

Buhari's victory will likely see him winning the commercial capital, Lagos, as well as racking up double digit gains in the Muslim north and single digit gains in the southwestern ethnic Yoruba states. Jonathan is set to maintain his very high margins in the oil producing Niger Delta south-south region, his home region, as well as strong margins in the eastern pan-ethnic Igbo states. Jonathan will likely also hang on to some religiously mixed middle- belt northern states adjoining the capital, Abuja. However abandoned by his political godfather, influential former President Olusegun Obasanjo, and beset by an active Boko Haram insurgency in the north eastern parts of the country that has sapped his middle class and female support even in many southern Christian states, Jonathan is poised to likely receive a cold Valentine's Day gift of ejection from the presidential palace at Aso Rock in Abuja. Jonathan's defeat, if it happens, will be unprecedented in Nigeria's political history.

A Buhari win on the 14th followed by a strong showing by the opposition All Progressives Congress (APC) party at the 28th February governorship races will see Nigeria edge closer and closer to a more normal bifurcated two- party system with the APC on the centre-left and the ruling People's Democratic Party (PDP) on the centre-right.

While the complex and tortured histories of both parties is too long to recount here, essentially while the

APC looks to the build a strong decentralised managed capitalist social democratic state, with a slight leftward Pan- African tilt towards China-Russia; the PDP looks to continue its generally centralised, pro-Western neoliberal free market capitalist democratic state, with a more insular Pan Nigerian nationalist neo colonial tilt.

In terms of policy changes, the shift will not be that dramatic. However Buhari will likely launch several corruption probes, target local oligarchs in a Putinesque way, push for a more interventionist central bank, prosecute an intense anti-Boko Haram counter insurgency strategy and tilt Nigeria's foreign policy towards Russia and China, if new entreaties to the US and UK for arms are rejected. If Jonathan surprisingly retains his presidential seat he is likely to do a major cabinet reshuffle and seek to co-opt the opposition. Either way, Nigeria is on course to finally enter the league of mature African democracies.

TABLE 2

DaMina Advisors VERITAS Frontier Markets Electoral Forecast Statistical Model Nigeria 2015 Presidential Election Comprehensive State-by-State Forecast

State	2006 Pop Census	2015 INEC Registered Voters	% of Pop registered	2011 Turnout	2003 Turnout	DaMina VERITAS Likely 2015 Turnout	DaMina VERITAS Likely 2015 PDP Vote Share	DaMina VERITAS Likely 2015 APC Vote Share	DaMina Advisors Comment
Abia	2,845,380	1,396,162	49%	77.95%	59.80%	68.88%	865,446	96,161	Abia and most of the pan-ethnic Igbo eastern states to firmly re-elect Jonathan
Abuja (FCT)	1,406,239	881,472	63%	42.19%	43.70%	45.00%	174,531	222,131	Capital Abuja to tilt towards Buhari and away from Jonathan
Adamawa	3,178,950	1,559,012	49%	49.98%	77.60%	60.00%	336,747	598,661	Boko Haram attacks; PDP elite confusion and unpopular Ribadu governorship quest to tilt state to APC
Akwa Ibom	3,902,051	1,680,759	43%	76.22%	80.50%	78.36%	1,185,338	131,704	Presidential stalwart Gov Akpabio to ensure PDP victory
Anambra	4,177,828	1,963,173	47%	57.52%	48.20%	55.00%	971,771	107,975	New Gov Obiano and pan-Igbo APGA party rooting heavily for Jonathan
Bauchi	4,653,066	2,054,125	44%	63.80%	81.60%	72.70%	149,335	1,344,014	PDP Party Chairman Muaazu's home state, but the anti-Jonathan wave strong
Bayelsa	1,704,515	610,373	36%	85.61%	97.00%	95.00%	521,869	57,985	Jonathan to win home state massively, but Buhari to make small in roads
Benue	4,253,641	2,015,452	47%	43.82%	71.10%	57.46%	648,524	509,555	Senate President Mark stays in PDP and rallies state
Borno	4,171,104	1,934,079	46%	49.46%	62.00%	40.00%	100,572	673,059	Heart of Boko Haram insurgency; PDP will get very few votes
Cross River	2,892,988	1,175,623	41%	63.24%	96.00%	79.62%	823,707	112,324	Cross Rivers and other pan-ethnic Igbo eastern states are firmly behind Jonathan
Delta	4,112,445	2,275,264	55%	68.82%	72.90%	70.86%	1,451,027	161,225	PDP Gov Uduaghan to assure Jonathan victory with large margin
Ebonyi	2,176,947	1,074,273	49%	47.87%	80.50%	64.19%	592,989	96,533	Ebonyi firmly behind Jonathan; but PDP Gov Elechi unpopularity to give APC breathing room
Edo	3,233,366	1,779,738	55%	37.52%	78.00%	57.76%	585,947	442,030	Popular Gov Oshiomole will pull large parts of state to APC, but PDP still strong
Ekiti	2,398,957	732,021	31%	34.24%	43.20%	45.00%	138,352	191,057	Ekiti despite recent PDP governorship gain will tilt towards APC

Appendixes

State	2006 Pop Census	2015 INEC Registered Voters	% of Pop registered	2011 Turnout	2003 Turnout	DaMina VERITAS Likely 2015 Turnout	DaMina VERITAS Likely 2015 PDP Vote Share	DaMina VERITAS Likely 2015 APC Vote Share	DaMina Advisors Comment
Enugu	3,267,837	1,429,221	44%	62.46%	77.40%	69.93%	899,509	99,945	Enugu, a major ethnic Igbo state is firmly behind Jonathan
Gombe	2,365,040	1,120,023	47%	58.41%	80.00%	69.21%	217,031	558,081	Buhari to carry Gombe as he did in 2011; Boko Haram sinks Jonathan further here
Imo	3,927,563	1,803,030	46%	83.56%	64.60%	74.08%	601,058	734,627	Opposition Gov Rochas Okorochas cattails to help Buhari
Jigawa	4,361,002	1,831,276	42%	56.64%	70.10%	63.37%	371,353	789,126	Gov Lamido is in PDP, but heart with Buhari/Obasanjo
Kaduna	6,113,503	3,407,222	56%	65.81%	83.60%	74.71%	890,878	1,654,487	Opposition to topple PDP in Kaduna with pro-Buhari Muslim wave
Kano	9,401,288	4,975,701	53%	53.17%	58.50%	55.84%	777,891	2,000,292	Emir of Kano and Gov of Kano implacable foes of President Jonathan
Katsina	5,801,584	2,827,943	49%	52.43%	66.60%	62.00%	333,132	1,420,193	Opposition leader Buhari hails from this state
Kebbi	3,256,541	1,470,648	45%	56.41%	65.50%	60.96%	358,573	537,860	Gov Dakingari and strong PDP leadership of state will prevent heavy losses in Buhari wave
Kogi	3,314,043	1,350,883	41%	42.66%	77.60%	60.13%	495,494	316,792	Jonathan to carry Kogi as he did in 2011
Kwara	2,365,353	1,142,267	48%	35.99%	62.70%	52.00%	326,688	267,290	Kwara despite strong APC winds will likely still see Jonathan winning there
Lagos	9,113,605	5,822,207	64%	31.84%	42.50%	45.00%	1,047,997.26	1,571,995.89	Heart of Opposition Empire, APC to win majority of votes
Nasarawa	1,869,377	1,242,667	66%	49.99%	86.90%	68.45%	416,766	433,777	State to split down the middle with just a small advantage for Buhari
Niger	3,954,772	2,014,317	51%	46.85%	65.50%	56.18%	294,201	837,342	PDP big wigs Babaginda, Abdusalami and Gov Babangida resigned to a Buhari wave
Ogun	3,751,140	1,829,534	49%	28.01%	86.60%	65.00%	440,003	749,194	Obasanjo home base; PDP in comatose state; Obasanjo may make late Buhari vote pledge
Ondo	3,460,877	1,524,655	44%	30.12%	66.10%	60.00%	548,876	365,917	Jonathan to carry Ondo, but by a smaller margin than in 2011
Osun	3,416,959	1,407,107	41%	39.62%	57.30%	55.00%	139,304	634,605	Osun under strong APC Gov Rauf Aregbesola to tilt strongly for Buhari
Oyo	5,580,894	2,415,566	43%	33.57%	49.00%	45.00%	391,322	695,683	State will flip to APC from PDP

State	2006 Pop Census	2015 INEC Registered Voters	% of Pop registered	2011 Turnout	2003 Turnout	DaMina VERITAS Likely 2015 Turnout	DaMina VERITAS Likely 2015 PDP Vote Share	DaMina VERITAS Likely 2015 APC Vote Share	DaMina Advisors Comment
Plateau	3,206,531	2,001,825	62%	62.46%	80.50%	71.48%	901,470	529,435	Retiring Gov Jang will marshal PDP votes in religiously divided state
Rivers	5,198,716	2,537,590	49%	76.33%	95.50%	85.92%	1,853,145	327,026	Opposition Gov Rotimi Amechi cattails
Sokoto	3,702,676	1,611,929	44%	40.12%	68.90%	54.51%	360,252	518,411	Feud between Gov Wamako and Ex Gov Bafarawa to split state; But Buhari to carry
Taraba	2,294,800	1,340,652	58%	55.31%	89.90%	72.61%	496,424	476,956	With no strong PDP governor in charge; Taraba will split tilting towards APC
Yobe	2,321,339	1,099,970	47%	45.28%	66.50%	55.89%	55,330	559,444	Yobe, under Boko Haram assault to vote heavily against Jonathan
Zamfara	3,278,873	1,495,717	46%	51.67%	73.00%	62.34%	139,853	792,502	Zamfara will fall vote even more decisively for Buhari than it did in 2011
Nigeria	140,431,790	68,833,476	48%		62.96%	20,902,705	21,615,393.89	
							49%	51%	
						PDP to win 25% in at least 31 states	APC to win 25% in at least 27 states	* The Nigerian constitution requires that a presidential election winner win at least 25% of the votes in 24 states.

The DaMina VERITAS model relies on traditional psychological assumptions that over time party voting patterns and preferences in any defined geo-political voting area remain largely consistent over time and differ only slightly from election to election in terms of voter turnout, new voters and slight changes in the heteroscedasticity of voter preferences for particular outstanding candidates. The model for Nigeria in 2015 is tilted to imply a large discount for ruling PDP votes in the Boko Haram insurgency states in the northeast; a strong surge in pan-Yoruba sentiment in the southwest for the opposition; only small voter shifts in the middle belt states against the ruling party and still strong support for the president in the southwest, south-south and the middle belt. The known unknowns relate to turnout in the northeast where Boko Haram may prevent a vote altogether and the level of pan Yoruba support that the opposition can garner away from the ruling party. Severe weather patterns and other exogenous variables may also skew the votes in some states especially where strong local races are also at play. Finally, with the constitutional mandate to win at least 25% of the votes in two-thirds of the states, and the high prospects that some states may not be able to hold the vote, it is not inconceivable that the winner, may yet not get 24 states required for outright victory and the loser may get more than 24 states - triggering an expensive acrimonious run-off.

Appendix 6

The Tom Ikimi/Bola Tinubu Exchange

Tom Ikimi's Resignation Letter To The APC
Wednesday 27th August 2014

1. Following my widely publicised statement made in the aftermath of the 13th June 2014 All Progressives Congress, APC National Convention, I took time off to reflect on the state of the party, the emerging re-configuration of the general political structure in the country, and the visionary effects on the state of our nation.

2. I have spent almost thirteen of the past fifteen years faithfully digging, in the trenches of the evolving democratic dispensations in our country, steadfastly pursuing my conviction that for true democracy to take firm root in Nigeria we should fall in line with the model being practised in successful democracies in the world, of a party in office and a scrutinising alternative party holding the Government to account. We all have watched with admiration how in those other countries through a process of hitch-free general elections, the baton of leadership changes hands from time to time from one party to the other to provide alternative policies

for their people. Therefore, I have never considered my location outside the ruling party, as being in an "opposition", rather as supporting an alternative platform. All that was necessary for me was the association with individuals committed to build and uphold that platform.

In this regard, my experiences during the era of the NRC and SDP in 1990-1993 are invaluable reference data bank in my quest to work to reincarnate the reality of two dominant political platforms in our country.

3. That is why in 2005, I was fully involved in the creation of the Movement for the Restoration and Defence of Democracy (MRDD), which transformed into the Action Congress (AC) in 2006. I worked with a few dedicated colleagues here in my Abuja residence to successfully achieve the project. Two groups, comprising those of us who broke away from the PDP and a breakaway faction from the AD (notably the former South West AD Governors) made up the foundation membership. For the benefit of political science students, I should now reveal that the original documents we prepared for registration bore the name All Peoples Congress (APC). We eventually settled for AC in order to locate the new party higher up in the ballot paper. In 2010, in pursuit of a bigger party ahead of the 2011 General Election, we changed the name from AC to ACN, in a very poorly constructed merger arrangement that failed. It was therefore an experience of great joy and satisfaction for me to host and lead the process that gave birth in February 2013, at my Abuja residence, to the All Progressives

Congress (APC) with the successful unification of the major opposition parties – ACN, ANPP, CPC and a part of APGA. I am aware of the well-known saying that success breeds many uncles, therefore the subsequent and recent claims of some persons as to the arrowheads of the creation of the APC does not surprise me nor will it surprise my devoted 89 colleagues who worked earnestly with me on the project.

4. The refreshing news of the entry of the All Progressives Congress (APC) into the Nation's political firmament was received across the nation and beyond with great joy and happiness. Our proclamation of a new party that would pursue democratic principles by example with particularly a culture of internal party democracy endeared us to the expectant public of teeming supporters who were all eagerly waiting to take up membership in the new party. For me, I thought we had finally broken the parochial boundaries of tribal and regional politics, which in my recent experience had stunted the growth of the now defunct Action Congress of Nigeria (ACN). Our clarion call for CHANGE reverberated across the country where all and sundry waited with high expectation to enrol in the new party. I myself looked forward eagerly to a wider frontier of comradeship and to once again recreate happiness, colour and pageantry in our national politics which in times gone by was so eloquently displayed in the legendary brotherly hand shake across the river Niger and river Benue by the founding fathers of our nation's politics.

5. It was my fervent hope that the emergence of the APC would bring to an end the sad and bitter experiences that I and some others endured in the ACN where one of the leaders from the South-West exploiting the narrow national success of the party in that region virtually hijacked the party, proclaiming himself Overall Leader. Five of the six governors in the Party at the time were all from that Region. Prominent leaders particularly from the North and South-East notably, personalities such as former Vice President Alhaji Atiku Abubakar, late Alhaji Abubakar Rimi, Alhaji Ghali Na'Abba, Alhaji Lawal Kaita, Alhaji Mohammed Shata, Amb. Yahaya Kwande, Senator Iyorchia Ayu, Otunba Fashawe, Senator Ben Obi, Chief Dubem Onyia, etc. who could not come to terms with the man's behaviour departed from the party back to the PDP. This mass departure of prominent members, from particular sections of the country, did not only seriously weaken the party but blemished it with an image of regional and tribal status. At that time I refused to quit the party despite the fact that my frequent solo protests against his behaviour were dismissively ignored as I was always told that the man was the overwhelming financier of the Party.

While I disagree stoutly with this bluff, it is true that the particular individual constantly boasted of his wealth and of his funding of the party. I on the other hand could recall that this was a man I knew who was an easily forgettable character in the 1990s when I was National Party Chairman and when my candidate Sir Michael Otedola of blessed memory, won the Governorship of Lagos State. It would come as no great surprise if Asiwaju Bola

Tinubu's boasted great wealth did not derive from any stupendous inheritance ancient or modern. Or that his sudden bragging as though Nigeria's Bill Gates is an accumulation of extraordinary hard work or financial wizardry. I would rather trust the informed whispers in the inner circles of the party which have it that having positioned himself as perceived leader in the most lucrative income sources of the party, he is recipient and dispenser of bags and bags of party funds. I am also aware that he is, too, a beneficiary of most of the lucrative contracts in all the ACN states without exception. To further bolster his image, it was also frequently said that Tinubu has control of all the votes from Southwestern Nigeria which, as has been currently touted, when added to the votes of Northwestern Nigeria would guarantee victory for the APC in the upcoming Presidential election.

6. This reckless and arrogant self-aggrandizement paved the way for the imposition of a strange leadership on the APC in July 2013 when the party obtained registration from INEC. Those of us who had worked so hard towards the successful merger and creation of the APC were manipulated out of the scheme of things. In the bizarre struggle to seize control of the party we were even openly accused by the self-proclaimed owners of the party, of wanting to steal "their" party. Many of us in the party as well as keen observers outside frowned at the skewed leadership image of the party that was being paraded; an image that blatantly ignored National sensitivities. The draft constitution prepared by the Merger Committee included an exit clause,

which provided a time limit of six months for the Interim Management of the Party. That clause mysteriously disappeared from the version of the constitution that was smuggled into INEC records. Chief Bisi Akande's national chairmanship was therefore primed to stay on in power *ad infinitum!* Asiwaju Bola Tinubu frantically constituted a group of friends and cronies which he proclaimed to be the APC leadership. The press, led by the *Nation* Newspaper, was made to propagate the aberration.

And so rather than allow the construction of a sound base for the party conducive to the free admission of members nationwide these self-proclaimed leaders embarked on a national travel spree all in a blaze of publicity, crisscrossing the country in private aircraft, visiting PDP State Governors to offer them the State branches of the APC if they would join the party. While they obviously but ridiculously assumed that the crisis then in the PDP would last forever, the details of the agreements they reached with PDP break away Governors, were never revealed to the authentic party leadership but they were such that they ignited the explosion of irreconcilable crisis in some states, particularly Kano, Sokoto and Adamawa, resulting in the instant loss of some valuable key members.

7. Major decisions said to be party decisions now started emerging from this select group whose ad hoc membership varied from time to time. They usually congregated at Tinubu's private parlour in his Asokoro – Abuja residence. Those who wanted to belong had to find or force their way into that parlour. Once initiated, your independence or

capacity to challenge the plots that emerged from that cult venue became seriously curtailed.

Rather than freely open up critical issues to free debate at the Interim Executive Council for democratic decisions to emerge, positions plotted at the notorious Asokoro parlour were being desperately foisted on the party for execution. A handful of us constantly challenged this trend with little success. Gradually, the direction of the Party assumed a focus on the contest for the Presidency. Then the images of presumed Presidential and Vice Presidential candidates as well as a privately cooked up Permanent Chairman for the party started emerging signalling a Muslim/Muslim Presidential and Vice Presidential ticket. The details of this issue I have sufficiently dealt with in my previous statement.

However, let me state again that their calculation that the Presidency in the 2015 General elections will be won by the APC through votes from the North West and South-West Nigeria became an obsession. Asiwaju Bola Tinubu who passionately believed in this theory and who arrogantly claimed custody of all South-West votes already picked an aspirant from Northwestern Nigeria who will run as Presidential candidate with him as Vice Presidential candidate. The National image of the party immediately plummeted.

8. This disastrous trend was worsened by the arrogant departure from observing the provisions of the Party's constitution particularly as it pertains to internal party democracy. Crisis broke out at uncontrollable levels

in the prosecution of the most undemocratic Ward, LGA, and State Congresses Nationwide. Machinery for managing this self-inflicted crisis was virtually non-existent and it was inside this mess that the controversial National Convention of 13th June was staged. The Constitution of the Party clearly defines the Party Organs and the Party Leadership. There is no provision for anyone to be named as the Party Leader. Asiwaju Bola Tinubu having paraded himself both at home and abroad as The Leader of Opposition and of the APC had great difficulty in descending from the fictitious throne. In order to continue manipulating the party from his parlours in Abuja and Lagos he struggled to retain Chief Bisi Akande as Chairman. He was further troubled by the growing influence of the Governors and panicked at the realisation that he and his South-West select caucus were losing their grip on "their" party to the Governors. His last minute efforts to rally a South West Leadership support for his absolute power over the party failed and chances of retaining Chief Bisi Akande as National Chairman also evaporated. In the circumstance as the only option was to find a successor National Chairman as well as other National Officers, an illegal process of horse trading between the Governors and Tinubu was initiated. The Interim Executive Council had no knowledge of all these processes. Chief John Oyegun, a Tinubu plan B project said to be favoured for his NADECO and SDP credentials and also as one who could be controlled now featured, came into the picture.

9. Until recently the APC had sixteen Governors who describe themselves as The Progressive Governors. They are made up of the original merging parties

governors and the breakaway PDP governors who as a group are determined to take control of the Party. This composition of Merging Party Governors and PDP breakaway Governors cannot in any realistic sense be described as PROGRESSIVE. They have come together with different personal agendas built around the central purpose of acquiring national power. Some of them nurse Vice Presidential ambition and some others are warming up for the Presidential contest. In the circumstance the project of taking control of the Party's national machinery became crucial and it was out of the Governor's caucus that the plan of zoning the national offices was initiated and concluded. The Interim Executive Committee had no input.

Although it is claimed that the National Chairmanship slot was zoned to the South South, the horse-trading to produce the beneficiary took place outside the zone. In order to secure the agreement of most of the Governors I understand that an agreement was extracted from Chief Oyegun that he would agree to step down as Chairman should a Governor from the region emerge as either Presidential or Vice Presidential candidate. And although the Governors may not have envisaged the present set back they now suffer in their numerical strength, the battle to take custody of the APC platform that they waged against the Tinubu structure signalled yet another twist in the tale.

10. Apart from the Tinubu Group and The Governors Group there is a third Group, of known Presidential Aspirants comprising in the main General Muhamadu Buhari and Alhaji Atiku Abubakar

who are both Northerners. The inclination of the party had always been to zone the Presidency to the North. Some Governors are now thinking otherwise and given the decisive role that they seek to play in the affairs of the Party as well as the tendency to ignore the principle of internal party democracy, a monumental disaster looms large in the selection of the Party's Presidential and Vice Presidential flag-bearers later in the year. The construction of the new National Executive Committee through horse-trading by the Governors and Tinubu has established a tool structure that is not in the interest of transparency or democracy. To whom will the newly installed National Chairman be finally loyal? Will it remain the Nadeco/SDP comradeship that will drive his loyalty to Tinubu or the current Governors ongoing tactics of dressing up the National Chairman that may become the game clincher?

Time will surely tell! How these known Presidential aspirants will make their way in the contest that may feature some Governors is better imagined. Can Tinubu dare to ditch Buhari? *I dey laf!*

11. Chief John Oyegun has made various statements since the 13th of June convention. He finally claimed that he emerged as National Chairman as a consensus candidate, which puts to rest his previous hasty announcement that I had stepped down for him. Needless to say, the process adopted at the APC convention for deciding on a new National Chairman was a sham in which I did not participate. The Chief knows very well that an even playing field, a fundamental requirement for sound intra

party contest did not exist. He also knows what I know that the conspiracy, with all the plotting and scheming to install him as National Chairman had been cooking long before the Convention process was revealed. The delegation that visited Benin City unceremoniously, last year, to admit him into the ACN party made no contact with the State Party Leadership. He was drafted into our State Party by outsiders who had ulterior motives.

I was away in Dakar, Senegal on a private visit two weeks or so before the convention. It was in the Senegalese capital I read on the Internet Chief Oyegun's press declaration of his candidature. When I returned home I was reliably informed that he had been instructed by his patrons to proceed and print campaign posters. All these manoeuvres taking place even before the emergence of convention guidelines were manifestations of a festering conspiracy. Having been secretly assured of the outcome, the chief not only ignored the position of the Edo State Party on the issue, he never bothered to campaign. On my part I did not approach any of the sixteen Governors or any Party leader to solicit for support to contest the National Chairmanship except for Governor Adams Aliu Oshiomhole of Edo State whom I saw in Benin City a few days to the convention when I became aware that the National Chairmanship had been zoned to the South-South zone. My State Party – Edo State APC naturally supported me unanimously but I printed no posters, did not campaign, did not return the nomination forms as there was to be no election.

12. I have read statements in the press credited to one of the Governors who claims knowledge of what transpired, to the effect that the allocation of National Chairman and other National offices of the Party was negotiated between the Governors and Tinubu. The late night event that took place at Eagle Square on the 13th of June was just a stage-managed ritual to satisfy INEC requirements and deceive the nation. I was never part of any talks that resulted in the allocation decisions and certainly could never have been in support of a strange process that replaced the democratic procedures enshrined in the party's constitution.

13. In the course of his maiden visit to Edo State Chief Oyegun, in his statement in the Governor's office referred to me as those "disgruntled" at his emergence as National Chairman. In a subsequent interview in the *Vanguard* and *Punch* News Papers widely advertised on the Internet under the caption "Ikimi made mistake threatening to leave APC" he said among other things: "It is unfortunate that when you feel hurt, you threaten your party. That alone creates suspicion about you in the party that you still belong to. Let me say it was a mistake for him to threaten to leave the party." Certainly the euphoria and relish of his new office may have taken possession of him, blurring his vision such that he does not see the deep wound inflicted on the party, which is now disintegrating rapidly across the country. For the record let me state that it was I who admitted Chief Oyegun into the APP in 1999. He joined the ACN a year ago in Benin City after he departed from the ANPP where in the 2011 General

Elections he was that party's Vice Presidential candidate. He certainly did not depart from the ANPP with great pleasure. Therefore moving from one party to another should not be so strange to him as his strange statement portrays. Let me state that notwithstanding my well known disagreement over the years with the conduct of Asiwaju Bola Tinubu, his actions within the AC, ACN and APC and notwithstanding the amazing retention of Chief Bisi Akande as National Chairman of all these parties since 2006, there was absolute mutual respect between me and Chief Bisi Akande. I have no difficulty in accepting any qualified member of the Party from any part of Nigeria emerging legitimately as National Chairman. Chief John Oyegun visits me regularly in Benin City and Abuja where I treat him graciously but I demand of him to clarify what he meant by "the suspicion" he claimed the Party he joined through ACN (a party he became a member of last year) would have about me, a founding foundation member of AC, ACN and APC. Is he speaking for himself or singing his master's tune?

14. Senator Ali Modu Sherriff, former two-term Governor of Bornu State enthusiastically supported the merger. In fact his influence as Chairman Board of Trustees of the defunct ANPP was crucial to bringing the party on board. Senator Sherriff achieved his first tenure as a Nigerian Senator in 1991 under the NRC party when I was the National Chairman. He always recalls the support I gave him in what was his maiden political outing. I appreciate the cooperation he gave to the merger committee,

which substantially helped us to overcome impediments put on our way during the merger talks, by some leaders of the ACN and CPC, who did not want the ANPP on board. To get the APC off the ground, Senator Sherriff made substantial contributions, which included huge finance. On the 7th of March 2014 the APC staged a National Summit at the Hilton Hotel in Abuja which was an elaborate event choreographed to officially unveil the new party. An extensive presentation was displayed to showcase how the party was formed. Most fair-minded persons who attended the event were shocked to observe that not even a word was mentioned of me as one of those who contributed to the creation of the APC. Film clips were shown of Bola Tinubu, Muhammadu Buhari, Bisi Akande, Ogbonnaya Onu and a few selected others who in most cases gave distorted accounts of the merger process.

Surprisingly it was Senator Ali Modu Sherriff who became so disgusted by the deliberate distortion of the facts that he had the courage to take the microphone and openly berated the injustice. Some were obviously embarrassed but it turned out that those who prepared the presentation, many of them high ranking members of the party, were working on the instructions of Asiwaju Bola Tinubu. For his noteworthy and courageous public intervention on this matter, Senator Sherriff was now marked down by Bola Tinubu as having opposed him so much so that shortly after the event both men almost engaged in physical combat at an expanded National Exco meeting in Abuja. Senator Ali Modu Sherriff may be a friend and long-time political ally but he is certainly not my sponsor. I read several fictional newspaper stories that said Senator Sherriff was sponsoring me for National Chairman. That is not true.

15. The merger talks of eight-nine members hosted by me, was managed by a leadership of four which included HE Ibrahim Shekarau of ANPP, Alhaji Garba Gadi of CPC, Senator Ani Okonkwo of the APGA faction and myself of ACN. I was unanimously nominated by the group to preside as coordinating chairman. We worked harmoniously together and on the 6th February 2013 the four of us signed the agreement for the merger of the three parties and a part of APGA. I announced the merger and presented the agreement to the world. We continued to the next and difficult stages of agreeing a name, flag, motto and symbol for the party. These were very intricate negotiations! Our sub-committees worked on the Constitution and Manifesto. After all these were accomplished Asiwaju Bola Tinubu prevented a smooth establishment of the party in accordance with our agreements. HE Alhaji Ibrahim Shekarau, former Governor of Kano State was sidelined in his State by a curious arrangement that ceded the party leadership in the state to the present Governor of Kano State with no defined role for the former Governor to play. He was compelled to withdraw his membership from the Party. He joined the PDP where he was recently appointed Minister of Education. Alhaji Shekarau possesses a very sound and critical mind. I found his contributions to our work most invaluable. Senator Annie Okonkwo

has also announced his departure from the APC. The popular will, prevailing at the time among a cross section of members was that the Merger Leadership should continue to mould the party for at least six months and bring it to fruition by diligently establishing all its structures. Regrettably this was foiled by hijackers who have now crashed the project.

16. Former Governor of Sokoto State Alhaji Atahiru Bafarawa could also not accept the shabby treatment meted out to him by those who seized the new party. Governor Bafarawa is very loyal and dependable. He is an astute politician with whom I have been associated for about thirty years now. He was NRC State Party Chairman of Sokoto State in 1991 when I was National Chairman. He has always been very keen on the unification of the opposition parties and consequently hosted several merger meetings prior to the 2011 General Elections. On this occasion he hosted the sittings of the Constitution committee. Alhaji Bafarawa suffered unprecedented humiliation in the ACN in 2011 in a kangaroo convention staged in Lagos to select the ACN Presidential candidate. He therefore withdrew from the party to return to the ANPP. This time as an ANPP delegate he enthusiastically participated in the merger talks. He has now withdrawn from the APC to join the PDP as he could not accept the sudden handover of the APC in Sokoto to the present Governor who during his tenure was his deputy.

Senator Ali Modu Sherriff has not hidden his very strong disapproval of the precarious direction that the Party is heading. The conduct of 13th June Convention was totally unacceptable to him. Following his open challenge of Tinubu it did not surprise me that Tinubu negotiated away all Sherriff's nominees from the newly constituted National Executive Committee. I understand that Sen. Ali Modu Sherriff is on his way out of the party, along with a very large slice of the party membership particularly from the North-East. It is not a coincidence to me that the prominent members of APC targeted by Bola Tinubu such as Alhaji Atahiru Bafarawa, Sen. Ali Modu Sherriff and myself are former NRC members or those perceived as Conservatives.

17. Since after the 13th of June APC Convention and after my post-convention statement, a few leaders of the APC have come to see me on their individual personal basis to plead with me not to abandon the party.

I have received quite a number of telephone calls as well, conveying similar views to me. None of these persons could disagree with my very strong views against the turn of events regarding the mismanagement of the party nor of the grave injustice that has been perpetrated against me through an unprecedented level of conspiracy and bad faith. All they are saying to me is that I should not abandon what I had helped so much to build. It is truly amazing that all who have spoken to me privately without exception agree with me that the image of the APC as is a Tinubu Party has severely damaged the party but each time I openly raise issues that challenge the consequences everyone keeps quiet. It is common knowledge that the vote against the very popular candidate Sen Chris Ngige in the Anambra governorship election and recently against one of the most successful Governors, Kayode Fayemi of Ekiti State, was indeed a vote against Tinubu. Tinubu's obsessive calculation of South-West/North-West votes is unproven and untested. It is in pursuit of a very selfish ambition that has seriously alienated block zones, such as South-East, South-South, North-East and most of North-Central from the party. The party has collapsed in very many states such as Adamawa, it is in distress in Edo, Ogun, Oyo, Lagos, Nasarawa.

18. In consideration of all the above I have come to the following conclusions:

    (i) I have lived to see one of my major political yearnings in place. Now there are two major Political Parties in my Country – The People's Democratic Party (PDP) and The All Progressives Congress (APC). I am satisfied that I have played an important and historic role in ensuring the emergence of an alternative platform to the party in office. There are many now claiming leadership of the APC who were very skeptical when we embarked on the merger project who openly dismissed the idea that it would never work. Yes, some of them tried several times in the past to unify some parties in order to achieve bigger platforms but in an atmosphere of prevailing dishonesty, greed, unbridled ambition, uncompromising and undiplomatic approaches to such delicate negotiations, their efforts yielded resounding failure. For my part I enjoyed the respect of all the 89 delegates who met with me for about six months because they were very confident I had no personal agenda not even taking sides to protect positions of the ACN, my own party then. But immediately we established what they had considered impossible to do, I became a prime target, as they believed that they could only control and manipulate the affairs of the party if I was not there. By my credentials in Political Party Leadership my claim to the top table in any party to which I belong is well earned!

In the present atmosphere of envy, plots and gossip the long-term satisfaction of a political comradeship and brotherhood anchored on shared principles and ideology, of honour, trust and confidence in pursuit of a common goal remain elusive.

(ii) I understand they claim that I possess a strong and independent personality as well as a mind of my own which cannot be bent and so I am said to be one that could not be controlled. On a rather mischievous note, my foremost assailant in that party, peddles in one breath a smear campaign that if I were to be in charge, I would sell the party while in another fowl breath that I am an enemy as I had served in the Abacha Government. My so called strong and independent personality sometimes misconstrued as an arrogant mien is merely the creation of nature and I have never ever been harmful at all to anyone around me but as for an independent and firm mind I believe it is an asset and an attribute which indeed is so direly needed for good and fair leadership in our society today and I apologize to no one for being so created. It is really ironic that I was not accused of going to sell the party over the past 13 years or so that I struggled in different recorded ways to make notable contributions in creating and building it up in its various forms but that I was now to sell the party after working successfully to achieve its present mega format. Who by the way is the buyer? Is it the PDP Government that opened its doors once more recently to one of the APC's foremost boastful and noisy leaders to consummate a mega oil deal on the eve of that controversial APC convention? Who then is really selling and who is indeed buying? Who sold Mallam Nuhu Ribadu's ACN Presidential candidature in 2011? Was it Chief Tom Ikimi? My tenure as Foreign Affairs Minister during the Abacha regime has turned out to be a befitting reference in patriotic diplomatic service in our country for which I am extremely proud! Why am I targeted for being that Foreign Minister that brought peace to Liberia, restored democratic governance in Sierra Leone, maintained the leadership of Nigeria in the OAU, ECOWAS and the UN, the first to turn to China with a trade delegation that opened up massive opportunities for our country but they fail to point even a feeble finger at others in their midst who benefitted immensely from the Abacha Government, some who ran the most lucrative agencies during that tenure, some others who made away with giant oil fields or are we blind not to see the giant, fancy lucrative projects currently being executed in partnership with well-known foreign friends of the same Abacha!

(iii) The recent mass exodus from the Party has effectively put the movement of the APC firmly in reverse gear. Those who have left include notables such as Alhaji Ibrahim Shekarau of Kano State, Alhaji Atahiru Bafarawa of Sokoto State, Alhaji Ali Modu Sherriff of Bornu State, Brg. Gen Buba Marwa of Adamawa State, Mallam Nuhu Ribadu of Adamawa State, Senator Annie Okonkwo of Anambra State and Pastor Osagie Ize Iyamu of Edo State. I understand that Chief Olusegun Osoba of Ogun State is on his way out too. The very weak National Leadership appointed for the Party in the last Convention is definitely incapable of restoring any positive movement to the party. The prevailing hostile atmosphere in the party does not present the opportunity for any intervention from me at this time at National, Zonal or State Level as I have done in the past.

(iv) I led the process of change in Edo State politics in 2006 when as National Leader of the Action Congress (AC) I brought the new party to the state. I worked with dedicated and courageous colleagues to establish the party in Edo State and we recorded a resounding success in the 2007 General Elections – our very first outing in the State. AC and eventually ACN has therefore been the Government in power in Edo State from 2008 to date and I am proud of the quality of peaceful, respectable and dignified leadership that I was able to provide to the party through these years.

Comrade Adams Aliu Oshiomhole who joined us in the middle of our preparation for the 2007 General Elections met me in firm control of the Party and its Leadership in the State at the time. We welcomed him warmly and with our support he was lucky to emerge victorious in the State Governorship election and I have over the years enjoyed an excellent working relationship with the Comrade. Now as he is the APC Governor of Edo State, I wish him good luck, good health and God's guidance as he proceeds to conclude his second term in office. But during the past seven years of performing my role as leader of the party in Edo State, my personal experiences of the relationship between the political party, the legislature and the executive at state level has instilled in me very useful lessons that would be immensely helpful in any future roles.

(v) I have no current or perceivable ambition to contest for executive power. My quest for an alternative political platform in the country is basically in pursuit of a credible political structure that would guarantee the vital checks and balances in the system so that our people may enjoy the benefits of alternative choices of National Government from time to time. It is certainly not for the creation of a vengeful ravaging army of flatterers and favour-seekers at the command of a desperate upstart with the hideous mission of stampeding an illusory enemy. While I have always regarded the entire country as my constituency, I am not oblivious of the reality of my circumstance as a South-Southerner, a Christian from a so called minority stock who will continue to align with the forces of change that would guarantee justice, prosperity, peace and happiness for all our peoples. The forces that have now seized the APC in a stranglehold are on a mission very much against my conscience and indeed my very being.

(vi) I have always viewed a political party as a congregation of like-minded persons who become welded together in a close-knit brotherhood in a manner beyond mere friendship. In a nation of two dominant political parties or even diverse political parties, the members, across party lines, who are all in politics need not be sworn enemies. After all they are citizens of the same Nation with I suppose a mission of service to their people. Therefore their hold to power has to be at the discretion of the people.

(vii) I am at the stage of currently critically re-examining the two dominant political parties in our country, which are the APC and the PDP, in both of which I have had close working knowledge. I have not ignored the other political parties but in the light of the foregoing I must now search to really ascertain where indeed my true political friends exist. I need to be, at this time of my life where I have friends who share a common vision with me and where my freedom, respect, honour and dignity would be guaranteed. Notwithstanding my enormous contributions over the past twelve years or so to building the alternative platform, after very deep thought and the widest consultations I have made the decision to withdraw my membership from the All Progressives Congress (APC) from today, inconclusive

Tinubu's Reply To Ikimi

Bola Ahmed Tinubu
— Sep 3, 2014 | 3 Comments

I ordinarily would not have responded to Tom Ikimi's lengthy chronicle of falsehoods, cheap blackmail and abuse. My only reason for this response is that I know Tom Ikimi's style. He subscribes to the view that no matter how unbelievable a lie may sound if you brazenly assert it and repeat it often enough you may persuade many that it is in fact true. I have seen Ikimi perpetrate this deviousness in his years in public life.

1. Regarding Ikimi's bid for the Chairmanship of the Party. It was clear to practically everyone who had the interest of the party at heart that we simply could

not have a man of Tom Ikimi's antecedents as Chair of the party. As chairman of the NRC, one of the only two political parties in the country under the military transition programme, Tom Ikimi not only connived with the then military regime to annul the elections, terminate the democratic process and sell off his party, he became Abacha's foreign minister, convincing the world that heinous state murders like the hanging of Ken Saro Wiwa were just acts! If Ikimi were the Chair of APC the party would have to sleep with both eyes open lest its chairman sell off the party before day break. No matter what anyone may say about me it is unlikely that I can be accused of supporting incompetent or morally light-weight individuals for important political positions. My philosophy is to put the best forward, men and women of competence and integrity, who can stand up to us politicians to challenge us and say no when necessary. Such people are not noisy or able to gain attention by being loud, I believe my role is to do all I can to project them. Who in their right mind would compare the highly principled Chief Bisi Akande, or Chief Oyegun with a Tom Ikimi? Either of these two men are known for their no-nonsense styles, not once in their careers would you hear that they betrayed a cause or were anybody's stooge.

2. Ikimi also concocts a story of a meeting he claims I had with Diezani on the Oando/ ConocoPhillips transaction on the eve of the APC Convention.

Only a Tom Ikimi can come up with the absurd falsehood that on the eve of the APC Convention when I was in crucial meetings practically round the clock I was meeting with the Minister for Petroleum!

What exactly would have been the point of such a meeting especially on the eve of the Convention? Was it to prevent Tom Ikimi from emerging as Chairman of the APC? To what end? Of what value would it be to anyone except Ikimi himself? Besides if this was so why he is back to the same party that purportedly planned his down fall?

What is the Oando/ConocoPhillips transaction anyway? For those who do not know this is a private sale of the assets of ConocoPhillips to Oando. It was not patronage of any kind from the federal government. The federal government's involvement was merely to formally consent to the sale. I was not involved and I have never been involved in any of Oando's transactions.

Typically he plays on the fact that Wale Tinubu of Oando is my nephew. Oando has been thoroughly investigated by South African and British authorities in the past five years as part of the process of listing the company on the stock exchanges of those countries. Those rigorous and comprehensive investigations conducted by the governments and risk control investigators are to discover the actual ownership of shares in the company. Politically exposed persons like myself are prime targets for those investigations. All these investigations have shown that I have no investments in Oando. My public position on the entire transaction is that if an indigenous Nigerian oil and gas entity run by young serious-minded Nigerians raise money transparently in the international capital markets to purchase private assets of a multi-national the federal government ought to give its consent. That it took so long is shameful. The ConocoPhillips transaction was a $1.7 billion dollars investment in Nigeria that would create more jobs, witness the establishment of allied industries and make the Nigerian economy more attractive. I would have been extremely proud to have made such a transaction possible.

3. Regarding the nonsense about selling out on Ribadu. I think common sense should dictate that if ever such a deal were reached we would have had to inform our members in all the States. How could that have been done secretly? How do you tell hundreds of thousands of people not to vote for your own party without it becoming public knowledge?

At the formation of the APC, a crucial debate ensued about what to do about persons like Ikimi who had done awful things in the past, but who were now minded to align with the progressive tendency in Nigerian politics. Should we forever blacklist them? This would have been the easiest route, but it would have kept rancour alive. It would have made us slaves to the bleakest chapters of our past. Instead we opted to extend the hand of brotherhood, reconcile and put the past behind us. This would enable a broader political consensus, while also giving the likes of Ikimi an opportunity to atone for their grievous wrongs against the people and be rehabilitated.

We recognised that many leading Nigerians had committed acts of shame. Some for private profit, others who were otherwise decent people who had become prisoners to a terrible system.

Not surprisingly, Ikimi acting true to type abuse that magnanimity. He was never sincerely committed to the party. He was always playing out a PDP script. He only wanted the chairmanship of the party as a bargaining chip for negotiations with his benefactors. His defection purportedly on account of the loss of the chairmanship of the party is a mere subterfuge, once his ploy failed he had no other objective within the party, I knew he would go back to his sponsors. He is back in the company he deserves. And APC is better for it.

— **Bola Ahmed Tinubu**

Appendix 7

APC Platform Document

All Progressives Congress Party
"Our Commitment" (Deliver happiness)

1. Our party will uphold a Nigeria bound in freedom, justice, rule of law and peace in a united nation.
2. Our party will uphold the democratic principle of one man one vote predicated on free and fair elections within the party and the nation.
3. Our party will uphold and respect the individual's choice of faith under one God.
4. Our party accepts the diversity of our Nation and will uphold and respect the interest of the various ethnic groups that constitute the Nigerian Nation.
5. Our party is committed to political and fiscal federalism as the most effective vehicle for harnessing the diversity and preserving the unity of Nigeria.
6. Our party believes that the human being is the most important asset of the Nation and thus will respect and do everything to protect and preserve human life and dignity.

7. Our party will be run on social democratic principles and as such its progressive and welfare objectives for Nigeria will be predicated on production and fair competition that promotes merit and bridges inequalities.

8. Our party will pursue these progressive and welfare objectives through a Government-led and private sector driven economy.

9. Our party commits to managing the Nigerian Nigeria's resources on principles of citizens responsibility, leadership accountability and the pursuit of the greatest good for the greatest number of people with no tolerance for corruption.

10. Our party fully appreciates Nigeria's strategic role on the African continent and commits to the pursuit of a foreign policy that promotes our national interest.

APPENDIX 8

Declaration Speech By General Muhammadu Buhari For Presidential Primaries, Abuja October 15th, 2014

PROTOCOLS

First I would like, Mr. Chairman, if I may, pay tribute to Nigerians as a whole who are enduring all sorts of hardships and deprivations on a daily basis. Many millions are grappling with extreme poverty and barely eking out a living. Nearly all are in fear of their lives or safety for themselves and their families due to insurgency by:

the godless movement called Boko Haram;
- marauding murderers in towns and villages;
- armed robbers on the highways;
- kidnappers who have put whole communities fright and sometimes to flight.

Ladies and gentlemen, it is everyone's duty to resolve and help the national effort to overcome these immense challenges. I would like us to place on record our appreciation for the efforts of our Armed Forces under new leadership and police in confronting these challenges.

I would like, secondly, to thank our supporters up and down the country for their perseverance and resolve in the face of an oppressive PDP government.

Mr. Chairman, this is an occasion to celebrate our efforts and to resolve to continue until victory is won. I humbly wish to present myself before you, before all of Nigeria and before God seeking to be elected as APC's Presidential candidate. Having appreciated that the only way to relieve Nigerians of the PDP, the main opposition parties decided to pool their strengths into one party. We have worked very hard in the last eighteen months to put up structures from the polling units to wards, local governments, states and the centre.

We have tried to ensure all processes in our party formation to be transparent and credible. These structures will lead to free and fair polls. There is no point in holding elections if they are not free and fair.

Interference in the form of rigging which PDP Government has practised since 2003 is the worst form of injustice – denying people their right to express their opinions. Whether they like it or not, injustice cannot endure.

Since 1999 PDP has presided over our country's decline. Nigeria in my experience has never been so divided, so polarized by an unthinking government hell bent on ruling and stealing forever whatever befalls the country. Mr. Chairman, we in APC are resolved to stop them in their tracks and rescue Nigeria from the stranglehold of PDP.

The last sixteen years of PDP Government has witnessed decline in all critical sectors of life in Nigeria

- There is now general insecurity in the land
Quite apart from Boko Haram, there is prevalence of armed robbery, kidnapping and killings, cattle rustling, market and farmland arson.

- These outrages have taken a new and a frightening dimension, disrupting economic and social life across whole communities.

- The economy continues to deteriorate while the Government continues to announce fantastic growth figures but manufacturing is down, agriculture is down, commerce is down.

- Simply because you sell oil and steal part of the money does not entitle you to cook figures and announce phantom economic growth when all the major indices, namely, employment, manufacturing, farming and trading are demonstrably on the decline.

- When PDP came to power in 1999 Nigeria was generating about 4,000 M/W of electricity. After 15 years and $20 billion spent we are generating between 3,000 – 4,000 M/W. No failure is more glaring than this.

We in APC are resolved to bring change to Nigeria. We plan to do things differently.

We plan to put priority on:

- Protection of lives and property.
- Pursuing economic policies for shared prosperity and immediate attention on youth employment.
- Quality education for development, modernity and social mobility.

- Agricultural productivity for taking millions out of poverty and ensuring food security.
- Reviving industry to generate employment and "make things" not just to remain hawkers of other peoples' goods.
- Developing solid minerals exploitation which will substantially attract employment and revenue for government.
- Restoring honour and integrity to public service by keeping the best and attracting the best.
- Tackling corruption which has become blatant and widespread. The rest of the world looks at Nigeria as the home of corruption. Nigeria is a country where stealing is not corruption.
- Last, (but not the least or final) respecting the constitutional separation of powers between the executive, legislatures and judiciary and respecting the rights of citizens.

Mr. Chairman, there, in outline are some policy proposals about the direction APC should take when, by the grace of God, we are given the responsibility of serving Nigeria in Government.

GENERAL MUHAMMADU BUHARI, GCFR

Appendix 9

Strategy Committee Report Presented On Wednesday 22nd Januray 2014

TABLE OF CONTENTS

S/NO		PAGE
1.	REPORT OF THE STRATEGY COMMITTEE	1
2.	ANNEX 1	6
3.	ANNEX 2	7
4.	ANNEX 3	15

Report of the Strategy Committee of the APC

1. Members
1.1 The membership of this committee is made up of people of like minds, led by Governor Babatunde Raji Fashola of Lagos State.

2. Terms of Reference
2.1 Its Terms of Reference are as Follows:

1. Design and develop an internal research capability for the Party to provide data and arguments that underpin and support its platform, policies and programs at federal, state and local government levels.
2. Develop a template for gathering and analysis of political, social and economic intelligence including but not limited to voter demographics, migration, anthropological diversity and socio-economic data as input for the electoral strategies of the Party.
3. Establish national and global network of resource persons and experts in various knowledge areas that will be volunteers or paid consultants to help articulate the Party platform, manifesto, policies, programs and plans for the federal, state and local government levels.

4. Develop strategies for the establishment of the Party's think tank – The All Progressives Institute, with the support of domestic and international donors, to serve as – the centre of research and policy excellence of the Party.
5. Submit monthly reports of progress, success and challenges to the National Executive Committee of the Party.
6. The Committee may wish to co-opt additional Members as it deems fit.

3. Meetings and deliberations
3.1 The committee has met in two full sessions and its representatives have met with the leadership of the party once.

4. Recommendations of the Committee

4.1 Having regard to the current developments in the national polity, the committee has thought it fit to give priority to Items 1 and 3 of its terms of reference, in order to provide quick wins upon which Items 2 and 4, are more continuous.

4.2 Some of the quick wins that the committee envisages include a clear messaging for the public about the purpose of the APC and also a clear summary of its management plan for the country.

4.3 Accordingly, the committee recommends that 2 (two) documents must issue from the party in order to achieve these quick wins.

4.4 The first document is a statement of commitment, in other words, the platform (Annex I) which helps the party present its ideology to the Nigerian public about the purpose of the APC.

4.5 The second document is a revised manifesto (which is in summary form for now) which helps the party present its management plan for the country, when it forms a Government.

4.6 In order to assist in the understanding of the need for 2 (two) documents, the committee wishes to stress that a political party such as ours, will do well to always bear in mind that it will always be addressing at least 2 (two) broad classes of people in any society.

4.7 The first class of people will be those members of the public, who want to join a political party.

4.8 It is our committee's view that such people will make the decision whether or not to join a party because of what it stands for in terms of ideology.

4.9 Some of the members of this class are often the society's intelligentsia who need an idea to galvanise them. To this group, we believe and recommend that the APC must present a platform message. (Annex I)

4.10 The other class, are those who in our view do not seek to belong to any party, but are interested in knowing what the party will offer them, if it forms a Government. To these people our Manifesto (Annex 2) must be presented.

4.11 In other words, while party members will affiliate and vote on the basis of membership and ideological commitment, non-party members will support and work on the basis of the expectation of public goods promised in our manifesto.

4.12 It must be emphasised that Annex 2 is still a summary and is still under development. It is only presented for information at this stage.

4.13 The plan is to present it when completed for consideration and approval, before it is presented to the National Convention when the party membership registration is concluded.

4.14 Accordingly we present Annex 1 and 2, and seek your approval of Annex 1.

5. NEXT STEPS

5.1 If the contents of Annex 1 are approved, we intend to organise a grand launch and presentation of the ideology and platform statement, by inviting some eminent people to speak at the launch for not more than 10 minutes. Each speaker will be allotted one of the 10 items we have committed to embark upon as a springboard for the media coverage that will then follow.

5.2 It is our belief that this will provide a final and well thought out answer to those who say we either have no ideology or we are the same as other parties.

5.3 It is instructive to observe that available records do not reveal that any political party has ever done something of the scale that we plan before now.

5.4 The closest we have come was the inauguration speech of the Action Group by Chief Obafemi Awolowo in 1951 (Annex 3)

5.5 If this framework is approved, it gives the committee more time to finalise a manifesto to be considered for approval and presentation at the National Convention.

5.6. We feel that it is relevant to also mention that while a few Governors were present at the meeting of December 2013 to make input into the platform document which have already been incorporated, the document was also presented to 9 (Nine) Governors of the APC who meet) under the aegis of Progressive Governor's forum in Lagos on Thursday 9th January 2014 and they have also given their blessing to the platform.

5.7 In closing it must be pointed out that Annex 1 has factored in recommendations of the party leadership when a draft was presented to them at an Extraordinary meeting convened by the Interim National Chairman in December 2013.

5.8 Finally we thank the party for the privilege of service.

Appendix 10

Jonathan sitting down for prayers with Obas
in the Southwest

Pastor Oritsejafor, former CAN President, leading other pastors in prayer for president Jonathan while in Israel for pilgrimage

Appendixes

Jonathan kneeling down before Pastor Adeboye for prayers

Appendix 11

Campaign Pictures With Mammoth Crowd

GMB in Adamawa State

The crowd at the Lagos Campaign Trail

The crowd at the Kano Campaign Trail

The Kaduna Crowd

The crowd in Katsina

Appendixes

The crowd in Maiduguri

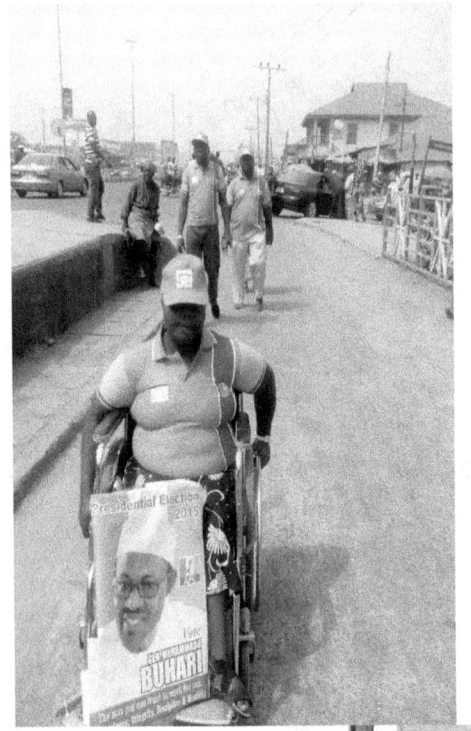

Change Network Initiative Volunteers, Ilorin, Kwara State

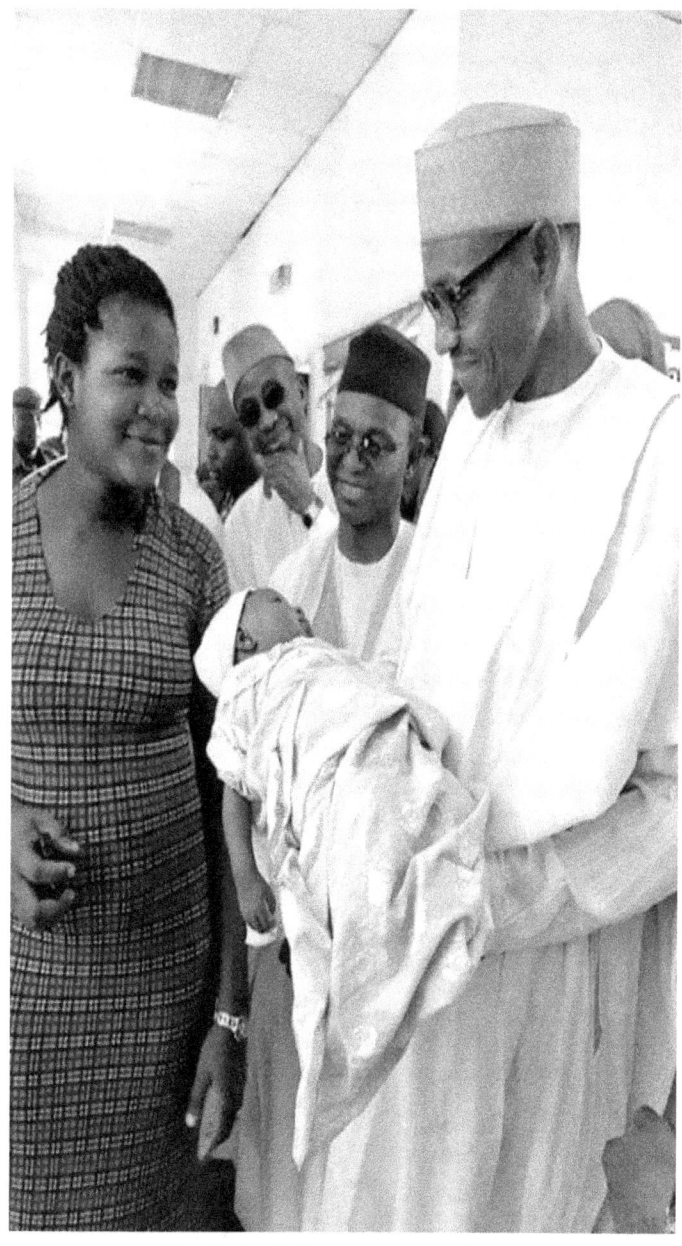

GMB holding a new born baby on a campaign trail in Benin City, Edo State

Appendix 12

Colour-Coded Surveys on Buhari's Chances

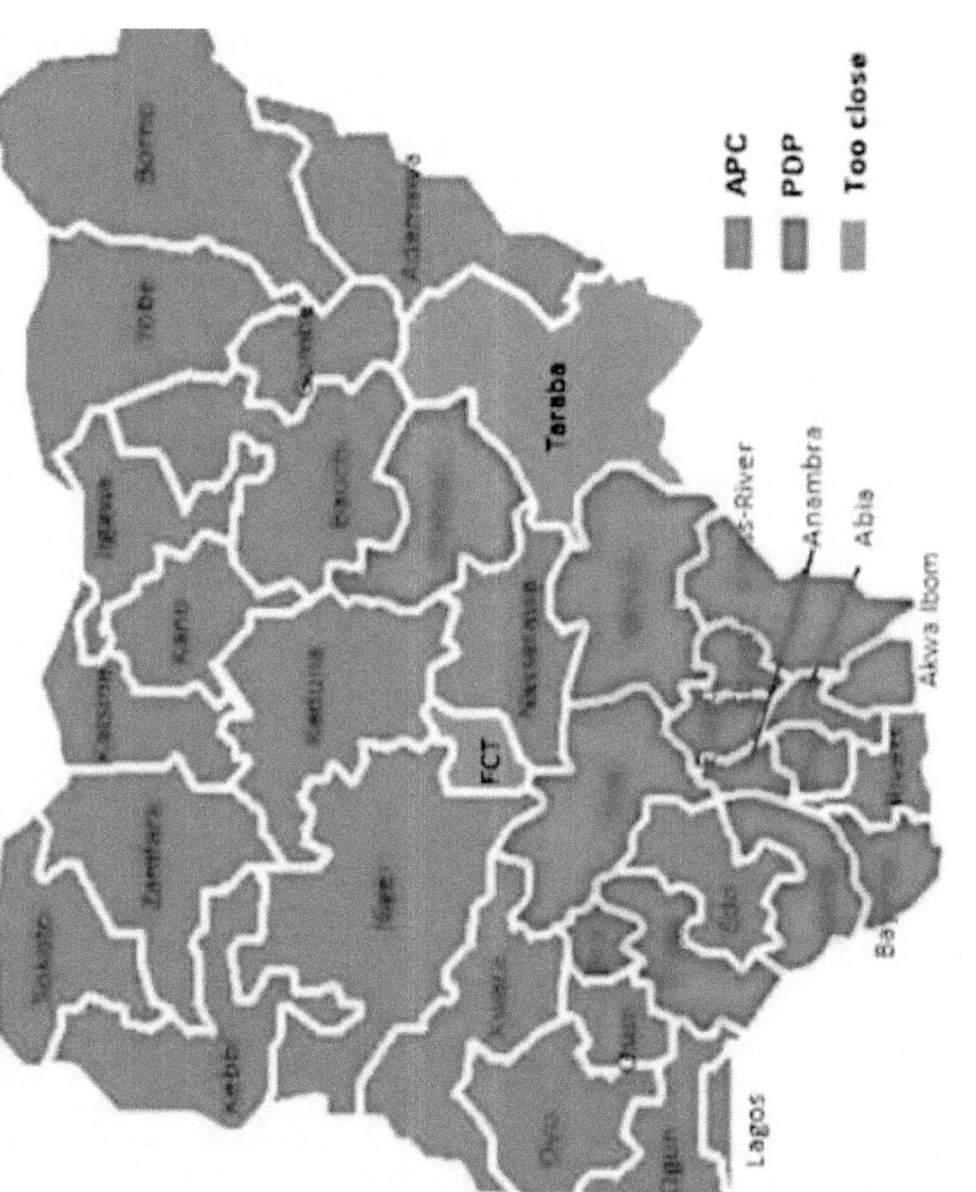

Appendix 13

Time To Rebuild Nigeria

Acceptance Speech By
General Muhammadu Buhari, GCFR
Presidential Candidate of the All Nigeria Congress
12th December, 2014

The National Chairman of the All Progressives Congress
National leaders of the APC
Members of the National Executive Council of the APC
Your Excellencies, State Governors
Distinguished Senators
Honourable Members of the House of Representatives and Assemblies
The Chairman and Members of the Convention Committee
State and Local Government Chairmen of the APC
Distinguished Delegates
Members of the Press
Invited Guests
Ladies and Gentlemen

ACCEPTANCE:

1. First of all, I wish to express my gratitude to the Chairman and members of the Convention Committee for planning and conducting a hitch free convention. The same appreciation goes to the chairmen of National and State Executive Councils of our party. Thank you very much for doing an excellent job.

2. I would like to pay tribute to Chief Bisi Akande the first chairman of APC and his National Executive for managing the party in its early stages.

3. I also wish to commend Lagos State Government and state party for hosting this convention. Time was when people feared to come to Lagos. Today, Lagos is the cleanest and dare I say safest city in Nigeria. This achievement is due to the leadership and strength of purpose of Asiwaju Bola Tinubu and Chief Babatunde Fashola the two Governors since 1999 and their team of professionals for this wonderful transformation Nigeria greets you!

4. The outcome of the presidential primaries of the All Progressives Congress is a demonstration of democracy at work. It is testimony to the fact that democracy as a concept is greater than the interests of individuals in a free and functional political system. What has just happened is not about winning or losing but about the triumph of liberty, freedom of choice and association, which are hallmarks of democracy.

5. To my fellow contestants; Alhaji Atiku Abubakar, Governor Rabiu Musa Kwankwaso, Owelle Rochas Okorocha and Mr. Sam Nda Isaiah, I wish to thank you for putting up a good fight. The keenly contested primaries we just had will help to strengthen our party and democracy, and ultimately send our message to Nigerian voters in the impending elections.

6. To you all, I pay my absolute compliments and congratulate you on the success of your respective campaigns. I extend my gratitude to you all for accepting the outcome of this convention and agreeing to support my candidature as we move forward. I shall meet with you all in the coming days to fashion out how we shall confront the challenge ahead.

7. My dear fellow countrymen and women, it is with a deep sense of humility that I stand before you today to accept the nomination of my party, the All Progressives Congress to be its candidate and flag-bearer in 2015 presidential elections.

8. My nomination is not because I am better than any of the other contestants. I see it as a tribute and mark of confidence to carry the torch as we all join hands to rescue our dear country Nigeria, from those who have led us into the current state of insecurity, poverty, sectarian divide and hopelessness among our people.

9. I stand before you today to ask that you join me in a common cause. My call to you is not to realise the personal fulfilment of one man. This Common Cause is nothing less than the love for our nation and concern for its present condition. And a resolve to make things better for Nigeria.

10. What I say today is for all Nigerians: Christian and Muslim, Southern and Northern, rich and poor, young and old, man and woman. We are all citizens of Nigeria. There is no dividing line among us that I care to honour. Either we advance as one or fail altogether.

11. My choice and my colleagues choice and wish is that we progress together. Preserving the nation's future is a scared obligation to all of us in this party. Leaders should be wholly committed to fulfilling this obligation otherwise they have no business being leaders.

12. Sadly, the current administration does not believe in this obligation. By their actions they are leading us to calamity.

13. At International Conferences, the Nigerian delegation is usually among the largest but at the same time the least effective. Our president should have the status and the voice of Africa's largest nation. But in political influence we are among the weakest.

14. Shall we at home continue to live in a condition where the Power Holding Company and its successors seem only to have the power to hold us in darkness?

15. Shall we continue in a situation where 250 of our daughters have been abducted and the government has been unable to rescue them or provide credible information about what steps they are taking?

16. Shall we live in a nation where several people were trampled to death in search of jobs in a stadium and yet no one has taken responsibility for the tragedy?

17. Shall we live in a nation where the ranks of the poor swell and their poverty increase while the consorts of the powerful enjoy unprecedented wealth? The lives of the poor are bled dry while those of the powerful soak in excessive abundance.

18. My answers to these questions are "No, No, No, No!"

19. It is time to close this demeaning chapter in our nation's history.

20. I ask that you join this effort, not for me, but to establish a better land for all of us.

21. I understand and accept the hard challenge ahead. When all is said and done, let it be written that Muhammadu Buhari gave his all for this nation.

22. As such, I make these five pledges regarding the government if we are elected next February;

    a. We will govern Nigeria honestly, in accordance with the constitution.
    b. We will strive to secure the country and efficiently manage the economy.
    c. We will strive to attack poverty through broadly-shared economic growth and attacking corruption through impartial application of the law.
    d. We will tolerate no religious, regional, ethnic or gender bias in our government.

    e. We will return Nigeria to a position of international respect through patriotic foreign policy.
    f. We will choose the best Nigerians for the right jobs.

23. Our government will be committed to the cause of the common man. Whether you are a Christian from Bayelsa State or a Muslim from Katsina State, you are first and foremost a Nigerian in my eyes. I shall treat you equally as my people, my national family, my brothers and sisters. There can be no genuine love of our country without loving all its people in our diversity.

24. Just as APC stands as a new party for a new Nigeria, our government will institute new policies to realise the new Nigeria.

25. We shall institute just policies that afford people the dignity of work and pay them a living wage for their sweat and toil. We intend to do this by instituting a national industrial policy, coupled with a national employment directive, that together shall revive and expand our manufacturing sector, creating jobs for our urban population and decreasing our reliance on expensive foreign imports.

26. We shall implement a national infrastructure master plan that will provide construction and related jobs across the land. Furthermore, by improving our transportation infrastructure through road, rail and port construction we expand the outer bounds of economic growth as no economy can grow beyond the capacity of its infrastructure.

27. Agriculture remains the backbone of the economy. Our government, when elected, will establish an agricultural policy that provides farmers a dignified living through improved input, improved extension services, access to credit and price support mechanisms.

28. On corruption, the government will enhance EFCC's powers to investigate independently. Moreover, we intend to plug the holes in NNPC accounting. There will no longer be two sets of books, one for public consumption and another for insiders who profit from this slick fraud. In an APC government, the public will know how much NNPC makes and where all the money goes.

29. No longer shall illegal flows of massive sums leave these shores to finance other economies. While our people languish in poverty, we effectively give financial aid to nations that is not justified. I am sick of this. It must stop. The money saved will finance jobs, health care and the provision of social safety net for the needy, weak and vulnerable of our land.

30. We will be a compassionate government, for out of compassion arises the truest forms of wealth and progress a society can attain. We shall open the door to tertiary education to excellent students who otherwise could not afford it. Pregnant and poor women and children shall be entitled to basic health care.

31. This is a Nigeria that I envisage but it is a far cry from the Nigeria that is now. Change is imperative if we are to avoid the impending national failure. Poor leadership placed us in the ditch. Continuation of poor leadership will only dig a deeper trench for all of us to fall in.

32. Let us join hands in progressive union to pull each other and the nation from the abyss.

33. I pledge to do my utmost to make this happen but cannot do it alone. I need your support. I need your help to become President of Nigeria so that government may come to serve you, so that it may bring relief to the broken and weary among us and so that it may usher in a new Nigeria meant for us all, a Nigeria that is the birthright of everyone but the exclusive possession of no one.

God bless you.
God bless our fatherland – Nigeria
Thank you.

GENERAL MUHAMMADU BUHARI, GCFR

Appendix 14

President Muhammadu Buhari's 2015 Inaugural Speech May 29, 2015.

I am immensely grateful to God who has preserved us to witness this day and this occasion. Today marks a triumph for Nigeria and an occasion to celebrate her freedom and cherish her democracy. Nigerians have shown their commitment to democracy and are determined to entrench its culture. Our journey has not been easy but thanks to the determination of our people and strong support from friends abroad we have today a truly democratically elected government in place.

I would like to thank President Goodluck Jonathan for his display of statesmanship in setting a precedent for us that has now made our people proud to be Nigerians wherever they are. With the support and cooperation he has given to the transition process, he has made it possible for us to show the world that despite the perceived tension in the land we can be a united people capable of doing what is right for our nation. Together we co-operated to surprise the world that had come to expect only the worst from Nigeria. I hope this act of graciously accepting defeat by the outgoing President will become the standard of political conduct in the country.

I would like to thank the millions of our supporters who believed in us even when the cause seemed hopeless. I salute their resolve in waiting long hours in rain and hot sunshine to register and cast their votes and stay all night if necessary to protect and ensure their votes count and were counted. I thank those who tirelessly carried the campaign on the social media. At the same time, I thank our other countrymen and women who did not vote for us but contributed to make our democratic culture truly competitive, strong and definitive. I thank all of you.

Having just a few minutes ago, sworn on the Holy Book, I intend to keep my oath and serve as President to all Nigerians. I belong to everybody and I belong to nobody. A few people have privately voiced fears that on coming back to office I shall go after them. These fears are groundless. There will be no paying off old scores. The past is prologue. Our neighbours in the Sub-region and our African brethren should rest assured that Nigeria under our administration will be ready to play any leadership role that Africa expects of it.

Here I would like to thank the governments and people of Cameroon, Chad and Niger for committing their armed forces to fight Boko Haram in Nigeria. I also wish to assure the wider international community of our readiness to cooperate and help to combat threats of cross-border terrorism, sea piracy, refugees and boat people, financial crime, cybercrime, climate change, the spread of communicable diseases and other challenges of the 21st century. At home, we face enormous challenges. Insecurity, pervasive corruption, the hitherto unending and seemingly impossible fuel and power shortages are the immediate concerns. We are going to tackle them head on. Nigerians will not regret that they have entrusted national responsibility to us. We must not succumb to hopelessness and defeatism. We can fix our problems.

In recent times, Nigerian leaders appear to have misread our mission. Our founding fathers, Mr. Herbert Macaulay, Dr. Nnamdi Azikiwe, Chief Obafemi Awolowo, Alhaji Ahmadu Bello, the Sardauna of Sokoto, Alhaji Abubakar Tafawa Balewa, Malam Aminu Kano, Chief J.S. Tarka, Mr. Eyo Ita, Chief Dennis Osadebay, Chief Ladoke Akintola and their colleagues worked to establish certain standards of governance. They might have differed in their methods or tactics or details, but they were united in establishing a viable and progressive country. Some of their successors behaved like spoilt children breaking everything and bringing disorder to the house. Furthermore, we as Nigerians must remind ourselves that we are heirs to great civilisations: Shehu Othman Dan Fodio's caliphate, the Kanem Borno Empire, the Oyo Empire, the Benin Empire and King Jaja's formidable domain. The blood of those great ancestors flow in our veins. What is now required is to build on these legacies, to modernise and uplift Nigeria. Daunting as the task may be, it is by no means insurmountable. There is now a national consensus that our chosen route to national development is democracy.

To achieve our objectives, we must consciously work the democratic system. The Federal Executive under my watch will not seek to encroach on the duties and functions of the Legislative and Judicial arms of government. The law enforcing authorities will be charged to operate within the Constitution. We shall rebuild and reform the public service to become more effective and more serviceable. We shall charge them to apply themselves with integrity to stabilise the system. For their part the legislative arm must keep to their brief of making laws, carrying out over-sight functions and doing so expeditiously. The judicial system needs reform to cleanse itself from its immediate past. The country now expects the judiciary to act with dispatch on all cases especially on corruption, serious financial crimes or abuse of office. It is only when the three arms act constitutionally that government will be enabled to serve the country optimally and avoid the confusion all too often be devilling governance today. Elsewhere relations between Abuja and the States have to be clarified if we are to serve the country better.

Constitutionally there are limits to powers of each of the three tiers of government but that should not mean the Federal Government should fold its arms and close its eyes to what is going on in the states and local governments. Not least the operations of the Local Government Joint Account. While the Federal Government cannot interfere in the details of its operations it will ensure that the gross corruption at the local level is checked. As far as the Constitution allows me I will try to ensure that there is responsible and accountable governance at all levels of government in the country. For I will not have kept my own trust with the Nigerian people if I allow others abuse theirs under my watch. However, no matter how well organised the governments of the federation are they cannot succeed without the support, understanding and cooperation of labour unions, organised private sector, the press and civil society organisations. I appeal to employers and workers alike to unite in raising productivity so that everybody will have the opportunity to share in increased prosperity. The Nigerian press is the most vibrant in Africa. My appeal to the media today – and this includes the social media – is to exercise its considerable powers with responsibility and patriotism.

My appeal for unity is predicated on the seriousness of the legacy we are getting into. With depleted foreign reserves, falling oil prices, leakages and debts the Nigerian economy is in deep trouble and will require careful management to bring it round and to tackle the immediate challenges confronting us, namely; Boko Haram, the Niger Delta situation, the power shortages and unemployment especially among young people. For the longer term, we have to improve the standards of our education. We have to look at the whole field of Medicare. We have to upgrade our dilapidated physical infrastructure. The most immediate is Boko Haram's insurgency. Progress has been made in recent weeks by our security forces but victory cannot be achieved by basing the Command and Control Centre in Abuja. The command centre will be relocated to Maiduguri and remain until Boko Haram is completely subdued. But we cannot claim to have defeated Boko Haram without rescuing the Chibok girls and all other innocent persons held hostage by insurgents. This government will do all it can to rescue them alive. Boko Haram is a typical example of small fires causing large fires. An eccentric and unorthodox preacher with a tiny following was given posthumous fame and following by his extra judicial murder at the hands of the police. Since then through official bungling, negligence, complacency or collusion Boko Haram became a terrifying force taking tens of thousands of lives and capturing several towns and villages, covering swathes of Nigerian sovereign territory.

Boko Haram is a mindless, godless group who are as far away from Islam as one can think of. At the end of the hostilities when the group is subdued the Government intends to commission a sociological study to determine its origins, remote and immediate causes of the movement, its sponsors, the international connexions to ensure that measures are taken to prevent a recurrence of this evil. For now, the Armed Forces will be fully charged with prosecuting the fight against Boko haram. We shall overhaul the rules of engagement to avoid human rights violations in operations. We shall improve operational and legal mechanisms so that disciplinary steps are taken against proven human right violations by the Armed Forces.

Boko Haram is not only the security issue bedevilling our country. The spate of kidnappings, armed robberies, herdsmen/farmers clashes, cattle rustlings all help to add to the general air of insecurity in our land. We are going to erect and maintain an efficient, disciplined people – friendly and well–compensated security forces within an over – all security architecture. The amnesty programme in the Niger Delta is due to end in December, but the Government intends to invest heavily in the projects, and programmes currently in place. I call on the leadership and people in these areas to cooperate with the State and Federal Government in the rehabilitation programmes which will be streamlined and made more effective. As ever, I am ready to listen to grievances of my fellow Nigerians. I extend my hand of fellowship to them so that we can bring peace and build prosperity for our people.

No single cause can be identified to explain Nigerian's poor economic performance over the years than the power situation. It is a national shame that an economy of 180 million generates only 4,000MW, and distribute seven less. Continuous tinkering with the structures of power supply and distribution and close on $20b expanded since 1999 have only brought darkness, frustration, misery, and resignation among Nigerians. We will not allow this to go on. Careful studies are under way during this transition to identify the quickest, safest and most cost-effective way to bring light and relief to Nigerians. Unemployment, notably youth unemployment features strongly in our Party's Manifesto. We intend to attack the problem frontally through revival of agriculture, solid minerals mining as well as credits to small and medium size businesses to kick-start these enterprises. We shall quickly examine the best way to revive major industries and accelerate the revival and development of our railways, roads and general infrastructure.

Your Excellencies, My fellow Nigerians I cannot recall when Nigeria enjoyed so much goodwill abroad as now. The messages I received from East and West, from powerful and small countries are indicative of international expectations on us. At home the newly elected government is basking in a reservoir of goodwill and high expectations. Nigeria therefore, has a window of opportunity to fulfil our long – standing potential of pulling ourselves together and realising our mission as a great nation. Our situation somehow reminds one of a passage in Shakespeare's Julius Ceasar *"There is a tide in the affairs of men which, taken at the flood, leads on to fortune; omitted, all the voyage of their life, is bound in shallows and miseries."* We have an opportunity. Let us take it.

Thank you

MUHAMMADU BUHARI
President Federal Republic of NIGERIA
and Commander-in-chief-of the Armed forces

APPENDIX 15

Offer of US$5.1 million from Ifegwu's Solicitors in London

AGREEMENT dated   1993

BETWEEN

(1)   LORD CHIEF DIKE UDENSI IFEGWU of 29B Bishop Oluwole Street, Victoria Island, Lagos, Nigeria (the "Lord Chief"); and

(2)   MR JIMI LAWAL of 188 Awolowo Road, Ikoyi, PMB 12882, Lagos, Nigeria ("Mr Lawal").

WHEREAS

A.   The Lord Chief and Mr Lawal together have an interest in an aggregate of 45,000,000 shares of N1 each in the capital of Afribank Nigeria Limited and an interest in shares in the capital of Afri Investments Limited (formerly Alpha International Bancorporation Limited) (the "Shares").

NOW IT IS AGREED AS FOLLOWS:

1.   Mr Lawal agrees that neither Alpha Merchant Bank PLC nor he nor any member of his family nor any company owned or controlled by him or Alpha Merchant Bank PLC or in which either he or Alpha Merchant Bank PLC has an interest has any interest whatsoever whether direct or indirect in the Shares and agrees that to the extent that any such interest exists it is hereby assigned absolutely to the Lord Chief.

2.   In consideration for the acknowledgement and agreement contained in paragraph 1 above, the Lord Chief agrees to pay to Alpha Merchant Bank PLC or to any person or company whom Alpha Merchant Bank PLC shall nominate in writing prior to the date of payment the sum of US$ 5.1 million (the "Consideration") payable in the amounts and on dates specified in the Schedule hereto.

3. The Lord Chief agrees that, at any time up to and including the date which is 12 months from the date hereof, Mr Lawal may by notice in writing elect to have transferred to him 14,062,500 of the shares in Afribank Nigeria Limited in consideration for the payment by Mr Lawal of the sum of US$ 5.1 million to the Lord Chief. In the event of Mr Lawal exercising such right the Lord Chief agrees to use all reasonable endeavours to procure that a transfer of such number of the Shares in Afribank Nigeria Limited to Mr Lawal is effected.

4. This Agreement shall be governed by and construed in accordance with the laws of England and the parties irrevocably submit to the exclusive jurisdiction of the English Courts.

5. This Agreement constitutes the entire agreement between the parties with respect to the matters dealt with herein and supersedes any previous agreement between the parties in relation to such matters. Each party hereby acknowledges that in entering into this Agreement he has not relied on any representation, warranty or undertaking save as expressly set out herein.

EXECUTED as a Deed by)
the said Lord Chief   )
in the presence of:)

Signature of Witness:

Name of Witness:

Address of Witness:

Occupation of Witness:

EXECUTED as a Deed by   )
the said Jimi Lawal in   )
the presence of:)

Signature of Witness:

Name of Witness:

Address of Witness:

Occupation of Witness:

THE SCHEDULE

Schedule for payment of the Consideration

Date	Amount US$
1.	1,100,000
2.	1,000,000
3.	1,000,000
4.	1,000,000
5.	1,000,000

Postscript

About the Author: *Baptism of Fire*

I was supposedly born as a special child, which symbol in line with Yoruba tradition manifests in my relatively long given names - Shakiru Olabosipo Olajimi Adebisi; so, if only for convenience I simply go by Jimi Adebisi Lawal. Mum and Dad were both from Ijebu-Ode, my city of birth and early childhood.

We were not born with the proverbial silver spoon or pampered but we were a comfortable middle class family. Dad was an educationist, a teacher, lecturer and part of the post-colonial first grade two teachers who also went to the University of Ibadan and became a principal of many colleges. These included the Teachers Training College, Ota and Ago-Iwoye Secondary School.

It was a very strict family upbringing. Dad believed that knowledge is power and so the best thing you could do was to sit down and read your books. He was also not one to spare the rod and spoil the child.

Growing up, I was called 'Omo teacher' or 'Omo 36.' The origin of the 36 reference was very simple; when you committed an infraction and were brought before Dad, you would almost be sure to receive 36 strokes of the cane in one go from him. And this he would usually do from one spot, and almost without blinking! So, most of the people that Dad taught in the South-West knew him very well; as it was practically impossible to pass through such a disciplinarian and forget about him.

We were also quite a mobile family. As a principal and later an education inspector, Dad would be posted from Oyo to Ogun this week and the other week to Lagos; all being part of the then Western Region. That was the structure of the school system at that time and that was how I grew up.

We were a family of eleven and Dad had three wives which was normal with most well-to-do homes then. And as I was later told, I was supposed to have been the first born child of my parents. My mother was the first wife and she is eighty-three years now. As the story went, their first son died. And this was on the same day that the second son – my brother, Remi - was born. Dad was very sad over the loss. He was consoled with a dream that the dead son would be replaced with a better one in the near future; which he believed and took to heart.

Eighteen months down the road, I was born. And in line with his belief, I had to be named Olabosipo Olajimi. Abbreviated, some called me Jimi while others preferred Bosipo. I also had nicknames from my classmates - Champion Bosi or Professor.

My name has a traditional meaning. It means "back to prime position" and I was literally named to compensate for the loss of the first son. So growing up, so much was being expected from me. This explains the toga of being a special child.

There also exists a second memorable complication in that I was born with asthma. Being asthmatic in those days was like living with a death sentence and it used to cost so much money then to raise an asthmatic child. In those days, when the attack came, it would feel like I was going to die. Even the memory of it now still haunts me but I have really been lucky and blessed in life. I had since stopped coughing and I'm now a nature therapist, with no medication whatsoever in over four decades. When I am tired I just go to sleep. I don't take any medicine whatsoever, be it Aspirin or Panadol. I just sleep and wake up and eat and there is no way I would not go to the gym within every two to three days.

But my ease with asthma now is a far-cry from my days growing up. Each time I see those with asthma today having attacks, I therefore empathise with them in a deeper sense, because I had been there.

Looking back, my disability turned out to be a blessing in disguise. Unlike other children, I had to keep to myself and take things easy to reduce the chances of having attacks that would significantly affect me. Out of boredom then, I took to reading and read constantly.

So, my being a life-long bookworm is as a result of the fact that I have had no choice other than to read. Till date the habit has stuck and I almost cannot do without reading. If you go to my bedroom now, you will find out that there will be at least two books that I am reading at the same time. It is really the source of who I am today.

The same situation was applicable to my Islamic education. The way Quranic learning was carried out was by memorising and it is more difficult than reading. I was trained in English and I understand the language but nobody really taught us the Arabic language. We just memorised all the verses of the Quran. Till date, I can remember by heart several of the verses of the Quran because I learnt them.

With this background, I find that I can repeat most of what I read as they stay in my memory. For me, it is like opening a page without seeing the page.

My early education was not typical. When I outgrew asthma and had to go to school, a special arrangement had to be put in place for me. Largely then, I was home taught by my teacher-father in my infancy and given the attention he gave to it, I caught up quite fast to the extent that Remi and I took common entrance jointly and on passing, were admitted to start Form 1 together at Muslim College, Ijebu-Ode.

In our Form 4, Dad had a near fatal accident and was bedridden for months without salary, such that he could not pay our school fees and we were asked to withdraw from school. However, on account of my outstanding academic records, I was allowed to take my School Certificate Examinations from Class Four, which luckily I passed. The same consideration was unfortunately not extended to Remi, even though he was also brilliant; so I left my elder brother in secondary school.

Banking finds me

Whilst growing up I had a single-minded ambition of being a banker. You know when a new wife is married into a family in Yorubaland; she is not allowed to call the younger ones in the family by name and uses pet names. It was in this way that the wife of my Uncle nicknamed me 'Doctor' but I refused and told her back then at age ten that I was not going to be a doctor but a bank manager. So, she calls me bank manager until tomorrow.

She asked me why I wanted to be a banker. I then told her about how I had come to like banking through the activities of my trader-grandmother, Mama Ode, who was the leader of the market women and fishermen in the community and would usually take me along with her to the bank to make her deposits. I was attracted to the profession by the tie and neat appearance of bank managers.

BARCLAYS BANK DAYS

My journey to getting into my dream career happened just like that. I had taken my visiting Uncle to the 40 Marina, Lagos head office of Barclays Bank for him to write an employment test and shortly after we got there, one of the invigilators suddenly asked all the candidates to get seated to begin the test. At this point, I made to go out but he stopped me and after confirming that I had sat for the school certificate exams stated that if I did not mind, I could also sit in and write the test; that there was no harm in trying! I did and when the scripts were graded, I had emerged as one of the top three best performers! It was such a dramatic turn of events that I remember being taken before the British Staff Manager, Ron Dietritch, who quizzed me some more, and upon his being satisfied, asked that I return on Monday for my letter. I had been offered a job!

On getting home, my dad asked me if all had gone well with my escort duties and I answered in the affirmative, adding that I had also gotten a job from the bank in the process. He laughed and thought I was joking. But when it later transpired that I was not, he still would not approve for me to take up the job as I was required to further my studies. So, I had to beg and cry for days before Dad relented.

My subsequent career rise was also meteoric as I was the regular beneficiary of promotions, bonuses and salary increases. But having my sights on something more, I knew I had to get a higher education.

When I told Dietritch, who had also become my branch manager of my further education plans, he seemed upset and he asked me to go and bring my dad.

When dad came with me, I was shocked by the tone of their exchange. "That's a very prized son you have there; please do everything to help him fulfil all of his goals. I will also be available to help out as much as I can." Rather than a rebuke, I was getting a commendation and expressions of even further support. And true to his word, he gave me all the support he had pledged.

On completion of my preliminary studies and the professional examinations at the City Banking College and the South West College, Dietritch sent me word that Union Bank, the successor to Barclays Bank in Nigeria after the 1977 indigenisation processes, was coming to set up shop in London and encouraged me to apply. I did and began work there as one of the pioneer staff of the Union Bank, London branch.

ONE GOOD TURN...

One of my more remarkable reminiscences of my days with Union Bank, London was on the day I met the then Colonel Ibrahim Babangida in 1983. He had walked into the branch to process a draft but was not being paid because the foreign exchange cover had not been received from Nigeria where the transaction was originated.

When the issue was brought to my notice, I reviewed the facts of the matter and concluded that he should be paid. When he found out how the headache had been cleared, he requested to see me. He asked why I had taken the decision to pay him and I explained that I was professionally satisfied. Besides, it was also, I told him, not very likely that an officer of his rank and standing who was still in the service of the Nigerian army, would travel all of those miles to come and play games in London. He was impressed and reached out to give me some money but I turned it down. He then gave me his card with a blanket invitation to call upon him anytime I was in Nigeria.

A couple of years later in 1985, I read from our regular supply of Nigerian newspapers that there had been a coup in Nigeria and the new military President was the same Ibrahim Babangida that had given me that invitation. So, I renewed the acquaintance by sending him a letter of congratulations; to which he responded promptly with a renewed invitation.

On getting to Dodan Barracks, my name was at the security gate and I was ushered in to see the President. Babangida welcomed me warmly and after pleasantries asked about my future plans. I told him I was interested in getting a banking licence. He responded, "From what I already know about you, you will surely do well in banking. Go and talk to my Finance Minister." President Babangida was truly charming.

I met Dr. Chu Okongwu who was the Minister of Finance then; we talked and the process was underway.

SETTING UP ALPHA MERCHANT BANK

While President Ibrahim Babangida had given his blanket support for the project, there were however nuts and bolts issues to work out.

One of these had to do with getting reputable shareholders, at least twenty, given the restriction of five percent per investor and then raising the statutory minimum share capital of ₦5 million - about five million US dollars. We then had to file a formal application with the Central Bank and fulfil all the stipulated conditions.

I went to all the people I could reach to interest them in the project. Obasanjo gave his words to come on board and did in fact effected payment of the initial deposit of ₦50,000 each for himself and Dr. Soleye. Babangida would not consent to being involved at this time because of his position. A prominent businessman, Lord Chief Ifegwu was a most generous supporter and there was also another investor, Chief Micheal Omisade, who I was favourably disposed at this time, to his serving as Chairman; but on hearing this, Obasanjo backed off and requested his money back. He was adamant and all my appeals and those of my father-in-law who facilitated the introduction fell on deaf ears. It was him or Omisade. Even Chief Omisade offered to apologise for having wronged him in the past but Obasanjo bluntly refused. So, I had to choose and decided to go on the basis of first-come, first-served. Of course, I was upset over this development but with the benefit of hindsight, I ought to have thought more deeply about it then.

At the subsequent meeting of shareholders, we were however still having something like a 20 percent equity shortfall to be raised; which made the loss of ten percent from Obasanjo and Soleye even more frustrating. But I had to stick to principle. At this point, the protem Chairman, Chief Omisade requested for a private audience with Ifegwu. He requested Ifegwu to loan him personally the sum required to pay up for the outstanding shares, pledging his house in Victoria Island - the venue of the meeting as collateral.

Rather than agree to this arrangement, Ifegwu returned to the meeting, agreed to give an advance for the shortfall for those that had not paid but then turned to me, requesting that I give him there and then a written undertaking that I, as the chief promoter and originator of the project would pay him back the said sum in future or in the event of a default, the shares would then revert to his nominees in lieu. Everyone was grateful and I was particularly touched and humbled, but Omisade expressed disappointment that Ifegwu turned him down for me.

Omisade and the troubles at Alpha Merchant Bank

I chose to be an Executive Director on account of age in spite of being the chief promoter and we had hired Macaulay Iyayi as the MD. The bank opened its doors for business on 6th June, 1988 and within three months had not only broken even but also posted a respectable profit. It was an industry record.

Shortly after the good fortunes of the bank had been announced at the board meeting, Omisade called me and asked that I arrange a loan in his favour to the tune of $2 million. It was an off-the-hook request and he was not willing to provide any collateral or pass it through the regular mill. I objected and he instantly threatened to get me out of the bank.

The first thing he did was to engineer my dismissal and arrest over the fact that I had not participated in the National Youth Service Scheme. Of course, I had not because I had only returned straight from the UK to start the bank. I reported the matter to Babangida who sent me to the NYSC Director, Col. Braimah. On getting to Braimah, I gave him the full picture and he stated that my options were between serving and being exempted. At this time, I was still under thirty and so could not lawfully be exempted. I therefore opted to serve. I wrote an application to serve on the spot and he immediately posted me to serve at Alpha Merchant Bank. One day, I was an Executive Director at my own bank; one of Nigeria's fastest growing and the other I was a Youth Corp member at the same bank, earning a paltry ₦200 per month in line with the usual allowance for other Youth Corp members. But Omisade would not be pacified.

Things got to a head and the issue had to be taken to the board to decide between Omisade and me. After an extensive deliberation and having heard from both sides, a vote was taken and by a margin of six to one (with Omisade's vote being the only one in his favour), the directors affirmed their belief in me and refused to work with Chief Omisade, so he was removed as the chairman.

We subsequently called an extraordinary general meeting of the shareholders who also voted by a margin of ninety-four to six percent to remove him as a director. The six percent he got were the five percent shares he owned and the one percent by a lawyer in his chamber. Otherwise, all the shareholders as with the directors supported me.

You would recall that initially Omisade had wanted to get the twenty percent extra shares which Lord Chief Ifegwu had then paid for. It was then that I realised the value of Lord Chief Ifegwu's standing by me and saying that he would rather give the loan to the promoters for us to get the licence in return for those shares in the event of a default. If those shares had gone to Omisade the bank would have been more or less destroyed.

Although Omisade had lost his place on the board as chairman and also with the shareholders in his futile bid to remain as a director, he did not give up. He went to court and also went public, making all kinds of wild allegations against me.

He wrote petitions to the State Security Service, the CBN and the Ministry of Finance, alleging that in addition to my not having a National Youth Service Certificate, that I had dropped out of Muslim College. For the latter charge, he had gotten a letter from Muslim College on this, which of course is the true position. But then, why did I compulsorily need to go to class five when I had passed my school certificate in class four?

He also went to Union Bank of Nigeria, London where I had at a point quarrelled with the manager, Mr. Jeffrey Efeyini over some infraction he had committed but would not own up to after I confronted him with the facts. Rather than do that, Efeyini had taken to transferring me around departments until I got fed up and resigned.

Omisade was now alleging that I had put in my resume that was sent to the CBN that I was a departmental manager at Union Bank, London. Of course he knew what had happened between Efeyini and me, so Efeyini also wrote saying that I was just his supervisor, not departmental manager. With those two letters and the fact that I didn't initially honour my youth service obligation, he went to court and got an injunction against me, that I should not be allowed to lead the bank, that I had bribed everybody and that was why the Director of the National Youth Service Corps, Col. Braimah had posted me to eventually go and serve in my own bank.

He was doing all of these because he wanted me out of the bank but he couldn't get me out. So he went to court and got an injunction against me. For the first couple of months, the judge was adjourning the case. Like I said before, I have been very lucky. The lawyer that I got was *pro bono*. He is Chief Frank Akerele who was our landlord when Alpha started trading at Awolowo Road, Ikoyi, Lagos. The old man liked me so much and when he got to know about my troubles with Omisade, said, "Jimi, you could have been Demola (Demola is his first son and we were close friends). There is no way I will allow anybody to cheat you. Omisade is a thug, he is my age mate but I won't allow it to happen." The old man went to court on my behalf, free of charge.

So after the judge had adjourned the case a couple of times, Akerele wrote a personal letter to the judge and said, "Listen, all I want is for you to just listen to the other side of the case. This young man called Jimi Lawal is one of the best brains I have met in my life. Just hear him out, if after you have heard him out and you believe Omisade, fine but I am taking on this case, not because of money but because I believe the young man is being cheated and it's not in our interest to allow it to happen."

The judge then agreed to hear us and Chief Akerele took the podium. He said,

> "My Lord, I just want to say three things to you; if Jimi Lawal was your son, you would be more than proud of him. The way the plaintiff, Chief Michael Omisade - who is my colleague in the legal profession, who I have respect for, but on this occasion, I don't think he has come to you with the truth of the position – is carrying on is simply not fair. He who seeks equity must come with clean hands. Omisade has not come with clean hands."

> 'I will give you just three examples my Lord. First, Omisade wrote to say that Jimi Lawal is not qualified to be Executive Director of a bank on the grounds that he has stated. But my lord, look at this letter."

At this point he brought out the letter of recommendation sent on my behalf to the CBN for them to exempt me from the age limit of thirty-five years as well as the requisite twelve years experience in the banking sector and it had been written by Omisade! I had even forgotten about this but Chief Akerele found the document during his investigation and now tendered it in court.

The judge then cut in to ask Omisade whether he indeed wrote that and he said yes, but that he did so when all of the facts were unbeknown to him then.

The second point had to do with a handwritten note that Omisade had written. This was on a day in August of 1988 when we broke even just after a few months of commencing operations and at the board meeting, he wrote me a note, affirming that I was 'a whizkid, a genius,' and that he was indeed 'very proud' of me.

So again, Akerele tendered it and said, "If you didn't know in 1988, after the bank started trading and you had seen Jimi's performance, you then wrote this, so what happened?" He couldn't talk, he had no words.

Akerele dug in. "So at that time, you had seen him in action, he had run the bank for a few months and you wrote this to him. Why is it that now in September/October because you were removed from the board, you are now denying your own testimony? I put it to you that it is because you were removed!" The judge was at this time shaking his head, but Akerele even had more ammunition.

> "My lord, that's not all. The third reason my lord is that Chief Omisade when he came to you and got this exparte injunction against Jimi Lawal said to you that he was giving an undertaking for damages, that he would post a bond for half a million naira to the court. But my lord, up until this morning, that I checked with the

registrar of courts, no bond has been posted and no such undertaking has been written which means that this injunction was procured by fraud. So without even going to the issue of whether or not Jimi Lawal did not go to class five or stole two million dollars as he initially alleged, or he did not do his youth service, this injunction should be vacated because this man has not come to equity with clean hands. We can then go to trial to determine the other facts he has stated, but for the three reasons I gave, I believe each of them is enough to vacate the injunction. First, he recommended the same man he is now coming out to say no to, and his answer is that it was because he didn't know him then. Second, even after he got to know him and the bank did so well, he wrote another statement of applause to him. And third, when he came to court to ask for injunction, the assurance he gave to the court to obtain it, he did not meet. So, why are we continuing to sustain the injunction, my Lord?"

The judge then asked Omisade what he would say to the points raised. He said, 'em...em....' The judge said, "Ok, the court will adjourn for one hour." He came back in thirty-five minutes with an order reversing himself and apologising to me. The injunction was lifted,

I almost cried in court that day. Again, I was not thirty when I went through that. It was in open court and the judge was saying that he was sorry and that he believed my lawyer; that the injunction was not fair that I should go back to the office, and the trial should continue.

In Aliyu Gusau's court

Omisade now petitioned the intelligence services. Thus, I was summoned by the head of the service, Brigadier Aliyu Gusau. I met him and they proceeded to investigate the matter.

They sent someone to Muslim College and someone else to London. When they all came back and reported to their boss, he then called Omisade and I to his office. So we went to his office in Ikoyi, Lagos and we all sat down along with two of his officers.

Then he said, 'Chief, you wrote this petition that Jimi Lawal stole two million dollars from the Dutch auction and took the money to London, but we have investigated and it is not true. You said he had no certificate; that he dropped out in class four? It is true he did not go to class five but he passed his exam in class four and we have the certified result here. And number three, you said he didn't do youth service, but he has been posted to his bank; he applied and got the posting, so what's the problem?'

Omisade responded, 'Ah! Jimi Lawal has done it again; he has done it again. The young man knows how to use money. Even here where I thought in the intelligence service he would not be able to do it, he has done it again....'

I had never seen such anger in my life. Aliyu Gusau lifted his desk and said, "Omisade, I will lock you up, you will never see the sun for the rest of your life. You are accusing me of being bribed, of being compromised by this young man who is not older than your son and my own son? Take that bugger and lock him up, take him in, lock him up!"

At this point, Omisade started begging. "Oh! I'm sorry sir, I didn't mean that sir, I mean, maybe your boys…"

That even incensed Gusau even further, "Hold it there! What did you just say? By accusing my men, you are accusing me. I am in charge of this investigation and even the president will never say that to me; lock him up!"

Omisade continued begging as he was being bundled away and I instinctively joined in the begging before remembering that he wanted me destroyed, if not dead. It took a while for Gusau to relent before we returned to our seats. We concluded with Omisade being cautioned to allow peace to reign and not destroy the new bank. Till tomorrow, General Gusau and I have remained close. If I call him, wherever he is in the world, he would be so happy to hear from me. If he is asleep, he will take my call or call me back thereafter.

Indeed, in a rather paradoxical way, Omisade did me a big favour by making all those wild allegations against me. Through the wild allegations and my high exposure to what I call 'my baptism of fire,' I got refined and also made life-long friends. So in the course of the Omisade persecution, those who actually got to know me got to like me even the more.

Awujale steps in

The dispute went on for a while more until Kabiyesi, the Awujale summoned us. At the meeting, Kabiyesi told him, "You know Jimi is my son, by fighting him you are fighting me. What has he done to you?" So he told Kabiyesi all that had happened, but conveniently failed to add that he had asked me for money and I said no. When Kabiyesi asked him about that, he said, "Sir, even if I asked him, what is that? It's just people who wrote petitions against him, that was my concern." Kabiyesi told him, "Chief, like I said, by fighting Jimi you are fighting me, now do you want to withdraw all these cases and find a way to work together?" He said yes, that he would go and think about it and come back the following week, but he never returned. Kabiyesi subsequently sent him a message saying, "You are fighting me by fighting Jimi and if I got onto this ancestral throne of mine by right, and if Jimi had done you no wrong, we will both survive you."

The case continued. By August 1989 when I finished my youth service, he had lost the substantive case and filed another one and eventually by the time I returned to the board of the bank in September 1989, Macaulay Iyayi had done some very dodgy stuff. He didn't steal money but he had granted bad loans that put the bank more or less in near-distress. So not quite two months after I got back – this was in November 1989 – the board got so upset with Macaulay after a report of what had happened in the bank, that five of the directors said they wanted Macaulay to go and that I should become the MD.

I refused. But when they put so much pressure on me, I had no choice. So, from being an ED that was hunted, and then a youth corp member; within two to three months of my getting back, I became the MD of the bank in late 1989.

HID Awolowo takes on Omisade

Then Chief Mrs. HID Awolowo, Mama as we called her, sent for me and I went to see her. I did not know if it was Kabiyesi or someone else that had spoken to her about my long-running battle with Omisade but that was the reason for her inviting me.

When I got there she said, "Jimi, who will not be proud of you as a son? I am not going to allow Omisade to destroy you the way he tried to destroy my husband." She never told me the entire story behind the treasonable felony trial and how Chief Awolowo got convicted but apparently, she hinted as much that Omisade was one of the moles used to rope in the sage. Again, she told me about how Omisade had insisted on contesting against Bola Ige in Oyo State and how that almost destroyed the party when Awolowo stood his ground that serving governors be allowed to fly the UPN flag, uncontested for a second term during the 1983 elections. So, Mama said that I should please give her the honour of intervening in the matter.

I replied that I could not refuse and told her how Kabiyesi, the Awujale had mediated between us but that Omisade did not show up for the follow-up meeting but she said not to worry, that I should leave that to her to address.

She subsequently called us and we went for the meeting. There, Omisade stated his own side of the story and then Mama asked me what the issue was. In my response, I told her that the issue was that Chief was lying, because he would not admit that the real cause of the problem was that he had asked me for two million dollars which I would not give him.'

"How can you say that?" Mama cut in, lashing at me, "you came from a decent home; you are well brought up, how can you say that the old man is lying? You shouldn't say that."

I replied, "Ok, I am sorry Ma."

At this point, Chief took up the matter. "You see it? You see the kind of boy he is? He has got a big head because..."

Mama now descended on Omisade. "Chief, please, you better stop your own. I have corrected him because I want him to be respectful, but you are a dangerous man.

From what I have heard now, I will curse you and fight with you to heaven. I will go naked in the market because of you. This matter must be settled. I will not allow you to destroy Jimi and Alpha Merchant Bank. This young man is a credit to Yoruba land, I will fight you the way Papa was not able to fight you. Anything I know about you, I will use it to fight you."

Omisade, now seriously shaken, asked what she wanted him to do. Mama said, "You should withdraw all your cases and make up with Jimi, I have corrected Jimi where he is wrong, but I have seen that you are lying. I have also heard that Awujale had called you and Jimi to make peace but you didn't agree. From this moment, if you fight Jimi, I will mobilize the whole of Yorubaland against you."

He then started saying, "em... Mama, but you are not being fair. You didn't ask what I want." She said,' Ok, what do you want?" His response was telling. "Jimi has humiliated me, I want to go back to the board of the bank, we started the bank together. I want to be back in the bank as chairman and then we can have peace."

Mama said, "Jimi what do you say to this?" I said, "Ma, I will not lie to you I can get him back as a director, but somebody is already chairman and that person ought to finish serving his term. Chief Omisade is a Yoruba man, I am a Yoruba man and the chairman is Igbo; I will not remove an Igbo and replace him with a Yoruba."

Omisade refused to be persuaded on this but Mama said, "Chief, Jimi is making sense to me. He didn't say he would not bring you back as director, he could have said he can't do it. But he has said he will convince shareholders to vote for you as a director, but he will not remove an Igbo chairman for you, and I think he is a very wise young man. If it is another Yoruba man, he can ask him to step down for you, but an Igbo person, let the man finish serving his term." She now turned to me. "Jimi, how many years?" I said, "Four years, ma. So when the man finishes serving from 1989 to 1993, he can come back." So he agreed.

On the way back to Lagos, Chief called me aside and asked if we could meet later in the evening, strictly one-on-one at a location of my choice, as he was anxious for the settlement that had been brokered to endure. I promptly agreed and offered to meet with him in his house in Victoria Island. He was surprised that despite the bitterness and enmity between us, I was willing to come to his house. He emphasised that I came alone and we agreed to meet at 8pm.

I showed up as appointed and Chief ushered me into his office in the back of the main house where we exchanged pleasantries. He proceeded to bring out copies of the Bible and Quran from one of his drawers and asked me to choose which I would like to swear by as he was aware that I was comfortable in church in spite of being a Muslim. I chose the Quran but asked to know what the subject of attestation would be before agreeing to swear as requested. He then informed me that he needed me to swear that I would stop 'washing my head with blood' every morning, as he had been reliably informed by more than two sources. I instantaneously returned the Quran to him and made it clear that there was no way I would stop the practice because it was a means of protecting and strengthening me rather than it being done to harm him or anyone else for that matter.

Chief protested vehemently and asked how I get my supply of blood, to which I responded that it was from my mother. He was agitated and enquired further as to how my mum was able to sustain the supply. I answered that she had assured me it was saved during childbirth; and I never asked why it hadn't ran out as I only used a drop at a time; and it also explained why my head is usually clean-shaven. Chief there and then conferred a nickname on me as *"eni ti a pa ti o ku"*; *"the person that we killed but refused to die."* In closing, I reaffirmed the assurance that the practice was not meant to harm him and I was willing to swear on that, consequent upon which we parted on that note.

MEETING EL-RUFAI

We revived Alpha, and it started growing, I was on top of the world again. I was shaken but restored back and in a better position as MD of the bank. We started building a five-star hotel in Victoria Island called Alpha Sofitel Hotel. Then we were also working on building a befitting head office for the bank, just after I got back.

We had recruited a legal adviser, a young man called Aminu Dikko. He was an assistant manager in Savannah Bank. The post of a legal adviser for the bank was supposed to have been a GM level appointment, but because he was so young, and indeed younger than me and an assistant manager, we brought him to the bank as a deputy manager and every year, he got promoted. He came to me in 1989 after I got back and said "Sir, this head office we are trying to build, I know a firm of quantity surveyors - El-Rufai and Partners. My brother's friend and partner is the managing partner and he is a young man called Nasir El-Rufai, you will like him. Please give them a chance to bid for the job."

I replied, "no problem, bring them. Get El-Rufai and Partners to apply." That's how I met Nasir El-Rufai when he came to bid for the job. I looked at his submission and it was by far the best. We invited them for an interview and I met a man that is smarter than me. People say I am smart but he is smarter. Every time I say he is smart, he says no, that I am smarter. But since that 1989 meeting we have been very close. He came to apply for his firm to be the quantity surveyor to do the bank's head office, but was so good that I asked him to join us as a staff and partner in our real estate development company.

At this time I was also making money with my properties in the UK. I also had other properties in Nigeria apart from those of Alpha Merchant Bank. So I said please join me in Alpha Properties as GM; come and run the property company for us. He replied that his family was in Kaduna but I told him that it didn't matter. I persuaded him and he joined. Since then we have been like brothers and we have been through ups and downs together. I thank God for His mercies.

So, by 1989, I was back in the bank as MD, Omisade had gone to withdraw all the cases and we had settled. We convened a shareholders meeting and he was restored to the board as a director, but not chairman. Alpha was peaceful and we were making progress and money, without problems.

We then went after Afribank. Because we were a merchant bank, the lesson to be learnt from what Macaulay had done with the bank being illiquid with bad debt was that you had to find ways of continually raising deposits. Merchant banks were restricted to taking hot money from the interbank market as deposits. We didn't have the branch network for current account operations, what we call checking accounts where people leave free money. That is the secret of banking success and we didn't have it. The moment it became clear to me, I decided we should go after a commercial bank.

Ordinarily, what people do here was to get a second license, Mike Adenuga for example had Devcom Bank and Equatorial Trust Bank but I refused to go that way. As luck would have it, whilst we were carrying out the Alpha Sofitel Hotel's site development in Victoria Island, the Managing Director of Accor Afrique informed me that the French conglomerate - Banque National de Paris had resolved to sell their controlling interest in Banque Internationale pour l'Afrique Occidental (BIAO) that was the predecessor of Afribank.

They were divesting their equity interest in all the countries they were into so their shares were up for grabs here in Nigeria. We went after the acquisition with vigour in 1990. Before going too far, I went and met with President Babangida and thanked him for his role in the progress Alpha Merchant Bank had made so far and told him that we needed a commercial bank, but that rather than taking a second licence I would prefer to acquire Afribank as it is available. He said, "why not? Go and see the Finance Minister and Abdulkadir Ahmed, Governor of the Central Bank and carry them along."

The Finance Minister at the moment was Alhaji Abubakar Alhaji. Dr. Okongwu had been moved to National Planning and I wished it was still him in the saddle there because Alhaji Alhaji or Triple A as he was more fondly called, took longer than necessary to grant us a formal approval in spite of having complied with all the requirements. He never asked us for bribe but just said, "Jimi, I know you are a good man. I am told that anything I want you will give me. I will work for you to make sure you get this bank." He went into alliance with us, we eventually got the approval and were making even more progress.

On getting the approval of the Minister of Finance, we bought the shares and at the point of taking over, the Governor of the CBN received fresh petitions which I later discovered were being engineered from Omisade's house. This was in 1993, and some two years into the purchase.

Instructively, when we went for the bid, the then Chief of Army Staff, General Sani Abacha had a finance company which also bid alongside us but we won the bid on merit and we actually proceeded to appoint two directors into the board of Afribank.

At the same time that we bought the forty-five percent shares from BIAO, Afribank was also being privatised locally. Taking advantage of this, Lord Chief Ifegwu, other friends and I also bought some more naira shares during the privatisation exercise. At the end, between us and Alpha, we had over sixty percent control of Afribank. Effectively it had become a subsidiary of Alpha but we had not gotten the final consent of CBN when we had our AGM in April 1993. It was like yesterday as it remains fresh in my mind; the event was at the Transcorp Hilton, Abuja and the place was packed.

Before then, in 1992 or early in 1993, Alpha had gone public and we became the first merchant bank to be publicly quoted on the Nigerian Stock Exchange. During that listing, our shares were over-subscribed by three times! We were doing more than well; we were building our head office, acquiring Afribank and the sky was the limit. The "wizkid" was back full time.

With Omisade's continuing efforts to undermine our progress however, we were not at this point very keen to push for his reinstatement as Chairman. When shareholders asked me who I wanted as the new chairman my answer was "we have had a Yoruba even if he was removed, we have had an Igbo, let's go for a Hausa person." So the following day we had an election and overwhelmingly, we voted for Dr. Audu Abashiya. So Omisade lost and became even more vicious. Perhaps I should have kept my side of the bargain with Mama, even though he did not keep his!

I was taking the OPM programme in Harvard then and was in my second year. I remembered that after the AGM I took off to Boston, Harvard, to return in May. By the time I returned, Omisade had written a petition again to the same places; The CBN, Ministry of Finance and SSS. He claimed that the shares we had acquired in Afribank were without board approval and it was all Alpha's money that was stolen. It was a total of sixteen million dollars that we had used to buy the shares. Five million dollars came from Alpha and was guaranteed by Lord Chief plus his own investment of three million dollars; two million dollars from me, which I had borrowed from Barclays Bank in London. We borrowed another six million dollars from Barclays. The sources of the funds turned out to be a life saver for me as we would later see.

In their response to Omisade's petition, the CBN came and said they didn't know who to believe. They however made the point that if Omisade was right then it means that the board which he was a part of had been negligent, so the whole board should go whilst they investigate freely. He didn't want that and went to court once again.

Unfortunately for us, this was happening at the same time of the June 12, 1993 electoral annulment. There was a huge confusion in the country, Babangida could not sleep, I could not sleep and the country was upside-down.

I remember then that I was trying to fly from Lagos to Abuja and protesters and 'area boys' were blocking the roads. Very few people could move about in Lagos as it was so bad, but because of my determination I was able to get through.

I got to the airport, flew to Abuja and booked an appointment to see the president. For the first time, it took me two days to see him. I didn't go to Abuja with a change of clothes. I wanted to fly in and fly back to Lagos, but there was so much tension in the country that I couldn't sleep for two days. Eventually I got to see him and said, "Sir I have a problem, you also have a problem and the country has a problem, but forget about my own problem, I am more concerned about Nigeria and you." I continued "unless you reverse the annulment, you would go down on the wrong side of history. I know you to be a good man, but we all make mistakes, I don't want your mistakes to be what will define you as a human being. I don't want that for you sir, please "de-annul" the annulment."

We had just gone through a very free and fair election and it was not a good way to conclude the process. By the way, I was very close to Chief MKO Abiola, who was the clear winner of the polls. Not only that, Chief Abiola had promised to make me the Minister of Finance but I didn't go to Abuja because of that, I went because it was not in Babangida's interest to not make amends at this time. When he responded, he said, "Jimi, your words have always been very powerful to me, how do I do it? We have convinced our colleagues in the military that we are not going back." I replied, "Sir, a man, given new information changes his mind. A wise general knows when to retreat, a foolish one fights to finish. I want you to be alive sir, and write your own history, I don't want history to be written against you."

His brother, Alhaji Mustapha Wushishi, his only half brother, later came over to see me as I was still in Abuja and couldn't indeed go back until the third day. He said, "Jimi, what did you say to my brother that he has now summoned a meeting of the Armed Forces Ruling Council?" I said it was because I wouldn't want him to end up on the wrong side of history.

Before then, Alhaji Mustapha had bought shares in Alpha when we went public. Therefore, I had become even closer to the family.

So because of the confusion in the country in June, we never got our bank back, the same way we never got Nigeria back for many years to come. Finally IBB had a meeting with the Military Council, but failed to persuade them to "de-annul" the elections. He then stepped aside, leaving former UAC Chairman, Ernest Shonekan to head a short-lived Interim National Government, ING. This did not last as the Army Chief, General Sani Abacha soon took over power for himself.

Abacha comes after me

Following Abacha's ascension into power, among other scorched earth battles that he fought, he was to wage a vicious war against bank chiefs under the aegis of the Failed Banks Tribunal. For us in particular however, the issue of his firm's loss to Alpha in the bid to buy controlling shares in Afribank was reopened. Abacha still wanted the bank and I was a stumbling block. He came after me and would almost have cut short my life had it not been for the feelers on this that the Awujale had received and passed on to me, advising an urgent flight to safety abroad. When I got to the airport to board a flight for this purpose, a very close acquaintance within the aviation sector who saw me approaching and had only moments ago seen Abacha's goons come to instruct that I must not be allowed to travel out of the country but that their attention should rather be called if I attempted to do so, ran down to meet me at the parking lot. After herding me back into the car, he explained the situation and urged me to scram. I did.

I decided to leave Nigeria immediately by road and that night headed for the Seme border. As we got close, panic returned to my heart; what if Abacha's goons had also gotten here ahead of me? But providence had an answer. It suddenly started raining very heavily, such that when we got to the border all the posts had been abandoned and the officers had gone to seek shelter. We drove past and out of the country.

I was still in exile for the whole of the Abacha years and even at that, his son Ibrahim had come over and tried to get me to sign away the Afribank shares to them for $5m. When that failed, they now proceeded to push harder with the 'failed banks' military tribunal processes and had me tried in absentia. Predictably, the regime secured a kangaroo conviction and proceeded to issue duplicate shares with which they now forcibly took over the investment in Afribank.

My erstwhile major investor partner in Alpha - Lord Chief Ifegwu also put considerable pressure on me to deny the bank's interest in Afribank in return for also $5 million, which I again refused; in spite of being threatened and being desperately broke. A copy of the written offer from Ifegwu's solicitors is attached, marked Appendix 14.

Subsequently, one of my uncles, Professor Adesanya, who also happens to be the lawyer who handled the settlement over the Afribank case, filed a suit for me to appeal the conviction while I was still in exile, and he built the case around two very simple legal principles. The first was that the decree of Abacha was backdated to an act that was not a crime when it was done. It wasn't a crime to have taken a loan on the directive of the bank. He (Abacha) now promulgated a decree to backdate the effectiveness. In criminology, it's a violation of human right.

The second ground was that I was not given a chance to defend myself. You could have a charge filed in court against me but you must wait for me or arrest me and bring me to face the charge. The case went up to the Supreme Court and the prosecutor lost, so I became a free man without paying a penny.

When the bank was eventually restored to the original owners, I got all the pounds and dollars I can imagine in my life without lifting a finger. But I had suffered. The settlement was effected in June 2003. From June 1993 when the Omisade/Abacha onslaught began, it was exactly ten years of my having been robbed. So, God decreed my life the way he wanted it to happen, from excelling in life, setting up a bank, closing the bank, being broke and now getting the money back. Most importantly also, I was now very free to return home and walk the streets unmolested even as closure had been brought on a very significant decade of stress for me.

Following our victory in the courts, El-Rufai whom I had advised *pro bono* when he had served as Director General of the Bureau for Public Enterprises, BPE was seriously instrumental in bringing the deeper facts of the Alpha/Afribank crisis to President Obasanjo's attention, which enabled him take executive action facilitating the reversal of the injustice done to us by Abacha. When Obasanjo got to know the full extent of what Abacha had done, he was so taken aback that he promptly signed off on it for the shares to be sold to the public.

One other reason why El-Rufai and the National Council on Privatisation were interested in the resolution of the crisis was because they also wanted to bring closure to the Afribank ownership crisis so that they could go on with the government's plan to fully divest its holdings in the bank. Along this line El-Rufai met with the various interested parties that had been contesting the ownership of the disputed 375 million shares representing 33.96 percent of the paid up capital of Afribank Nigeria Plc. This was in order to ascertain the true ownership of the shares before they could be put up for sale under the privatisation programme of the Federal Government.

El-Rufai and his team met with a few of us officially on this matter, including in the course of a visit to Paris, France, that also involved meetings with the liquidator of the original owner of the shares, Banque Internationale pour l'Afrique Occidental (BIAO), and a lawyer representing Lord Chief Ifegwu.

At the end, we got back about $33.5 mllion from our initial $16 million invested. It came to a 105 percent return, thus our money was more than doubled! Alpha Merchant Bank also got back about $10.1 million, in return for investing just over $5 million; Lord Chief Ifegwu got back the most, I got back about just over three million dollars. We paid off the Barclays loan and I was like a baby, free and content with real cash in the bank.

When my share of the money hit my personal account, I remember, for the first ninety days or so, I didn't touch the money. I would wake up at night and call the automated banking services and listen just to hear the balance in my account - "The balance on your account was two million, nine hundred and ninety-nine thousand, nine hundred and ninety-eight dollars, fifty two cents." Bank managers were calling me, how can you leave this kind of money in your current account? Let's invest it for you. I was not going to invest that money, I just left it there. For ninety days, I was just waking up and thanking God.

OBASANJO AGAIN

Before I returned fully to Nigeria, El-Rufai had now been offered the position of FCT minister.

He came to me in London and said, 'I know that you can now go to Barbados and lie over in the beach for the rest of your life but I can't do this FCT job successfully without you. I need your brain, I need your support.' He continued:

> Obasanjo gave me this job because two ministers had failed him, we can't afford to fail.' I replied, 'I can advise you from here,' but he would not agree. 'No, you cannot advise me from here this time around, it's not possible. You could advise me from here on BPE but on this one, I am running the federal capital not selling parastatals. I am running a 'state.' Everybody sees Abuja, everybody comes to Abuja, I need you there.

I gave in but said it would be on two conditions. 'I won't take any penny and no formal title'. I will just do any special assignment you want me to do.' He consented so I moved back to Nigeria in late 2003, after I had made some more investments in the UK. I joined him in the FCT and we initiated a couple of major projects that I won't forget in my life. For example, what is now known as the Abuja Technology Village (ATV), including the African University of Science and Technology (AUST), was started by us. I wrote the business plan, Mallam took it to the cabinet and when it was approved by the Federal Executive Council (FEC), we started the ATV. Secondly, I chaired the sale of federal government houses in Abuja, where we sold about 32,000 housing units and got back about ₦32 billion. The sale was successful largely because we got the Federal Mortgage Bank to issue the first mortgage backed bonds of ₦100 billion to provide loans at single digit interest rate for the buyers.

Meanwhile, NDIC had since declared and paid two interim dividends totalling ₦7 for each 50 kobo share in Alpha Merchant Bank from the proceeds of sale of shares in Afribank. Many of the shareholders had expressed gratitude to me for ensuring the safe return of their investments, even though some had prematurely condemned me when the bank was put in liquidation.

And one final point. There was no amount of pressure that was not put on me by some shareholders to write a petition and get the bank's licence back, but I was not interested. I was done, I thank God for his blessings. There are many of them like that, and it was because of them that I refused to sell out.

INDEX

Index

Adamu, Abdullahi 110
Abacha Government, 275, 277
Abacha, Ibrahim 360
Abacha, Sani 11-13, 16, 18 ,90, 204, 277, 356, 359-362
Abashiya, Audu 357
Abiola/Kingibe
- slate, 106
- ticket, 131

Abiola, M.K.O, 21, 358
Abubakar, Abdulsalami 187, 189, 195
Abubakar, Atiku 105, 109, 116, 120, 122-126, 128-130, 206, 260, 265, 314
Abubakar, Sa'ad 188
Abuja Technology Village (ATV), 364
Action
- Congress of Nigeria (ACN), 30, 33-35, 39, 43-45, 51-52, 59, 63, 65-66, 68,71, 74-75, 77, 79, 86, 91-93, 113, 116, 193, 120-121, 215, 221, 258-261, 267, 268-275, 227- 278
- governors, 114
- governed states, 106
- Group, 296

Activate the constitutional provisions for the suspension of election, 164
Adeboye, Pastor, 301
Adedeji, Dokun 238-241, 244
Adegbenro, Adedunni 205-206
Adejuwon, Adebayo 237-240, 245
Adenuga, Mike 355
Adeola, Fola 33, 45
Adeosun, Kemi 200
Adesanya, Professor 361
Adetunmbi, Bunmi 96
Adoke, Mohammed Bello 162-163, 184-185
Advertising Practitioners Council of Nigeria (APCON), 174

Afenifere Renewal Group (ARG), 27
African
- democracies, 251
- Independent Television (AIT), 174
- People's Congress, 79
- University of Science and Technology (AUST), 364

Afrik Network Groups, 245
Agbaje, Jimi 33, 36
Agricultural Productivity, 290
Ahamba, Mike 221, 230
Ahmed, Abdul-Fatah 82
Ahmed, Abdulkadir 355
Ahmed, Hakeem Baba 179
Ajimobi, Abiola 107
Akande Bisi, 71, 85, 92, 106, 114, 133-134, 200, 262, 264, 269-270, 281, 314
Akeredolu, Rotimi 110
Akerele, Frank 344-345
Akintola, Ladoke 323
Akinyemi, Bolaji 188
Akume, George 110
Alake, Dele 113
Alhaji Abubakar Alhaji 355
Ali, Ahmadu 22, 185
Aliero, Adamu Mohammed 26, 213-215, 221 227-228, 233
Alison-Madueke, Diezani 32,171
Alkali, Zainab 188
All
- Nigerian Peoples Party (ANPP), 17, 19-20, 23-24, 27, 42, 66, 68-69, 71, 74-79, 86, 91, 93, 107, 114-116, 221, 259, 268-272
- Patriotic Citizens, 79
- Peoples Party (APP)., 17,268
- Progressive Congress (APC), 48, 59, 63-79, 81-89, 93, 96-98, 100-101, 103, 106, 108 111-116, 119,

Index 367

122-123, 129, 132, 141-143, 145, 150-151, 156, 158, 160, 171, 173-174, 179-180, 183, 200-201, 205-207, 240, 250-251, 257-264, 266, 270-274, 276-285, 288-291, 293-296, 314-315, 318-319
- Election Winning Management System, 144
- governors, 99
- platform document, 285-286
- report, 291-297
- strategy committee, 89-103
- Progressive Institute (API), 95, 293

APGA, 51, 68, 74-75, 79, 82, 93, 259, 271
Alliance for Democracy (AD), 82, 258
Alliances and Mergers 221
- Task Tem, 233-234
Allison-Madueke Diezani 281
Al-Makura, Tanko 66-67, 71, 76-77, 108, 110
Alpha Merchant Bank, 19
Amaechi, Chibuike Rotimi 81, 83-84, 87, 108, 110, 132, 141-144, 158
- as Campaign Director, 141-144
American Constitution, 22
Amnesty programme, 326
Amosun, Ibikunle 107, 114, 200
Anenih, Tony 22
Annulment of June 12 1993 elections, 11, 184
Anti-Boko Haram counter insurgency strategy, 251
Anti-rigging, 57
Aondoakaa, Mike 26, 185
Approach to renewal assignment, 213-215, 227
Aregbesola, Rauf 44, 107, 120-122, 133-134
Armed Forces Ruling Council, 359

Army Mechanical Transport School, Borden, United Kingdom, 3
Association for Democracy and Good Governance in Nigeria (ADGN), 11
Awolowo H.I.D. 349-353
Awolowo, Obafemi 54, 239, 244, 296, 323, 350
Axelrod, David 98, 142
Ayu, Iyorchia 260
Azikiwe, Nnamdi 323

Babangida regime, 11
Babangida, Aliyu 86
Babangida, Ibrahim B. 8, 34, 90, 113, 162, 184, 204, 207-208, 338-341, 358-359
Bafarawa, Atahiru 272, 277
Bakare, Tunde (PTB), 25-26, 38-41, 44-45, 49, 52-53, 56, 65, 70, 75,-76, 120-122, 161-163, 167, 172, 204, 212, 226, 237, 239, 244
Bala–Usman, Hadiza 96
Balance of Power, 31
Balewa, Abubakar Tafawa, 323
Ballot paper stuffing, 155-156
Banking License, 339
Baraje, Kawu 81
Barewa College, 2
Bayero, Prince 125
Belgore, Dele 86
Bello, Ahmadu 323
Benin Empire, 323
Biometric
- based identity card system, 216
- data of members, 118
- register of APC members, 116
Birth of CPC, 24
Blair, Tony 21
Board of Trustees (BoT), 65, 93, 212, 219, 221, 223, 226, 232, 269
Boko Haram, 111, 167, 169, 131, 137-140, 254, 287, 289, 322, 325-326
- challenge, 170
- fighters, 138

- insurgency, 102, 138-139, 169, 250, 254, 325
- meaning of, 139
- sect, 137

Braimah, Col 342-343

British
- Government, 171
- Shipping Line, Elder Dempster, 2

Buhari
- Administration, 8
- and Obasanjo's 3rd Term Drive, 21-24
- Band" 212
- /Idiagbon administration, 92
- Presidency project, 69
- reaches out to Bakare, 39-43

Buni, Mai Mala 115

Bureau for Public Enterprises (BPE), 362

Cadet corps, 2

Campaign
- manifesto, 61
- message, 141, 144, 176
- strategy, 221

Campbell, John 163, 187

Card reader
- jammer scheme, 158, 173
- jamming device/machines, 155-168, 191, 193
- project, 157

Central Working Group (CWG), 213-215, 219-228, 233-234

Chad encounter, 6-11

Change
- Agenda, 178
- Nigeria Project (CNP), 26

Chibok girls, 325

Civil
- rule, 6
- war, 16
- years 204

Clinton democrats 21

Clinton, Bill 21

CNP/SNG model manifestor, 38

Coalition for change, 35

Code of Conduct Tribunal, 63

Conduct accurate census, 165

Conference of Catholic Bishops, 131, 134

Congress for Progressive Change (CPC), 24, 26-27, 30, 35, 37, 40-41, 44, 49, 51-52, 55-56, 65-68, 71-72, 74-79, 91-93, 101, 112, 114 121, 123, 141, 211, 221, 225-235, 240-248, 259, 270-271
- birth of, 24
- constitution, 214
- Presidential Campaign Manifestor, 38
- Renewal Committee, 48-54, 56-57, 63, 65, 211-223, 226
- interim report, 211-223

Constitution, 1999, 31

Constitutional separation of powers, 112

Contest, 2015 102

Cooperative political action, 25

Corruption, 8, 35, 52, 103, 112, 139-140, 175, 203, 324

Council of
- States, 6
- Ulamas 123

Create a Transitional Government, 165

Dag-Ellams, Idris 26

Dangote, Aliko 188

Danjuma, Theophilus 6, 204, 207

Dare, Sunday 143

Dasuki, Sambo 169-170

David-West, Tam 110

Davies, Stephen 137

Democratic
- People's Party (DPP), 74-75
- principles, 259

Dietritch, Ron 337-338

Dikko, Aminu 353

Index 369

Direct Data Entry (DDE), 117-119
- demerits of 118,
- merits of 119-120

Dividends of economic progress, 204
Doctrine of Necessity, 28
Dubai consensus, 30
Duke, Donald 33, 42

Economic and Financial Crimes Commission (EFCC), 25, 319
ECOWAS, 276
Edun, Wale 141, 199-200
Efeyini, Jeffrey 343
Election
- 1983, 350
- 2011, 30, 32, 37-45, 55-56, 67, 101, 107, 193
- 2015, 57, 122, 188
- 2019, 102
- Campaign Council 2011, 132, 178
- day 158
- Management
  - and Monitoring, 179
  - Committee, 144-151
- Monitoring, 144, 178
  - Analysis and Reporting System, 144
  - centre, 181
  - Directorate, 142
  - platform, 42
- petition, 50
- primaries, 105
- Reporting Platform, 56
- results, 194
- rigging, 42, 57
- season, 111,137

Electioneering process, 50, 112, 187
Electoral
- calendar 162-163
- contests,136
  - for offices, 115
- cooperation, 221
- fairness, 18
- manipulations, 211, 225
- process, 23, 163, 171, 190
- season, 187
- votes, 39

Electronic Voting System, 194
El-Rufai, Nasir Ahmad (NAE) 8, 19,21-22, 25-37, 40, 42, 45, 48-53, 60, 63-70, 75-76, 78, 96, 108, 112-115, 126, 133, 158, 161, 167, 200, 205, 207, 211-212, 221, 223, 226-227, 235, 241, 353-354, 362-362

Emir of Borgu, 72
Eseagu, Emma 219
Esin, Larry 213-214, 227-228
Eurasia Group, 180-181
Executive Ministers Council, 6
Ezeazu, Emma 233
Ezekwesili, Oby 33

Failed Banks Tribunal 359-360
Fashakin, Rotimi 222-223- 234, 241
Fashawe, Otunba 260
Fashola, Babatunde Raji 33, 72, 95-96, 102, 106, 110 114, 126, 132, 135, 141,199-200, 292, 314
- led Strategy Committee 94-98
- workplan and recommendations, 96-98

Fayemi, Kayode 107, 127, 132, 135-136, 200, 274
Federal Executive Council (FEC), 27, 364
"Fifth columnists" 70
Fika, Adamu 22
Fika, Wazirin 22
Financial task team, 234
First Republic, 203
Food security,111
Forthcoming Elections, 221-222
- Task Team, 234

Fraud-proof mechanism, 119
Free and fair elections, 193

G 53 , 26-27

G 54, group 172
G 57, 26-27
Gadi, Garba 79, 91, 96, 271
Galadima, Buba 37, 65, 75-76
Gambari, Ibrahim 108, 188
Gates, Bill 261
General Election, 211
- 2011, 101, 109, 156, 258, 268, 272
- 2015, 263
Global Political risk research, 180
"God Factor" 65, 73, 136, 149
Good Governance Group (3G), 26, 139, 215
Government of National Unity, 23
Gowon, Yakubu 54, 204
Gubernatorial election, 221, 214
Guobadia, Ameze 188
Gusau, Aliyu 31, 204, 207-208, 346-348

Habib, Mustapha 110
Hamma, Sule 37, 65, 77
Hanga, Rufai 221, 230
Harvard Business School, 237, 357
House of Commons, 171

Ibori, James 26
Ibrahim Babangida era, 90
Ibrahim, Abba Bukar 110
Ifegwu, Chief 340-342, 361-362, 356, 360
Ige, Bola 350
Igietseme, Joseph 26
Ikeazor, Sharon 110, 213, 219, 227, 229
Ikechukwu, Osita 221, 234
Ikimi, Tom 79, 89-92, 276, 280-284
Impeachment proceedings, 27
Independent
- electoral body
    - establishment of, 166
- National Electoral Commission (INEC), 24, 70-71, 75, 77-79, 91, 101, 120, 146-148, 155-157, 170, 183-184, 187, 189-190, 196, 235, 261-262, 268
Indigenisation processes, 338
Interim
- Executive Council, 263, 265
- Government, 162
- National Executive Committee, 94
- National Government (ING), 163, 359
Internal
- democracy, 81
- party democracy, 259
- Party Documents, 219
- security, 218
- selection process, 31
International
- Capital markets, 282
- Community, 43, 138, 322
- Conference, 316
- Election observers, 170
- Media organisations, 223
- Republican Institute (IRI), 179
Iriase, Parry 96
Isa Kaita, Abdul Malik 2
Islamic education, 335
Ita, Eyo 323
Iyamu, Osagie Ize 277
Iyayi, Macaulay 349, 354
Izunaso, Osita 96

Jang, Jonah David 87
Jankada, Salome 213-215, 227-228
Jega, Attahiru 170, 183, 186-187, 191, 196
Job creation, 204
Joda, Ahmed 196
Jonathan Administration, 69, 88, 138, 141, 171, 188, 195, 197-198
Jonathan, Patience 185
Jonathan, Goodluck President, 27, 31-32, 34, 41, 52, 61, 63-64, 70, 77, 83, 99, 101, 125, 129, 150-152, 158,

Index

160-171, 173, 176, 178, 180-181, 184-185, 187, 190, 193, 195-198, 204, 206, 249-251, 299-301, 321
June 12, 1993 elections, annulment, 21, 162, 358

Kabiyesi, The Awujale of Ijebu land, 64, 72-74, 160, 167, 207, 348-351, 360
Kaita, Lawal 260
Kanem, Borno Empire, 323
Kano, Aminu 203, 323
Katsina Foundation, 9-10
Kerry, John 167, 171
Koki, Nasiru Aliko 96
Kukah, Matthew Hassan 188-189
Kumo, Suleiman 22
Kuye, Priscilla 188
Kwande, Yahaya 260
Kwankwaso, Rabiu Musa 82, 84, 109-110, 116, 120, 123-126, 129, 143, 314

Labour Party, 30, 33-34
Lamido, Sule 82, 84, 86
Lawal, B.D. 110
Lawal, Hassan 213, 215, 218, 227, 229
Lawal, Jimi (Shakiru Olabosipo Olajimi Adebisi a.k.a. "Omo teacher" or "Omo 36" or "champion Bosi" or "Professor")
- Abacha after him, 359-363
- As
  - M.D. Alpha Merchant Bank 349, 353-354
  - Pioneer staff at Union Bank, London branch, 338
- At
  - City Banking College, 338

  - Muslim College, Ijebu-Ode, 336, 343
  - South-West College, 338
- Barclays Bank days, 337-339

- Birth, 334
- Executive Director, Alpha Merchant, Bank 341-342
- in
  - Aliyu Gusau's Court, 346-348
  - banking, 336-349
- Meeting El-Rufai, 353-359
- NYSC posting to Alpha Merchant Bank, 342
- Setting up Alpha Merchant Bank, 339-341
- Taking OPM programme in Harvard, 357
Lawal, Remi 334, 336
Leader of Opposition, 264
Leadership
- selection, 60
- succession planning, 204
Local Government
- Joint Account, 324
- Collation Centre, 147
- duties of, 147-148

Macaulay, Herbert 323
Maduekwe, Ojo 22
Mama Ode (author's grandmother), 336
Mamman, Yusuf 223
Mamora, Olorunimbe 110, 113, 144
Mandela, Nelson 35
Mantu, Senator 22
Marwa, Buba 77, 277
Masari, Aminu Bello 32, 110
Media
- and Communications task Team, 234
- and communications, 222-223
- group, 151
Membership
- cards, 216
- Mobilisation, 219-221
  - Task Team, 229-230

- Registration, 51
  - mode, 117
  - Task Team 215-217, 230
Merger
  - Committee, 71-72, 74, 89-91, 94, 233, 261, 269
  - partners, 67
  - process, 67
  - Project, 77
  - Resolution, 79
Merging
  - parties, 91, 93, 101, 264
  - partners, 91
  - Party Governors, 265
Militarised occupation, 225
"Military
  - Boko Haram" 137
  - occupation, 61
  - presidency, 204
  - service, 2
Minimah, General 160-161
Modu, Timothy 26
Mohammed Murtala 8
Mohammed, Lai 30, 200
Momoh, Tony 37, 49, 75, 110, 212, 226, 247
Movement for the Restoration and Defence of Democracy (MRDD), 93, 258
Muazu, Adamu Ahmed 190
Muazu, Aliyu Babangida 82
Muhammed, Murtala Ramat 4, 204
Muoghalu, 110
Musdafa, Muhammad 188
Muslim–Muslim
  - ticket, 106, 130-32, 134-135
  - Presidential ticket, 263

Na'Abba, Ghali 260
NADECO, 264, 266
Nahibi Basirat, 213, 222, 227, 234
Naija politics, 245

National
  - Assembly, 27-28, 149, 156
  - Collation Centre, 148,183
  - Conference 2014, 165, 99-100
  - Conventions, 105-136
    - and primaries proper, 109-112
  - Council on privatization (NCP), 175, 362
  - Democratic Institute (NDI), 179
  - Economic Council (NEC), 175
  - Economy, 8
  - Executive committee, 212, 226, 293
  - mediation and conciliation, 190
  - Peace Committee, 188
  - political
    - development, 98
    - turf, 94
  - politics, 259
  - Reconciliation Committee, 187
  - Republican Convention, 90
  - Rescue Mission, 161, 203
  - wealth, 5
  - Working Committee, 116
  - Youth Service Scheme, 341, 343
Nationwide electioneering campaign 144
NCC SIM Registration Front-end project, 117-118
Nda-Isaiah, Sam 126, 129, 314
NDIC, 364
New People's Democratic Party (New PDP), 81-88
  - entrants, 81-88
  - governors, 109, 141-143
Ngige, Chris 274
Niger Delta situation,325-326
Nigeria
  - Governors Forum (NGF), 87
  - Immigration Service (IMS), 140
Nigerian
  - crisis, 137
  - Military Training College,

Kaduna 3
- political
  - history, 203
  - landscape, 98, 211, 225
  - space, 204
- Stock Exchange, 356

Nigerians in the Diaspora 26
Nnamani, Ken 32
Nomination to CPC Renewal Committee, 247-248
Northern elite, 2
NPN, 21
NRC 93, 258, 269, 273, 281
Nwabuchi, Nwankwo 221, 230
Nyako, Murtala 81, 83, 85, 125, 142

Obiagbena, Nduka 126, 152
Obama, President, 98, 142, 171
Obasanjo, Olusegun 5-6, 11, 14-16, 18, 21-23, 40, 61, 67, 113, 199, 204-206, 250, 340, 362-363
Obi, Ben 188, 260
Obuah, Felix 84
Odidi, Isa 26
Odigie-Oyegun, John 92, 96, 114, 264-269, 281
Odumakin, Yinka, 27, 33, 36, 171-173, 213, 222, 227-228, 234
Official results, 183
Ogbeh, Audu 110
Ojudu, Babafemi 113
Okechukwu, Osita 110, 213-214, 227-228
Okocha, Tony 84
Okoh, Nicholas 188
Okongwu, Chu, 339, 355
Okonjo-Iweala, Ngozi 33, 40
Okonkwo, Annie 79, 271, 277
Okorocha, Rochas 125, 129, 314
Okoye, Festus 219, 233
Okupe, Doyin 77
Oluwa, Oluwatayo 110

Omisade, Michael 340-351, 354, 356-357
Onaiyekan, John 188
Ondo State Gubernatorial Election, 2012, 121
Onu, Ogbonnaya 270
Onyia, Dubem 260
Operation wetie, 54
Opinion polls, 9, 102, 106, 159
- results, 106
- surveys, 101-102
Organisation of African Unity (OAU), 276
Oritsejafor, Ayo 188, 300
Orubebe, Godsday 183, 186-187, 190
Osadebay, Dennis 323
Oshiomhole, Adams 107, 110, 114, 132-133, 135, 267, 278
Osinbajo, Yemi 132, 134-136, 141,
Osoba, Olusegun 277
Osun, Wale 33
Otedola, Michael 260
Over voting, 57
Oyinlola, Olagunsoye 199
Oyo Empire, 323
Ozieh, Victor 26

Palace coup, 8
Party
- agents
  - roles of, 145
  - specific duties on the day of election, 145
- Constitution, 219
- manifesto, 26
- to-party transition, 203
Peace committee, 190
Pemu-Amuka, Sam 188
People's constitution–creation of, 166
People's Democratic Party (PDP), 15, 19-20, 23, 32, 42-44, 48, 67, 77-78, 81-85, 87-88, 93, 98-100, 102-103, 107, 111, 124, 126, 129, 139, 149-

150, 156, 158-162, 167, 169, 171, 173, 176-178, 180-183, 186, 190, 215, 242-243, 250-254, 258, 260, 262, 265, 271-272, 274, 276, 280, 284, 288-289
- Reform Committee, 32

Periodic polls outcome, 180

Permanent Voters Cards (PVCs), 57-58, 156-157, 173-173

Petro-dollars, 5

Philippe de Pontet, 180

Political
- action, 25
- actors, 20
- alliances, 49
- allies 124, 271
- aspirations, 142
- capital, 23
- career 113
- challenges, 56
- circuit, 23
- class, 21, 25
- climate, 18
- collaboration, 30
- competition, 47
- conduct, 321
- control, 88
- development and conduct, 98
- disputes, 189
- economy, 218
- elite, 47
- expressions, 49
- fall-outs, 8
- field, 16
- fortunes, 24
- games, 99
- gesture, 100
- history, 57, 65, 98, 203
- landscape, 211, 225
- map, 99
- mediation team, 1878
- muscle, 43
- nests, 82
- observer, 57

- options, 33
- outing, 269
- parties, 18-19, 49, 79, 92, 155, 170, 173, 189, 269, 278-279
- party leadership, 275
- platform, 258, 278
- players, 8, 92
- practices, 99
- process, 36
- risk, 99, 132
- scenario, 34
- scene, 34
- situation, 36
- space, 47
- structure, 257, 278
- tempers, 195
- tempo, 33
- transition programme, 90
- watchers, 127

Police action, 4

Policy Development, 218-219
- Task Team, 232

Polling
- agents, 144, 178
- outcomes, 103
- results, 103
- stations, 155
- unit agents, 56, 177-178
- Units, 194
  - information, 144

Post-election
- litigation processes, 49
- problem 195
- vacation, 50
- violence, 43

Post-electoral disputes or crises, 190

Post-registration tests, 89

President Muhammadu Buhari (PMB)
- Acceptance speech by presidential candidate, 313-320
- As
  - Class Monitor 1
  - Commander, 2nd Division, Ibadan, 6

Index

- Chairman, Nigerian National Petroleum Corporation (NNPC), 5
- Executive Chairman, Petroleum (Special) Trust Fund (PTF), 11-13, 16
- Federal Commissioner for Petroleum and Natural Resources, 5
- General and Team Leader of the Commanding Forces Divisions, 6
- Head of State, 7
- Leader, Association for Democracy and Good Governance in Nigeria (ADGN), 11
- Military Administrator, North Eastern State, 4
- Peace Enforcer during post-independence crisis in the Congo, 4
- Platoon Commander at the 2nd Infantry Battalion, Abeokuta, 4
- School prefect, 1
- attended
    - Katsina Model School, 1
    - Katsina Provincial Secondary School (Now Government College, Katsina), 1
    - Mechanical Transport Officer's Course, 3
    - Officer Cadet Training, 3
    - Platoon Commander's Course, 3
    - U.S. Army War College, Carlisle, Pennsylvania, U.S.A. 3, 5-6
- beneficiary, countrywide merit-based competition of Elder Dempster, 1
- birth, 1
- call to be a soldier, 2-3
- campaign pictures 303-309
- Chairman
    - Katsina Foundation, 9
    - Nigerian National Petroleum Corporation (NNPC), 5
- commander, 2nd Division Ibadan and Jos, 3rd Armoured Division, 6
- declaration speech for presidential primaries, 287-290
- enlisting in the Nigerian Army, 3
- enrolled in primary schools, 1
- fought valiantly for Federal Forces during the Nigerian Civil War, 4
- in the Federal forces during the Nigerian Civil War, 4
- Inaugural speech, 321-327
- involvement in non-governmental community development, Katsina Foundation, 9
- leadership qualities, 3-4
- leading Ministry of Mines and Petroleum Resource, 16
- Love for outdoor activities , 2
- member, All Peoples party (APP), 17
- Military Administrator, North-Eastern State, 4
- Northern Region beneficiary of country-wide merit-based competition, 1
- obtained Master's Degree in Strategic studies, 3
- post-war deployment, 4
- professional and leadership capacities, 4
- schooling, 1
- training,
    - at Defence Services Staff College Wellington, India, 3

- at Nigerian Military Training College (NMTC), Zaria 3.
Presidential
- Campaign Council (PCC), 40, 49, 142
- candidate, 113
- contents, 61
- contest, 82, 149-150, 170
- election, 148-150
- Debate Organising Committee, 152
- Election, 182, 196, 261
  - level, 66
  - results 2015, 129, 141
    - analysis of, 191-193
    - predicted 311
- Results, 2003, 2007, 2011 and projection for 2015, 249-255
- Elections, 167, 183
  - campaign season, 2015 140
- 2015 315
  - primaries, 314
- Primaries, 59, 105-136, 150
  - Organising Committee, 200
- primary election, 109
Primary election, 115
Pro-democracy initiatives, 26
Progressive Governor's Forum 93-94, 264, 296
PTF
- challenge, 11-15
- era 18, 204
Puritanism versus Pragmatism, 53, 237-245

Quality education, 289
Quranic learning, 335

Rebranding Buhari and the APC, 151-152
Red Media Africa 143
Rehabilitation programmes, 326

Renewal Assignment –approach to, 213-215
Ribadu, Nuhu   25, 33-34, 36, 44, 152, 276-277, 283
Rights of citizens, 112
Rimi, Abubakar 260

Salihu, Mustafa 75-77
Sani Abacha era 90
Sanusi Lamido Sanusi 125
Saro Wiwa, Ken 281
Save Nigeria Group (SNG), 26-29, 34, 172
School system, 334
SDP, 93, 258, 264, 266
Second Republic, 203
Self-exile status, 31
Separation of Powers, 112
Shagari, Shehu 7, 16
Shata, Mohammed 260
Shehu Othman Dan Fodio's Caliphate, 323
Shekarau, Ibrahim   34, 79, 91, 152, 271-272, 277
Sherriff, Ali Modu 269-271, 273
Shettima, Kashim 108
Shonekan, Ernest 359
SIM
- registration, 118
- technology, 159
Social development and infrastructure, 12
Social disorder, 8
Soleye, Dr. 340
Specific Duties of the Party Agents on the Day of Election, 145-146
State
- collation agents, 148
  - specific duties of, 148
- Collation centre, 148
- creation exercise, 4
- of emergency, 125, 163
- Renewal Teams (SRTs), 219

Index

Supreme Military Council, 6
SW Global LTD (SWG), 215-218, 230-231
Sylva, Timipre 89, 91-92, 110

Tafida, Dalhatu 22
Talakawas, 38, 43, 48, 151, 178, 203
Tambuwal, Waziri Aminu 120, 123, 206
Tarka, Joseph S. 131, 323
Teasonable felony trial, 349-350
Technology, 216, 231
Tenure elongation project, 22
Territiorial integrity of the Nigerian nation, 7
The Abuja Accord" 188-190
The Buhari Organisation, (TBO), 20-21, 37-39, 55-56, 65, 74, 207, 212
The Lagos Group, 177-178
3rd Armoured Division, 6-7
Third Term Agenda/ debacle/project, 21 – 22, 61
This Day Interview 126-129
3G 29-31, 50
3G Steering Committee, 27
Tilley-Gyado, Terfa 96
Time to rebuild Nigeria, 313-320
Tinubu, Bola Ahmed 43, 45, 52-54, 63-66, 71-74, 83, 85-86, 93, 98, 105-107, 112-116, 120-127, 129-136, 141-143, 172, 174, 199-201, 205, 260-266, 269-272, 274, 280, 284, 314
Tinubu, Wale 282
Tom Ikimi/Bola Tinubu Exchange, 257-284
Traditional alliance model, 65
Transition
   - committee 196-198
   - process, 196, 321
Tribunal processes 211
Tuggar, Yusuf 213, 218-219, 227
Tukur, Mahmood 22
Tumsa, Tijjani 114

Ukeje, Rose 188
Ukiwe, Ebitu 188
Ulama's Intervention, 123-126
Ulamas 125
Ume-Ezeoke, Edwin 20
Unemployment, 103, 140, 325, 327
United Middle Belt Congress, 131
University of Ibadan, 333
UPN 350
Usman, Hadiza Bala 110, 144, 213-214, 227-228
Usman, Ismaila 60
Utomi, Pat 33, 141

VERITAS Frontier Markets Electoral Forecast Statistical Model, 249-250, 252, 254
Vice Presidential
   - Candidate
      - Choice of, 105-136
   - issues, 129-136
Vote counting, 183
Voter demographics, 57, 59
Voters
   - card, 155
   - education, 156
   - register 56-57
   - registration exercise, 57
Voting
   - delegates, 113
   - for Buhari 34-36
   - materials, 144
   - period, 155

Wammaka, Aliyu 82
War against
   - corruption, 175
   - Against Indiscipline campaign, 8
Ward
   - Collation agents, 147 –
      - specific roles of, 147
   - Collation Centre, 147

Web-based platform, 216
Western education, 139
Williams, Adebola, 143
Working with AKPD 98-99
Wushishi, Mustapha 359

Xiaoping, Deng 35

Yar'Adua administration, 20
Yar'Adua, Shehu Musa 2, 5-6, 204, 207
Yar'Adua, Turai 26
Yar'Adua, Umaru, 18, 23-24, 26-28, 61, 96, 172
Yari, Abdulaziz 108
Yerima, Ahmed 110
Youth employment, 111
Yusuf, Mohammed 137

www.ingramcontent.com/pod-product-compliance
Lightning Source LLC
Chambersburg PA
CBHW070805300426
44111CB00014B/2432